By Robbin F. Laird

THE USMC TRANSFORMATION PATH

Preparing for the High-End Fight

CONTENTS

Foreword 1

Preface 4

Chapter 1: The Shift from the Land Wars to Preparing for the High-End Fight ..8

    Escalation Management.. 13

    The C² Piece... 17

    The ISR Piece... 21

    The Basing Piece 26

    The Logistics Piece... 30

    The Training Piece 33

    The Pace of Conflict Piece 42

    Shaping a Way Ahead... 45

Chapter 2: The Marine Corps in the Strategic Shift 48

    The Tiltrotor-Driven Transition 49

    The F-35-Driven Marine Corps Transformation 62

    The Next Phase: The 2020s 69

    Enter Force Design 2030... 71

Chapter 3: The View from MAWTS-1..81

    Col Gillette, CO of MAWTS-1.. 82

    Working Mobile Basing 89

    Moving Forward with Mobile Basing 91

    The Role of Heavy Lift.. 94

    Forward Arming and Refueling Points (FARPs) 97

    MAWTS-1 and the F-35 99

    Expeditionary Basing and C² 103

    The Evolving Amphibious Task Force 105

    The Ground Combat Element in the Pacific Reset................................. 109

Blue Water Expeditionary Operations..111

The F-35 and USMC–U.S. Navy Integration...113

Unmanned Air Systems and the USMC..116

Chapter 4: The View from II MEF and Norfolk **121**

The Perspective of VADM Lewis 123

The Perspective of the Commanding General of II MEF.....................................127

The Perspective from II MEB...135

Working II MEF Operations in Transition 138

The C² Piece..140

The ISR Piece..143

II MEF Information Group 146

The Logistics Piece..149

The Challenge of Preparing for Future Operations..152

Shaping a Way Ahead 156

Looking Back and Looking Forward for the USMC 160

Chapter 5: The View from 2nd Marine Airwing **164**

Multiple Basing, Kill Webs and C²: Shaping a Way Ahead 170

Further Thoughts on the C² Piece 174

Working the Distributed Operations Piece...177

Working the Light Attack Helicopter Piece 182

The Osprey Piece 185

The Heavy Lift Piece...191

The Coming of the CH-53K..194

The Impact of the CH-53K...198

Visiting MAG-26 204

The Tactical Fighter Piece MAG-14 Preparing the Transition 208

Nordic Training...210

Visiting the Warlords 214

The Training Piece 218

Shaping a Way Ahead for the Assault Support Community 224

Chapter 6: The View from the Pacific **229**

The Perspective of LtGen Rudder, the MARFORPAC Commander 238

The Perspective of LtGen Heckl, I MEF Commander 245

Three Key Weapons Systems for the Marines in the Pacific 248

The F-35 Piece 249

The Osprey Piece 251

The C^2 Piece 252

Seam Warfare, Exercises and Deterrence 253

Allies, Partners and Marines in the Indo-Pacific 254

Operations in the Information Environment 258

The Logistics Challenges 261

Shaping a Way Ahead for Force Design 2030 in the Pacific 265

Chapter 7: The MARSOC Case **269**

MARSOF 2030 270

Shaping a Way Ahead for MARSOC 276

A Discussion with Major General James F. Glynn 281

Chapter 8: Challenges Facing the Way Ahead for the USMC **287**

The Way Ahead for the U.S. Military Strategy and the Joint Force 288

Adversaries and Allies: How Will They Shape the Dynamically
Evolving Strategic Environment? 290

The Configuration of the USMC Going Forward 295

Challenges Going Forward: The Perspective of LtGen (Retired) Robling ... 302

Afterword **307**

Dr. Robbin F. Laird **312**

This book is dedicated to my father Bradley Clayton Laird, in honor of his service in the Pacific during the Second World War, including his time in Japan after the defeat of the Empire of Japan. He taught me much about the true nature of the brutality of war and the threat which a determined adversary to our democracy truly poses. He was part of the fight against the Empire of Japan and now we face at least three determined adversaries in the Pacific challenging our way of life.

FOREWORD

LtGen George J. Trautman III, USMC (Ret)
Former USMC Deputy Commandant for Aviation

My first experience with Robbin Laird occurred almost fifteen years ago when I was assigned as the new U.S. Marine Corps Deputy Commandant for Aviation. Facing the daunting task of introducing the MV-22 Osprey into combat operations, we deployed the first of three Osprey squadrons to Iraq beginning in the fall of 2007. Of course, our rabid and largely uninformed critics predicted abject failure and even I had to admit the stakes were extremely high. During that tense period, one of the key intellects I turned to for advice was Robbin Laird.

From that initial relationship grew a bond between Robbin and a succession of USMC Deputy Commandants (both Air and Ground) that helped the Marine Corps not only achieve incredible success with the Osprey, but also the F-35 Joint Strike Fighter, the Venom and Viper helicopters, and state-of-the-art command and control systems such as the TPS-80 G/ATOR radar.

So, what has Robbin's main contribution been to the Marine Corps? He always asks the right questions, and he is doggedly determined to examine new warfighting concepts and equipment — not just from the perspective of the upper echelons of the Pentagon, but from a broad cross section of tactical operators serving in the fleet. He interviews Marines who come to work every day with a passionate dedication to improving the Corps. They are always thinking, and sometimes struggling, to translate the ideas and equipment given to them in ways that take maximum advantage of the tools of their trade. Sometimes all they need to excel is a knowledgeable listener who can help coalesce their thought processes into action and Robbin fulfills that niche perfectly.

Unlike many of the "gotcha" defense journalists and think tank elites writing today, Robbin is happy to play the role of a facilitator who shines the spotlight on the active-duty sailors and Marines who are actually serving in the arena. In this book Robbin uses this technique to explore three primary objectives. First, is the fact that Marine aviation has been at the forefront of post Iraq and Afghanistan operations for at least two decades. While the rest of the Corps was bogged down in small unit tactics and nation building, USMC aviation introduced capabilities that are ideally suited for 5th generation warfare and the potential near peer adversaries of the future. Second, is the sometimes-overlooked fact that the Marine Corps occupies the "vortex of the dynamics of change" being pursued by the U.S. Navy and the U.S. Air Force. Marines must not be myopic in how they envision their future contributions to the joint and combined force. And, finally, he provides an examination of the 38th Commandant's sweeping changes as delineated in Force Design 2030 (FD 2030). Almost everyone agrees that service wide transformation is required following two decades of stagnation and the evolution of new global strategic priorities, but the harshest critics of this new path believe "the cart has been put before the horse" and the future relevance of the Marine Corps is at stake.

Robbin is careful not to join the chorus of Force Design 2030 naysayers. Instead, he burrows into the thinking of those who are dealing with the coming changes and inspires them to think through the impacts – positive and negative — that lie off our bow. In that way, this book contributes directly to a principal element of Force Design that is often overlooked because of the premature ax that has been taken to service end-strength and force structure (including cuts to infantry battalions, aircraft squadrons, tanks, and cannon artillery). That is, that the transformation being thrust upon the Corps today must "rest upon a solid analytical foundation." As John P. Kotter,

Harvard Business School, is quoted on the opening page of the document, "Transformation is a process, not an event."

After Former Navy Secretary James Webb blasted Force Design 2030 in an op-ed for *The National Interest* well over a year ago, there has been little intellectual curiosity or constructive criticism expressed by the defense establishment, including relevant members of Congress about the plan. Is this because FD 2030 is so sound that it stands above criticism or is it because the changes, as eloquently described by Secretary Webb, will make the Marine Corps largely irrelevant? Only time will tell how the Marine Corps navigates this treacherous transformation journey, but it's not the equipment that will make the Corps successful on the future battlefield – it's the Marines. Their imaginations, ideas and creativity will lead to innovative employment of the tools they are given. That's true of every piece of equipment in use today and it will remain that way in the future. *The USMC Transformation Path: Preparing for the High-End Fight* makes a valuable contribution to the professional dialogue that must occur by giving voice to those who are charged with managing the change.

George J. Trautman III
LtGen, USMC (Ret) Former USMC Deputy Commandant for Aviation

PREFACE

Last year, I published a book on *Training the High-End Fight: The Strategic Shift of the 2020s*. This book is a continuation of that effort. My colleagues and I have focused on the strategic shift from the Middle East land wars to the return of Great Power competition for a number of years, certainly before it became a more general focus of attention.

The strategic shift is much more than that—it is a strategic shock as well. We have trained and battle tested a whole generation of warriors who have operated in the deserts of the Middle East and the mountains of Afghanistan. The U.S. Army has been the bedrock force to which all the other services have provided capabilities, and even though what went on in the past twenty years was called joint warfighting, what really was happening was the United States Marine Corps (USMC) was becoming an adjunct to the U.S. Army; the United States Air Force (USAF) was providing fire support, intelligence and lift for the ground fight; and the Navy was providing amphibious and carrier support to the ground scheme of maneuver.

Many innovations in warfare occurred during these twenty years, but they were in support of U.S Army operations and the ground scheme of maneuver. The focus was on counterinsurgency, counterterrorism, nation-building and stability operations. This period came to a dramatic end with the Biden Administration's Blitzkrieg withdrawal from Afghanistan in August 2021. That withdrawal has significant and lingering effects on the U.S. military and our alliance policies and approaches. I have written about that elsewhere.

And to be very clear, the dramatic withdrawal from Afghanistan represented the failure of twenty years of U.S. Central Command (CENTCOM) policies and of the U.S. Army's dominating role in defining forces and shaping strategy. The conflicts involving peer competitors have little to do with the force structures and strategies pursued in the past twenty years.

But how effective will be the rebound? How effective will the political and military leadership in the beltway be in understanding how dramatically different the strategic shift really is? Will the U.S. Army's leading role be jettisoned to allow for a fresh redesign of the joint force, one appropriate to the nation's defense?

When I worked for Secretary Wynne, first when he was head of acquisition and then Secretary of the Air Force, it was abundantly clear to him and his team that going down the rabbit hole of the land wars was going to lead to a significant reduction in high-end warfighting capability. That has clearly happened. Both Defense Secretary Gates and President Obama attacked the F-22 as a "Cold War" airplane, and the fifth-generation revolution was slowed to a crawl. The U.S. poured its operational resources into support for the land wars and struggled to keep up its other warfighting skills. For example, anti-submarine planes turned into land support assets, and skill sets finding enemies on land replaced those of prioritizing finding enemies underwater.

There is a real danger that the nation does not recover rapidly enough and shape a force more appropriate to the world in which we live. To do so requires significant reworking of how the joint and coalition forces work together. That strategic shift is discussed in the first chapter.

The second chapter highlights the core focus of the book, which is highlighting the transition of the USMC within the overall strategic shift. The Marines have unique air, ground and sea capabilities which put them at the vortex of the dynamics of change being pursued by the U.S. Navy and the USAF.

And many coalition partners look to the USMC as a relevant benchmark for the kind of multi-domain operations which they can pursue. For many allies, their force structure approximates the size of the USMC, and they find the fit better than emulating the total force which the United States has built. It is also the case that the legacy force coming out of the land wars which the United States deploys today is distorted in terms of its warfighting relevance to the approaches for combat with the peer competitors.

The second chapter focuses on the Marines and their transformation, which really started with the introduction of the Osprey into the land wars and has continued with the deployments of the F-35, to the return to more focus on amphibious operations and the latest phase of transformation, the one being shaped by the current USMC Commandant.

The remaining chapters bring together my discussions with Marines over the past two years as they shape their transition within the overall strategic shift. Those Marines certainly understand the gravity of the situation and the challenges they face. I have had a wide range of interviews over the past two years, which are included in this book.

I spent time with MAWTS-1 and 2nd Marine Air Wing in 2020. In 2021, I returned to 2nd Marine Air Wing and visited II Marine Expeditionary Force twice. I then went to Hawaii, where I spent time with the commander of U.S. Marine Corps Forces, Pacific or MARFORPAC and his staff. As I spent time there in 2014 and 2015, I have included interviews from those visits as well, which provide a good sense of how the transition which the Marines launched in 2014 is playing out now. My final look at the Marine Corps transition focuses on the Marine Special Forces Command as a case study in the transition from the land wars to the peer competitor fight, and includes my interview with the Commanding General of MARSOC.

In other words, the reader can learn first-hand how Marine Corps combat leaders see the transition and the challenges they face to making that transition. All of these interviews are taken from our two websites, *Second Line of Defense* and *Defense Information*. I have indicated the date published to provide the time horizon to the judgment being made by Marines.

I conclude by taking a look at the challenges being faced by Marines to make their transition within the broader strategic shift which U.S. forces are undertaking. These challenges are significant and if not met will leave the Marines exposed to threats and dangers which will impact their combat success. Success in making the strategic shift is not guaranteed, but failure is not an option.

CHAPTER ONE:

THE SHIFT FROM THE LAND WARS
TO PREPARING FOR THE HIGH-END FIGHT

It cannot be overstated how different the decade ahead preparing for the high-end fight and engaging in full-spectrum crisis management is from the past twenty years of Middle East land warfare. In my interviews over the past few years, I have talked with a number of officers in the USMC, U.S. Navy or the USAF as well as several allied militaries who entered the service towards the end of the Cold War. There are few remaining officers who have served in this period, but they are a very precious commodity because they bridge back to the peer fight with the Soviet Union to the current 21st century authoritarian competitors.

It is not the Cold War, of course. Russia is not the Soviet Union, and China is a very different animal than the Soviet Union. But the experiences of the 1980s were rooted in dealing with a core peer competitor. Air and sea dominance could not be assumed as it has been in the period of the past twenty years of engaging in the U.S. Army–led approach to counterinsurgency and stability operations.

We began to see movement towards the peer fight with the shift in the Middle East required to destroy ISIS strongholds and with the Russians bringing their naval and air forces to Syria and engaging in shadow war with the United States and its allies. But it was just a foreshadowing of how different the decade ahead would be from the past two decades.

The use of airpower against ISIS-held territory saw the beginnings of a return to what airpower really is all about as opposed to supporting the ground scheme of maneuver. I interviewed my colleague Ben Lambeth, who wrote a very important book about this transition and how hard it was for the Army-led CENTCOM. And it took the election of a new president as well to authorize the kinds of air strikes which are more relevant to peer warfare than the past twenty years of the use of airpower.

In his book entitled *Airpower in the War against ISIS*, Lambeth provided his assessment of the shift from the pure dominance over airpower of counterinsurgency operations to the fight against ISIS, a fight which required airpower to remove the Army's shackles on its proper use against a state-like competitor.[1]

Lambeth noted: "Clearly, as counterinsurgency operations became the predominant American way of war after 2003, the USAF lost a lot of muscle memory for doing much of anything else by way of higher-end force employment. And the predominant Army leadership at U.S. Central Command continued to apply its long-habituated Army thinking going forward into an entirely different situation that was presented by the rise of ISIS. A more assertive leadership in CENTCOM's air component at the time would have pressed for a different response to the challenge it was handed in 2014 by arguing for targeting ISIS not as an insurgency, but rather as a self-avowed state in the making.

"However, CENTCOM's commander, U.S. Army General Lloyd Austin III, simply assumed ISIS to be a regenerated Islamist insurgency of the sort that he was most familiar with, which it was not at all, and accordingly proceeded to engage it as just another counterinsurgency challenge. Eventually, his air component's second successive commander, then-Lieutenant General C. Q. Brown, finally prevailed in arguing for deliberate strategic air attacks against critical ISIS infrastructure targets in both Iraq and Syria, not just for on-call air 'support' to be used as flying artillery for the ground fight.

"One must remember that the vast majority of today's serving U.S. Air Force airmen are only familiar with Operation Desert Storm from their book reading. And even much of the USAF's more senior leadership today has

---

1.   Benjamin S. Lambeth, *Airpower in the War against ISIS* (USNI Press, 2021).

never really been exposed to higher-end aerial warfare as we last experienced it over Saddam Hussein's Iraq in 2003. Only now are we slowly coming to realize the opportunity costs that were inflicted by this neglect for nearly two decades, during which time we fixated solely on less-intense counterinsurgency warfare."

The other transitional moment was when the U.S. and its closest allies conducted a strike on Syrian chemical weapons facilities. This was done within the threat envelope of potential Russian counter-engagement against those forces. Ed Timperlake provided his assessment of this event from the side of the United States: "… the surface Navy can also undertake independent offensive operations, as the Russians in combat support for the President of Syria recently found out, after the Syrian President used chemical weapons on his opponents:

"When President Trump gave the go order to attack Shayrat Air Base Syria, where a chemical attack had been launched, two U.S. Navy surface warships stood ready to implement the order. In one shining moment with Tomahawks fired from *USS Porter* and *USS Ross*, the world knew a new Commander-in Chief was at the helm. It was reported that 59 of the 60 Tomahawks hit the intended target. Our way of war was to actually warn the Russians to minimize any chance of Russians being hit or killed — how nice for them."[2]

Murielle Delaporte reported on the French engagement in the operation, which also presages how the allied engagement changes as the strategic shift begins to unfold. "France was in charge of hitting two facilities assembling and stockpiling chemical weapons near Homs. They were hit simultaneously by a combination of airborne and sea-based missiles: a total of 12 out of the 105 fired by the three countries, which, when added to the British salvo of eight Storm Shadows, constitutes the usual percentage of the French and British contributions to coalition operations (roughly 20 percent)....

---

2.   Ed Timperlake, "The Impact of a 'Ready on Arrival' U.S. Navy on Crisis Management," *Second Line of Defense* (March 5, 2019), https://sldinfo. com/2019/03/the-impact-of-a-ready-on-arrival-us-navy-on-crisis-management/.

"Being able to strike every 10 minutes from different platforms using different types of missiles meant working in perfect synchronicity on a tri-lateral basis (the U.S., the UK and France) and among the three countries' different services, something that cannot be improvised.

"Political meetings beforehand and constant contacts and coordination among the three countries' ministers of defense and military chiefs were crucial to prepare a pretty risky mission both politically and technically, but what counted to achieve that kind of success have been the decades of mil-to-mil relationship and training among the three allies. Building the trust necessary so that a French mission commander based in the Mediterranean could direct part of the strikes in an autonomous manner did not just happen overnight. This is the result of years and years of flying and sailing together and operating together whether in Afghanistan or over Libya or in Niger. It is also the result of the joint planning done in 2013, albeit in a very, very different threat environment."[3]

In a way these two developments framed the transition. But a brutal transition it is and a difficult one. As the United States was focusing on the Middle East and pouring treasure, manpower and equipment into those wars, the Chinese put their money on shaping their version of a 21st century combat force and their version of the revolution in military affairs. The Russians are somewhat different in terms of their investments and their approach, but they seized Crimea and refined new methods of warfare central to the challenges of direct defense today in Europe. The Russians had already experienced their Afghan nightmare and were no going to go down that rabbit hole again.

And the latest version of their military doctrine released on July 2, 2021, provides a very clear statement of how they are approaching the conflict with the liberal democracies. What is asserted is the priority for Russian values against Western values. And in this defense of Russian values, infor-mation war is highlighted as a key reality facing the Russian federation as the West using the various modern means of information, such as the internet,

---

3.   Murielle Delaporte, "French Quick Reaction Force Key to Syrian Missile Strikes," *Breaking Defense* (May 2, 2018), https://breakingdefense. com/2018/05/french-quick-reaction-force-key-to-syrian-missile-strikes/.

to seek, in the Russian view, to disrupt the Russian value system and way of life. This means that the Russians see themselves as free to do the same, and to use information warfare to do the same. Indeed, the document does not use the word cyber warfare whatsoever. It focuses on political warfare and information security.

And in the Russian military mind, information war is an ongoing element of the global competition which allows them to get inside the adversary's decision-making cycle, and inside the debates and conflicts within Western societies and in their alliances, and to do so in ways that weaken the West and lead to disintegration of Western values.

It is not just about intrusion for classic military effect; it is about a much wider agenda of undercutting Western values, protecting the "Russian way of life," and preparing the way for the Russians to use various lethal means to achieve their objectives short of widespread direct armed conflict. It is about using lethal force to achieve their objectives without triggering a wide-ranging conventional confrontation but being prepared to master escalation control.[4]

The peer fight has little to do with how to manage a slo-mo counterinsurgency control the ground campaign. It is about the right tools, managed in the right way, to achieve escalation control. It is about compressed time operations; it is about understanding that when dealing with nuclear powers, the counterinsurgency model has really no relevance whatsoever.

In this chapter I will address a number of the key factors driving the redesign of U.S. forces to deal with full-spectrum crisis management and escalation control and an ability to engage and prevail in the high-end fight. I will deal with what I think are the most central ones, which will allow one to understand how different the challenges are facing our forces as they transition. It is not an exhaustive or comprehensive list, but in the interviews, which follow in the book, a wide range of such challenges are identified by the Marines I have interviewed over the past two years.

---

4.   http://publication.pravo.gov.ru/Document/View/0001202107030001.

In particular, I will discuss seven elements which highlight the character of the strategic shift, strategic shock or strategic transition. These elements are escalation management, the Command and Control (C^2) piece, the Information, Surveillance, and Reconnaissance (ISR) piece (I prefer this over intelligence, surveillance and reconnaissance), the basing piece, the logistics piece, the training piece and the pace of conflict piece.

It is important to realize that our core adversaries, China and Russia, are engaged in political warfare as well as military operations against us and our allies. Terms like "gray zone conflict" and "hybrid warfare" have been created to explain that our competitors are working to leverage the perceived weaknesses in the liberal democracies and exploit seams within our societies and as well with our alliance relationships.

That is why it is a full-spectrum crisis management set of challenges and not a race to get to World War III as fast as possible and win. At the same time, we live in a world where counterterrorism is a reality, and we have to expend our efforts and use forces and allied working relationships to manage those threats as well. But it is not about occupying territory and building new societies, which then will in the ideal world not breed terrorists. It is about understanding the limits of what we can do and prioritizing core defense tasks and not frittering away our resources leaving us unable to provide for the most salient and significant defense challenges facing the nation and our allies.

Escalation Management

The Russians face three nuclear powers in the West—the United States, France and the United Kingdom—and the United States and its allies face three nuclear powers in the Pacific—China, Russia and North Korea. This means that any peer competitor conflict is embedded in a wider consideration of escalation management, which entails at a minimum shadowboxing with regard to the nuclear warfare dimension. It also means that a number of developments in conventional warfare, such as degrading an adversary's C^2, the excessive use of artificial intelligence decision-making systems and errant use of autonomous systems, can have significant consequences for approaching the nuclear threshold much more rapidly than intended.

One of the legacies of the land wars is that we have a generation of officers who have NEVER had to consider this problem. That legacy is a very negative one. Conventional force modernization needs to be done in such a way that its integration within the real world of dealing with nuclear powers is a sine qua non for shaping a way ahead for deterrence.

What certainly cannot be done is to shape a way ahead with regard to high-end warfare as if it is primarily or solely a conventional engagement. Even a conventional engagement has nuclear consequences, notably with regard to embedded C^2 systems and networks being relied upon in conflict. Notably any U.S. Army or USMC thinking about the way ahead in the Pacific needs to return them to their Cold War roots, where there was no expectation that one could do land engagements without considerations for the overhang of nuclear operations.

As Dr. Paul Bracken, the author of *The Second Nuclear Age* and a noted strategist, put it in a 2018 piece: "The key point for today is that there are many levels of intensity above counterinsurgency and counter terrorism, yet well short of total war. In terms of escalation intensity, this is about one-third up the escalation ladder. Here, there are issues of war termination, disengagement, maneuvering for advantage, signaling, — and yes, further escalation — in a war that is quite limited compared to World War II, but far above the intensity of combat in Iraq and Afghanistan....

"A particular area of focus should be exemplary attacks. Examples include select attack of U.S. ships, Chinese or Russian bases, and command and control. These are above crisis management as it is usually conceived in the West. But they are well below total war. Each side had better think through the dynamics of scenarios in this space. Deep strike for exemplary attacks, precise targeting, option packages for limited war, and command and control in a degraded environment need to be thought through beforehand.

"The Russians have done this, with their escalate to deescalate strategy. I recently played a war game where Russian exemplary attacks were a turning point, and they were used quite effectively to terminate a conflict on favorable terms. In East Asia, exemplary attacks are also important as the ability to track U.S. ships increases.

"Great power rivalry has returned. A wider range of possibilities has opened up. But binary thinking — that strategy is either low intensity or all-out war – has not."[5]

Ed Timperlake and I interviewed Bracken on the challenges of conventional force modernization in the context of engaging with the nuclear powers in conflict. According to Bracken: "When considering how to go after the adversary's C^2 systems with whatever new technology system you have in mind, you have to do so from the standpoint of a broader warfighting strategy that considers how you can exercise escalation control and war termination. From the outset, we need to structure options from an escalation control point of view, rather than simply coming up with conventional options driven by new technologies which are pursued WITHOUT thinking through how such change works for rather than against escalation management…."

"In other words, if we do get into a major conventional conflict with a nuclear power, we want escalation control, we want to get to a point where we can bargain a solution to end the conflict on favorable terms. It is not simply a race to build up new conventional forces built without any consideration of how nuclear weapons are woven into escalation control.

"We agreed that there is need for an ongoing and robust debate about how best to do so, and when new weapons are introduced into the conventional forces, it is crucial to focus on how force structure change augments

---

5.   Paul Bracken, "One-Third Up the Escalation Ladder," *Second Line of Defense* (April 25, 2018), https://sldinfo.com/2018/04/one-third-up-the-escalation-ladder/.

rather than diminishes escalation control. It is not an add on, but an integral part of the force modernization strategic process."[6]

When thinking about reshaping U.S. and allied forces for the Pacific, the nuclear dimension is not an add-on or bolt-on to the strategy; it is an integral part of any credible warfighting strategy. In an April 2020 interview with Dr. Bracken, we discussed the nature of the challenge to do so. According to Bracken: "China is a major nuclear power. And they are one which has missiles of various ranges within the Pacific region. What they have done far exceeds what the Soviet Union had against NATO Europe during the Cold War. With the end of the INF treaty, an end driven in part by Chinese missiles which would have been excluded by an INF treaty if they had been party to it, Beijing's long-range missile threat needs to become a focus of attention, and not just by counter military responses."

The nuclear dimension is too frequently considered by contemporary military strategists as a subject separate from warfighting. As Bracken put it: "It is treated as a problem of two missile farms attacking each other. This perspective overlooks most of the important nuclear issues of our day, and how nuclear arms were really used in the Cold War. It should be remembered that China is the only major power born in a nuclear context. The coming to power of the Communists in China was AFTER the dawn of the nuclear age. And Beijing learned early on the hard realities of a nuclear world. Soviet treatment of Beijing in the Taiwan Straits crises and in the Korean War with regard to nuclear weapons, taught China the bitter lesson that they were on their own. This led directly to China's bomb program....

"When discussing defense strategies, it is crucial to understand the nature of escalation. One of the fundamental distinctions long since forgotten by today's military leaders and in academic studies is the zone of the

---

6.   Robbin Laird and Ed Timperlake, "Conventional Forces and Technology: What Is Their Impact on Escalation Management with Nuclear Powers," *Defense.info* (March 27, 2021), https://defense.info/re-thinking-strategy/2021/03/convention-al-forces-and-technology-what-is-their-impact-on-escalation-manage-ment-with-nuclear-powers/. Also, see, Paul Bracken, *The Second Nuclear Age: Strategy, Danger, and the New Power Politics* (St. Martin's Griffin, 2013).

interior, or ZI. As soon as you hit a target inside the sovereign territory of another country, you are in a different world. From an escalation point of view striking the ZI of an adversary who is a nuclear, crosses a major escalation threshold.

"And there is the broader question of how we are going to manage escalation in a world in which we are pushing forward a greater role for autonomous systems with AI, etc. Will clashes among platforms being driven by autonomous systems lead to crises which can get out of control? We need a military strategy that includes thinking through how to go on alert safely in the various danger zones."

I noted that his point raises a major question for strategy: How to manage military engagements or interactions in the Pacific without spinning crises out of control? How does the nuclear factor weigh in? He underscored: "The first thing is to realize it is woven into the entire fabric of a Pacific strategy. You don't have to fire a nuclear weapon to use it. The existence of nuclear weapons, by itself, profoundly shapes conventional options. The nuclear dimension changes the definition of what a reasonable war plan is for the U.S. military. And a reasonable war plan can be defined as follows: when you brief it to the president, he doesn't throw you out of the office, because you're triggering World War III."[7]

The C² Piece

In today's world, full-spectrum crisis management is not simply about escalation ladders; it is about the capability to operate tailored task forces within a crisis setting to dominate and prevail within that crisis. If that stops the level of escalation, that is one way of looking at it. But in conflict with peer competitors, full-spectrum crisis management is about the ability to operate and prevail within a diversity of crises.

---

7. Robbin Laird, "Paul Bracken on China, Nuclear Weapons, and Pacific Defense," *Defense.info* (April 19, 2020), https://defense.info/interview-of-the-week/paul-bracken-on-china-nuclear-weapons-and-pacific-defense/.

This means that a core legacy from the land wars and Counter-Insurgency (COIN) efforts needs to be jettisoned if we are to succeed—namely, the OODLA loop. This is how the Observe, Orient, Decide and Act, or OODA, loop has worked in the land wars, with the Lawyers in the loop, and hence the OODLA loop. The OODA loop is changing with the new technologies which allow distributed operators to become empowered to decide in the tactical decision-making situation. But the legalistic approach to hierarchical approval to distributed decisions simply will take away the advantages of the new distributed approach and give the advantage to our authoritarian adversaries.[8]

In my recent book *Training for the High-End Fight: The Strategic Shift of the 2020s*, a major element of the shift focused upon was how command changes with the crafting of a distributed but integrated force. The book started by quoting Rear Admiral Manazir, then head of N-9, in an interview which I did with my colleague Ed Timperlake in 2016. "The key task is to create decision superiority. But what is the best way to achieve that in the fluid battlespace we will continue to operate in? What equipment and what systems allow me to ensure decision superiority?

"We are creating a force for distributed fleet operations. When we say distributed, we mean a fleet that is widely separated geographically capable of extended reach. Importantly, if we have a network that shares vast amounts of information and creates decision superiority in various places, but then gets severed, we still need to be able to fight independently without those networks.

"This not only requires significant and persistent training with new technologies but also informs us about the types of technologies we need to develop and acquire in the future. Additionally, we need to have mission orders in place so that our fleet can operate effectively even when networks are disrupted during combat; able to operate in a modular-force approach

---

8.   The concept of the OODLA was developed by my colleague Ed Timperlake.

with decisions being made at the right level of operations for combat success."[9]

The C^2 piece is a key element of reshaping the forces to be able to distribute for geographical reach and being able to operate in flexible sanctuaries to operate within a contested battlespace with a peer competitor. The assumption is that from the outset the peer competitor will seek to disrupt our and our allies' force integration, and C^2 systems are crucial to be able to overcome that threat.

In a March 2021 discussion with industrial expert Mike Twyman, who has worked for many years on the evolving C^2 technologies, we focused on the C^2 part of the strategic shift. We started by discussing how he saw the co-evolution of the command shift with the technological dynamics for enabling technologies in the C^2 domain.

Twyman said, "I love the concept of co-evolution because, what you're seeing now with what the Navy's doing is they're leading with ideas. And they're basically developing the plans and the tactics with existing capabilities. They're integrating the F-35. They're integrating the Triton. They're integrating the P-8. They're integrating all these great capabilities and really, in very novel ways, to build this distributed integrated task force. That's going to be what they go to the fight with today but are positioning themselves for what new technologies can enable down the road."

The C^2 evolution within the strategic shift is Concept of Operations (CONOPS) informed. According to Twyman, "That is a great way of putting it. Co-evolution is a key element of how to understand what is happening in the C^2 domain. In my view, there are three streams of activity shaping the way ahead. The first is how the adversaries are working C^2 for themselves and shaping tools for disruption and contesting the C^2 space. Second, there is what our warfighters are doing to shape operational art and innovation.

---

9.   Robbin Laird and Ed Timperlake, "The Deputy Chief of Naval Operations for Warfare Systems Looks at the Way Ahead: Rear Admiral Manazir on Shaping Kill Webs," *Second Line of Defense* (October 13, 2016), https://sldinfo.com/2016/10/the-deputy-chief-of-naval-operations-for-warfare-systems-look-at-the-way-ahead-rear-admiral-manazir-on-shaping-kill-webs/.

Third, there are the dynamics of change in the C^2 domain globally, such as the emergence of 5G systems. It's really the co-evolution of operational art and technology that leads to new solutions to counter the threat, both today and in the future."

We then discussed what is happening in terms of developments in the C^2 and ISR space. "I see three critical areas that are evolving and offer capabilities which can reinforce and accelerate the shift to the integrated distributed force," Twyman said.

"The first is in the digital domain. Here there is a major shift underway in how the warfighter sees the battlespace and to leverage that vision to deliver decision superiority. I am intrigued by the U.S. Navy establishing MISR (Maritime ISR) officers whose role is to deliver to the maritime force what can be leveraged from the joint and coalition force to get the information to the right place at the right time.[10] Another digital example is the Defense Advanced Research Projects Agency's (DARPA) Adaptive Warfighting Architecture. Here the focus is upon micro-modularity in C^2 and the importance of being able to push processing and decision capabilities to the tactical edge. You need the ability to move the command post as needed to provide for the flexibility to commander where the force is operating in an area of influence. You need flexibility in terms who you can integrate at that point of influence. I like to call it composing the force for a particular mission or effect that you're trying to achieve. DARPA's Adaptive Warfighting Architecture, I think is going to help move that along in the next evolution of capability.

"The second is in the embedded Internet of Things domain. High-performance, secure computing is being brought to the tactical edge. With the evolution of sensor networks, there is a major opportunity to integrate sensor networks into the distributed task force operational approach. With flexible C^2 and ISR systems, one can both pass and integrate information, and get it to the right people to achieve the desired effects.

---

10.   I discussed MISR officers in my book *Training for the High-End Fight*.

"Additionally, there is the coming of artificial intelligence (AI) and machine learning. This is in its infancy for military ISR and C² decision-making. What AI solutions will be part of is strengthening information processing at the edge? What we're going to need to do is more processing at the tactical edge.

Thirdly, with contested environments, driven by the near peer threat, we need the ability to maneuver throughout the spectrum. We're really seeing the importance of protected communications in both the space and aerial network layers, to allow the force to communicate and make necessary connections. Reducing the need to over manage information in centralized centers of decision making is a key element of change."[11]

In other words, a key element of the technological innovations underlying the strategic shift is in the domain of command and control. Here the shift in the command structure leverages technological developments in connectivity as well as how ISR systems can generate information for decision superiority.[12]

The ISR Piece

ISR-led operations are becoming a key part of the reworking of 21st century warfighting, which enables modular task forces to operate at the tactical edge. And to do so with enough information and to make decisions and to be able to continue to operate effectively in their area of responsibility in the battlespace.

But this is ISR better understood as Information, Surveillance and Reconnaissance than as Intelligence, Surveillance and Reconnaissance, where ISR collectors are pushing information to decision makers somewhere else in the battlespace. An example of this shift in focus is highlighted in the U.S.

---

11. Robbin Laird, "C², the Kill Web and Concepts of Operations," *Second Line of Defense* (March 10, 2021), https://sldinfo.com/2021/03/c2-the-kill-web-and-concepts-of-operations/.

12. For more on the evolution of the C² piece in the strategic shift, see "C²/ISR and the Integrated Force," *Defense.info* (August 12, 2020), https://defense.info/highlight-of-the-week/c2-isr-and-the-integrated-distributed-force/.

Navy's Resolute Hunter exercise. I visited the exercise held in November 2020 at NAWDC, or the Naval Aviation Warfighting Development Center, located at Air Wing Fallon near Reno, Nevada.

The exercise was shaped around a crisis management scenario. In a fluid political and combat contested area, where friendly and hostile forces were operating, ISR assets were deployed to provide proactive capabilities to assess that fluid situation. A number of U.S. Navy and USAF assets were deployed along with USMC intelligence capabilities to operate in the crisis scenario.

The assets were working together to assess the fluid situation, but the focus was on fusion in the battlespace by assets operating as decision nodes, not simply as collectors for decision makers elsewhere in the battlespace.

What the exercise was working was the importance of assets being used in a broader ISR lead role which evolving sensor networks can provide, as well as training the operators to both work the networks and consolidate what these asset operators judged to be happening in a fluid battlespace. It was about how ISR and C^2 are evolving within a fluid battlespace with the ISR assets moving from a subordinate role to hierarchical decision-making to becoming key members of the overall tactical process itself.

The joint and coalition aspect of this exercise is a key one. Because of COVID-19 neither the Brits nor the Aussies were there but it is planned that they will be at the next one. This exercise will provide a key input to the Brits working their "integrated operating concept" and the Aussies their fifth-generation warfare approach. The Marines were there in terms of an expeditionary intelligence unit operating with their core equipment which had been delivered by a KC-130J. The package which was deployed could be delivered by CH-53s as well, notably by the new CH-53Ks. I MEF (Marine Expeditionary Force) was part of the pre-planning process and will be there for the next iteration of Resolute Hunter.

This is a walk, run and sprint exercise approach but rooted in the clear understanding that the role of ISR in an integrated distributed force is significantly changing now and accelerating in the future as a diversity of sensor networks are deployed to the battlespace, notably through the expansion of maritime and air remote systems.

Not surprisingly, this is MISR-led exercise. Frankly, until I went to San Diego in February 2020 and met with VADM Miller, the Navy Air Boss, I had never heard of MISR Weapons and Tactics Instructors (WTI). But now NAWDC is training MISR weapons instructors, and they have their own warfighting patch as well. The importance of MISR cannot be understated. As Vice Admiral Miller, the recently retired Navy Air Boss, has put it: "The next war will be won or lost by the purple shirts. You need to take MISR seriously, because the next fight is an ISR-led and enabled fight."

CDR Pete "Two Times" Salvaggio is the head of the MISR Weapons School (MISRWS) and in charge of the Resolute Hunter exercise. MISR prides itself in being both platform and sensor agnostic, along with employing an effects-based tasking and tactics approach that allows for shaping the ISR domain knowledge, which a task force or fleet needs to be fully combat-effective. What is most impressive is that CDR Salvaggio has been present at the creation and is a key part of shaping the way ahead in a time of significant change in what the fleet is being asked to do in both a joint and coalition operational environment.

What is entailed in "Two Times" perspective is a cultural shift. "We need a paradigm shift: The Navy needs to focus on the left side of the kill chain." The kill chain is described as find, fix, track, target, engage and assess (F2T2EA). For the U.S. Navy, the weight of effort has been upon target and engage. As "Two Times" puts it, "But if you cannot find, fix or track something, you never get to target."[13]

There is another challenge as well: in a crisis, knowing what to hit and what to avoid is crucial to crisis management. This clearly requires the kind of ISR management skills to inform the appropriate decision makers as well. The ISR piece is particularly challenging as one operates across a

---

13. Robbin Laird, "Resolute Hunter: Shaping a New Paradigm," *Second Line of Defense* (January 25, 2021), https://sldinfo.com/2021/01/resolute-hunter-shaping-a-new-paradigm/.

multi-domain battlespace to be able to identify the best ISR information, even if it is not contained within the ISR assets and sensors within your organic task force.

And the training side of this is very challenging. That challenge might be put this way: How does one build the skills in the Navy to do what you want to do with regard to managed ISR data and deliver it in the correct but timely manner and how to get the command level to understand the absolute centrality of having such skill sets?

"Two Times" identified a number of key parameters of change with the coming of MISR. "We are finally breaking the old mindset; it is only now that the department heads at NAWDC are embracing the new role for ISR in the fight. We are a unique weapons school organization at NAWDC for we are not attached to a particular platform like Top Gun with the F-18 and F-35. The MISR school has both officers and enlisted WTIs in the team. We are not all aviators; we have intel specialists, we have cryptologists, pilots, aircrew-men etc."

As "Two Times" underscored: "This is the only place within the Navy where we are able to pull all of these ISR assets together to work the collaborative assessment and determination space. (And) we need to take what we have today and make it work more effectively in a collaborative ISR effort."

But to underscore the shift from being the collectors and delivering data to the decision makers, he referred to the goal of the training embodied in the exercise as making the operators in airborne ISR "puzzle solvers." Rather than looking at these airborne teams as the human managers of airborne sensors, "we are training future Jedi Knights."

And to be clear, all of the assets used in the exercise are not normally thought of as ISR platforms but platforms that have significant sensor capabilities. It really was about focusing on sensor networks and sorting through how these platform/networks could best shape an understanding of the evolving mission and paths to mission effectiveness.

The ISR role is expanding and changing. In one sense, the ISR sensor networks with men in the loop can deliver decisions with regard to the nature of the evolving tactical situation, and the kinds of decisions which need to be made in the fluid combat environment. It may be to kill or to adjust judgments about what that battlespace actually signifies in terms of what needs to be done. And given the speed with which kill decisions need to be made with regard to certain classes of weapons, the ISR/C^2 network will operate as the key element of a strike auction.

Which shooter needs to do what at which point in time to degrade the target? How best to determine which element of the shoot sequence—not the kill chain—needs to do what in a timely manner when fighting at the speed of light?

The evolving role of ISR in a contested fluid battlespace also raises the question of rules of engagement. As noted earlier, in the legacy land wars, the rules of engagement were shaped around a certain understanding of the OODA loop, which allowed for the OODLA loop, with the lawyers entering the cycle to determine the validity of a targeting sequence. With ISR systems determining the where and nature of how to execute a mission in a rapidly unfolding battlespace, the need to think through information engagement really pulls apart the inherited notion of rules of engagement as well.

Put another way, there is not going to be a carefully constructed common operating picture for the political-military commanders located far away from the moment of decision with regard to the dynamically unfolding contested battlespace. What the ISR capabilities can deliver are "moments of clarity" about how to deliver decisive actions.

Resolute Hunter is about shaping new capabilities, skill sets, and training for the evolving kill web fighting navy, one embedded in and capable of leading the joint force. It is a question of evolving the relevant skill sets by the ISR teams of operators and decision makers and not some automated network. And a key part of the challenge facing the ISR teams is to understand adversary intent and not misread the red side's ISR actions or chess moves with weapons into the engagement area.

In addition, with the joint and coalition forces. the challenge will be to be able to work together as collaborative teams operating in the battlespace to shape appropriate "moments of clarity" for combat decisions and mission effectiveness. Clearly, Resolute Hunter is an example of how ISR is changing in the context of the strategic shift.

The Basing Piece

In the strategic shift to engage peer competitors, a key concern is to have deployment flexibility in order to reduce the ability of the adversary to destroy force concentrations with their evolving weapons capabilities. This means that basing flexibility is a crucial part of the strategic shift.

The USAF is pursuing agile employment; the Navy is pursuing distributed maritime operations (DMO) and the USMC is adding expeditionary basing to its tool kit of mobile basing capabilities. And together these efforts shape the integrated distributed force, which is emerging from the various reworkings of joint and allied concepts of operations.

As the Navy rethinks how to use its aircraft carriers, how to use its amphibious forces and how to use the whole gamut of its surface and subsurface forces to fight as a fleet, an opportunity for change is clear: why not rework how air assets move across the sea bases to provide the fleet a wider variety of combat capabilities tailored to specific combat scenarios? Notably, moving helicopters and tiltrotor assets across the fleet provide for a wider variety of options than simply having a set piece of equipment onboard each class of ship.

The mobility of the fleet is a baseline capability which the sea base brings to a more agile combat force. Ships provide for presence but mobility at sea, with variable degrees of speed and stealth. But added to this are a range of other mobility capabilities.

The first is the use of land either as protected base from which air assets, manned or unmanned (for that is what weapons are), can operate as reachback forces to enhance the scalability of a modular at sea task force. Or from which the U.S. Army's missile and air defense capabilities can be deployed as part of an integrated air and sea force.

The second revolves around how the Marines can leverage their expeditionary history and capabilities to operate more effectively with the DMO fleet. One way is to enhance how they can operate off of the amphibious fleet to play an expanded role in sea control and sea denial at sea. Rather than looking at the amphibious fleet as providing greyhound buses to jump off to fight at land, the focus is upon how the amphibious fleet today and redesigned into the future can be part of the wider DMO sea control and sea denial mission sets.

A second way is to enhance their capabilities to operate their crisis management integrated forces, such as marine expeditionary units or marine expeditionary brigades to operate from mobile bases. These capabilities have clearly expanded as they are building out the Osprey–F-35B–CH-53K triad. The focus here is upon having an integrated modular force capability survivable and lethal enough to fight as an integrated combat force while operating from distributed bases.

The third way is what the current Commandant has labelled expeditionary basing. This is the Commandant's version of a wider focus by navies on how to deploy an inside force to support the outside force. By the inside force, one is referring to a small force operating inside an adversary's weapons engagement zone.

An example of how one service is relooking at basing within the context of the strategic shift is the USAF. Pacific Air Forces (PACAF) is working the agile employment concept as a key part of shaping the ability of the Air Force to operate across the expanse of the Pacific and to do so in a more survivable mode. When I met General Kenneth Wilsbach, the current PACAF Commander in Australia, he was the commander of 11th Air Force. And during a 2018 Williams Seminar, he discussed the need for what would now be called Agile Combat Employment. I wrote about his assessment in my book on the evolution of Australian Defence strategy published in 2021.

LtGen Kenneth Wilsbach, 11th Air Force Commander, at 2018 Williams Foundation Seminar, Canberra, Australia. March 2018. On his left is Vice Admiral Tim Barrett, then Chief of the Royal Australian Navy. Credit: *Second Line of Defense*.

At the Williams Foundation Seminar in Canberra in March 2018, the 11th Commander, LtGen Kenneth Wilsbach, highlighted the nature of the challenge requiring the shift to mobile basing as follows: "From a USAF standpoint, we are organized for efficiency, and in the high intensity conflict that we might find ourselves in, in the Pacific, that efficiency might be actually our Achilles heel, because it requires us to put massive amounts of equipment on a few bases. Those bases, as we most know, are within the weapons engagement zone (WEZ) of potential adversaries.

"So, the United States Air Force, along with the Australian Air Force, has been working on a concept called, Agile Combat Employment, which seeks to disperse the force, and make it difficult for the enemy to know where you are, when are you going to be there, and how long are you are going to be there.

"We're at the very preliminary stages of being able to do this but the organization is part of the problem for us, because we are very used to, over the last several decades, of being in very large bases, very large organizations, and we stovepipe the various career fields, and one commander is not in charge of the force that you need to disperse. We're looking at this, and determining of how we might reorganize, to be able to employ this concept in the Pacific, and other places."[14]

Now PACAF Commander, Wilsbach has made this a core effort. During my visit to PACAF in August 2021, I had a chance to discuss with Brigadier General Michael Winkler, Director of Strategic Plans, Requirements and Programs at the Pacific Air Forces, the evolving USAF approach to basing.

This is how BGen Winkler underscored the effort: "PACAF has done a pretty decent job over the last three years of getting the Air Force to embrace this idea of agile combat operations and to export it to Europe as well. The whole idea, if you rewind the clock to the mid 80s, early 90s, was that every single base in the United States Air Force that was training for conflict would do an exercise where you'd run around in chemical gear. At that point in time, there was a large chemical biological threat, and the Air Force recognized that it needed to be able to survive and operate in that chemical threat. So, we trained to it.

"I think the new version of that chemical biological threat is the anti-access area denial umbrella. The idea of agile combat employment is our capability to survive and operate and keep combat momentum underneath the adversary's anti-access area denial umbrella. Basically, we are focusing on our ability to survive and operate in a contested environment.

"PACAF has taken a realistic approach that is fiscally informed because it would be very difficult for us to go try to build multiple bases with 10,000-foot runways, and dorms, and ammunition storage all over the Pacific. What we've done instead is concentrated on a hub and spoke mentality, where you build a base cluster. That cluster has got a hub that provides quite a bit of logistic support to these different spoke airfields. The spokes are more expeditionary than most folks in the Air Force are used to.

"The expeditionary airfield is a spoke or a place that we operate from. It's not 10,000 feet of runway, it's maybe 7,000 feet. We're probably not going to have big munitions storage areas, there's probably going to be weapons

---

14.   Robbin Laird, *Joint by Design: The Evolution of Australian Defence Strategy* (2021), chapter six.

carts that have missiles on them inside of sandbags bunkers. And we're going to look a lot more like a Marine Expeditionary base than your traditional big Air Force base. It'll be fairly expeditionary."

We then discussed the challenge of reducing the number of USAF personnel necessary to sustain air operations, along the lines which the Marines have focused upon. "The Military Occupational Specialties (MOS) challenge is a very real problem for us. And I think we're starting to figure out how we're going to get around that. We're calling it multi-capable airman, where we do some degree of cross training. So, your average crew chief now can actually do other flight line tasks like load missiles, and vice versa, your fuels folks actually can do some minor maintenance tasks. It is very much more along the lines of the USMC model. The goal is to have airmen do more things, which then means we don't need to deploy as many of them to one location to still get the job done. And then, we'll work a logistics schema maneuver from the hubs to the spokes to do the things you'd mentioned previously, the fuel resupply, the munitions resupply, any other expendables."[15]

Basing and the appropriate ecosystem to support agile employment are key challenges which would complement the reinforced fixed basing being undergone in the region as well. Clearly, agile employment cannot be the dominant operational approach for the USAF, but it is a toolset giving it greater survivability and lethality.

The Logistics Piece

The basing piece certainly highlights how dramatically the change is from the land wars to full-spectrum crisis management against peer competitors. Defending fixed bases during the land wars was always a concern, but what was not of concern were peer competitor air and naval strikes against such installations.

---

15.   Robbin Laird, "Shaping a Way Ahead for Pacific Defense: The Evolving Role of the USAF," *Second Line of Defense* (September 21, 2021), https://sldinfo. com/2021/09/shaping-a-way-ahead-for-pacific-defense-the-evolving-role-of-the-usaf/.

And no greater gap between the land war era and the new one is to be seen than in the logistics era. The U.S. Army built large scale supply depots, which functioned in effect as WALMARTS to support the force. All of the services had significant depots in the area. Commercial services such as container ships and FedEx could bring supplies in a steady stream. The services could even rely on just-in-time logistics to provide for parts that needed to be replaced.

In the fluid battlespace, supplying a distributed force is a very different challenge. Logistics is a weapon system; if you do not have supplies delivered to the right platform at the right time in combat, the ability of that force to achieve its objectives is seriously compromised.

The core challenge is for pre-positioned equipment and supplies along with the various forms of lift—ground, sea and air—to be positioned to resupply rapidly in the context of conflict. For the sea base, how can the Military Sealift Command provide support in a contested environment? How best to use the tanking and lift assets of the USAF and how to defend them in a contested environment? How do the mobile land forces, which both the Marines and Army can adapt to more rapid movement, do so and be sustained?

The Australian Defence Force has been working significantly on force integration for a number of years around a concept of building a fifth-generation force. I am a research fellow at the Williams Foundation in Canberra, Australia, and have written the seminar reports for the foundation since 2014, usually two a year.

In the second seminar in 2019, the focus was upon "the requirements for fifth generation manoeuvre." A leading logistics thinker and officer in the Australian Army, then LtCol David Beaumont, then Commanding Officer and Chief Instructor at Australian Army School of Logistics Operations and now Col Beaumont, head of the Australian Army Research Centre, highlighted the challenges of providing logistics in the context of the strategic shift.

According to Beaumont: "Fifth generation manoeuvre is about accelerating the speed to deliver the desired combat effect through a greatly improved decision-making process. It's important that this speed is felt across the force and not just in the combat forces. As we build a force structure capable of this speed, we must ask how best can we sustain the pace? How do we direct this combat power where and when it is needed, with the resources it needs to win?

"The promise of speed requires will inevitably create a significant logistics demand. Thinking simplistically, sustaining operations at a higher speed tempo will require a greater fuel and munitions supply, repair parts etc. We will need to ensure that we can surge those stocks to the engagement force either by ensuring the force is mobile from existing bases, or with an operational force posture that leverages, or accesses supply closer to the combat zone.

"This will require a significant rethink to Australian strategy, where military forces might be based, where they might 'stage' their operations from, and how the force prepares itself more broadly. Assured supply will be key to this. This particularly applies to contingency stocks, and the supply chain that supports the force when it is in combat.

"When we are facing a crisis, it is inevitable that partners who are using the same combat systems will be putting demand on the stocks and the supply chain. Maximizing self-reliance is key. And, of course, it is not hard to see that adversaries will seek to disrupt our supply chains as part of their approach to crisis dominance.

"Our operational tempo will reduce with every interdiction. And this raises the significant question of the tradeoffs between the stocks and supplies you need to deal with short warning crisis and the investments in the force itself. How to manage the tradeoff between sustainability and buying and building your platforms for the force is a significant management challenge?"

In effect, what Beaumont was focusing on was the question of the durability of the force, i.e., the ability of the force to operate long enough to prevail in a crisis situation. Logistics is a weapon system in such an effort.[16]

The Training Piece

As my colleague Ed Timperlake often reminds me, the legendary Admiral Arleigh Burke underscored that training started with the core requirement, "know your platform." Training clearly must start with ensuring that the warrior knows how to fight effectively from the ground up with the platform he operates from.

But in today's training, knowing your platform is clearly not enough. What the U.S. military is shaping is a distributed but integratable force. They are taking their resources, dispersing them and operating with a mix-and-match modular task force capability. Learning to fight with a distributed force is part of the new training challenge. Being able to cross-link platforms within evolving task force packages is another part of the challenge.

In a 2020 interview with Lt. Jonathan Gosselin, a P-8 Weapons and Tactics Instructor at the Maritime Patrol Reconnaissance Weapons School, during a visit to Jax Navy, the challenge of learning cross-platform targeting was highlighted as an example of the new training challenge posed by shaping maritime kill webs. When he first deployed, the P-8 was an anomaly. Now it is deployed to all of the Combatant Commanders (COCOMS) worldwide.

The P-8 global fleet provides ISR, ASW and Surface Warfare products to the combatant commanders. In his current position, Lt. Gosselin serves as an innovation, cross-functional team lead where he works with innovation experts, defense industry and the Navy to shape projects which are then generated for implementation by industry. He works on process changes as well, where advances in tactics, techniques, and procedures (TTPs) can be enabled.

---

16.   Robbin Laird, *Joint by Design: The Evolution of Australian Defence Strategy* (December 24, 2020), Chapter Seven, https://sldinfo.com/books/joint-by-design-the-evolution-of-australian-defence-strategy/.

For Lt. Gosselin, at the heart of the effort is really understanding, training for and executing third-party targeting. He argued that moving from a stove-piped mentality, where one is both the sensor and the shooter, to a kill-web perspective, where the P-8 could provide the sensors for a firing solution, or whether the P-8 would deliver a weapon provided by another asset to perform the firing solution, is at the heart of the change.

In effect, dynamic targeting across a distributed integrated force is the goal. As Lt. Gosselin put it, "We're talking about taking targeting data from one domain and quickly shifting to another, just like that. I have killed a target under sea. I am now going to go ahead and work the surface target and being able to understand the weapon-sensor pairing network and being able to call in fires from different entities using commander's intent to engage the target. That's what we're trying to do. Get our operators to understand that it is not just a one-piece answer. There may be a time when you have to transfer the action to another shooter."

To do so, he is engaging significantly with the Triton squadron as well to shape a way ahead for kill-web dynamic targeting.[17] Lt. Gosselin noted: "With the P-8 and Triton we are able to expand our envelope of Situational Awareness (SA). We can take that and now take the baseline concepts from what the P-3 did and apply them to a more advanced tactics, techniques, and procedures in the form of integrating with the B-21, the B-1, the F-18's, the F-35 joint strike fighter in a dynamic targeting kill web."

And with regard to the cultural shift, this is what he added: "It's important to talk not about how can I defeat this target, but really it should be, how can we defeat this target? Let's break ourselves out of this stovepipe and understand that I may not always be the best shooter. I may be the best sensor, but I'm not be the best shooter."[18]

---

17.   For a look at the Triton and its evolving operational role for the U.S. Navy, see Robbin Laird, "Triton and Orbit Con-Ops," *Defense.info* (May 31, 2020), https://defense.info/defense-systems/triton-and-orbit-con-ops/.

18.   Robbin Laird, "O.K. I am a P-8 Operator: But How Do I Train to Work in a Kill Web," *Second Line of Defense* (June 29, 2020), https://sldinfo.com/2020/06/o-k-i-am-a-p-8-operator-but-how-do-i-train-to-work-in-a-kill-web/.

With the development of flexible multi-mission platforms, there is an ability to flex between offensive and defensive operations within the distributed battlespace. It is clearly challenging to operate such a force and delegate decision-making at the tactical edge, and still be able to ensure strategic and area-wide tactical decision-making.

The strategic thrust of integrating modern systems is to create a grid that can operate in an area as a seamless whole, able to strike or defend simultaneously. This is enabled by the evolution of C^2 and ISR systems. By shaping an evolving ISR-enabled C^2 system inextricably intertwined with platforms and assets, which provide for kill-web integratable forces, an attack and defense enterprise can operate to deter aggressors and adversaries or to conduct successful military operations.

How do you train to do this effectively? Part of the answer is given by training through exercises and then proliferating lessons learned from exercises back into the evolving training regime. But the nature of the systems being built and integrated into the force creates another problem. Systems like the F-35 outpace and outreach physical training space. And shaping a kill-web approach to cross-linking platforms to deliver the desired crisis management or combat effect needs to be part of training as well. How much do you want to show the adversary in exercises? And if you do not do that training in an exercise, where are you doing so?

Air Marshal (Retired) Geoff Brown put that challenge succinctly in an interview I did with him in 2019. "I believe it's safe to say it is impossible to deny an adversary entirely of the ability to shape aspects of the information environment, whether it's through spoofing or sabotaging ICT-based warfighting systems. As a result, our goal should be to sustain military operations in spite of a denied, disrupted, or subverted information environment."

He underscored the challenge this way: "The requirement is that warfighters need to be able to fight as an integrated whole in and through an increasingly contested and complex battlespace saturated by adversary cyber and information operations. But how to do this so that we are shaping our con-ops but not sharing them with an adversary in advance of operations?

The battle for information control needs to drive our training needs much more than it does at the moment. We need to provide warfighters with the right kind of combat learning."

We then discussed current approaches such as at Red Flag and how we might change the approach to get closer to the kill-web capability. "During large-scale exercises like Red Flag, cyber training is often employed in parallel with traditional kinetic training programs and is not fully integrated. Non-cyber war fighters do not necessarily experience the effects of 'cyber play' while it is ongoing.

"When cyber effects are integrated into live training events, my experience is that they are often 'white carded.' Although this does provide war fighters some insight into how their systems or platforms may be affected in the event of a cyberattack, the lack of realism precludes them from experiencing and subsequently troubleshooting that attack."

He cautioned that there are good reasons why this is not done. "The integration of these effects into a live training environment could sabotage the other goals of the exercise, present safety risks to war fighters, and reveal platform vulnerabilities to inquisitive adversaries." In spite of the limitation, "these live training challenges can't preclude us from training for a future contested and complex battlespace."

He argued, "We definitely need to train as we fight—so we need to develop tactical level cyber and information effects for simulators and to develop adversary cyber and info effects into our evolving concepts of operations." In other words, Brown argued that live training remains very significant for organizing a strike and defense force and working the physical pieces of the task force or air group. But the virtual world is now a key area in which you will shape, work on and exercise your information force concepts of operations.

"One of the foundational assumptions I've always had is that high quality live training is an essential to producing high-quality warfighters, but I believe that's changed. Even if you don't take cyber into account and look at an aircraft like an F-35 with the AESA radar and fusion capabilities, the reality of how we will fight has changed dramatically.

"In the world of mechanically scanned array radars, a 2v 4 was a challenging exercise—now as we have moved more towards AESAs where it is not track while you scan, but its search while track, it's very hard to challenge these aircraft in the live environment. And to be blunt about it, the F-35 and, certainly the F-35 as an integrated force, will only be fully unleashed within classified simulations. This means that we will achieve the best training outcomes for aircraft like the F-35 only if we have a more comprehensive virtual environment."[19]

The training function is facing significant challenges to be effective and realistic and to ensure that the joint and coalition forces leverage the full capability inherent in the force, rather than prioritizing what platforms do in stove pipes with whatever organic capability is on that particular platform. Training is becoming redefined as a driver of combat development and platform changes in the context of evolving concepts of operations and tactics. With the new generation of software upgradeable platforms, training driving combat development is part of then rewriting code and determining how platforms can cross-link and operate more effectively as flexible modular task forces.

In a discussion with Paul Averna from Cubic Mission and Performance Solutions, who is an experienced naval aviator and who has worked on training systems for many years, the role of training in the strategic shift was highlighted. Averna highlighted some key features of the skill sets required for training in the new strategic environment. The first is the team nature of delivering the desired combat effect. According to Averna: "Force capability is taking the key elements of the force and blending them together to deliver the desired effect at the right time and the right level. And to be able to

---

19.   Robbin Laird, "From Legacy Training to Training a Crisis Management Force: 5th Gen and the Kill Web," *Second Line of Defense* (April 4, 2019), https://sldinfo.com/2019/04/from-legacy-training-to-training-a-crisis-management-force-5th-gen-and-the-kill-web/.

anticipate reactions from the red side, and to evaluate how the red side has been impacted by the combat effect delivered."

The challenge is to not only work proficiently with one's platform but also be able to work in an integrated, coherent, mutually supportive manner in delivering the desired combat effect while staying inside the reactive enemy's ability to respond. The peer fight revolves around the competition to disrupt each side's ability to aggregate, integrate and deliver effects enabled by secure C^2 and ISR networks.

The use of joint and coalition exercises as a training venue is a key part as well. The goal of exercises expressed in training is to demonstrate to adversaries the blue side's capabilities to operate effectively in the high-end fight. As Averna put it, "Training is a lever for the combatant commander because he is able selectively to demonstrate that he can deliver effects when and where he wants with a team which is both U.S. forces and coalition in character.

"Understanding how rapidly to integrate and deliver multi-domain effects, particularly when those capabilities are distributed is a critical feature of the needed skill set. For the last 20+ years we have had the luxury of conducting operations at will from a persistent sanctuary. This battlespace sanctuary afforded us the time and space to observe, target, mass effects, and assess results in a manner with little concern for the threat's ability to disrupt, degrade, or otherwise hold us at risk.

"When facing a peer threat, we will have to consider how to create sanctuaries dynamically in both space and time as a precursor to or in conjunction with our afore mentioned operations. That adversary will work to constrict or pressure the blue side 'sanctuary' understood as a maneuver force."

How to aggregate effective force within dynamic sanctuaries? Operating within sanctuaries to be able to generate force to get a desired combat or crisis management effect requires integration of non-kinetic and kinetic capabilities and an ability to operate with resilient and effective C^2 and ISR connectivity. A significant part of the fight as the blue side sanctuaries operate as a maneuver force is keeping combat integrity and disrupting the peer competitor's ability to fight while maintaining signature control and superior understanding of the environment.

Another core skill set is to be able to deliver effective dynamic targeting.[20] As Averna put it, "A key challenge for operations in the sanctuary context is to be able to develop effective targeting. The goal here may not be to destroy kinetically, but to disrupt, and disaggregate the adversary's ability to fight. It is not just a classic kill chain; it is dynamic targeting within a kill web."

As Averna highlighted, "I may not want to destroy, I may want to just disrupt and degrade him long enough for the crisis management situation to de-escalate. This is a huge problem for lots of the people I've talked to who are still thinking the goal of the kill chain is a kinetic kill. And in an all-out war, I get that. But if we're really talking about is crisis management and controlling the escalation, we need to train for cross domain effects appropriate to control the crisis."

An additional set of required skills is learning how to operate your platform within the context of flexible and agile modular task forces. Rather than working a set piece task force, the platform operator needs to become accustomed to working in almost Lego block-like task forces which may well contain ground, air, space, cyber, and maritime elements to deliver the desired combat or crisis management effect.

As Averna noted: "We are now able to aggregate information from a variety of air, sea, land, and space platforms to give us a better picture of what's going on in the environment and to shape effectively the grand scheme of maneuver and leverage capabilities such as the electronic order of battle that will determine the limits of my operational sanctuary? How quickly can I aggregate capabilities and deliver the desired effect, and then measure whether or not I was successful in delivering that effect?"

---

20.   Robbin Laird, "The Strategic Shift and Dynamic Targeting: Meeting the Challenge," *Second Line of Defense* (May 28, 2020), https://sldinfo. com/2020/05/the-strategic-shift-and-dynamic-targeting-meeting-the-chal-lenge/.

Another key skill set is to operate in a C^2 environment where the decisions to be taken at both the tactical edge and at the strategic level operate in a very fluid and dynamic way. On the one hand, tactical decision making at the edge is being empowered by new capabilities such as F-35 wolfpacks. On the other hand, C^2 at a more strategic level is crucial to shape the deployment (long lead time) tasks and evaluate overall combat effects.

How do we train to ensure effective decision making at the tactical edge and a strategic level as well? The C^2 and ISR revolution we are now facing is reversing the logic of platforms to infrastructure; it is now about how flexible C^2 and available ISR systems can inform the force elements to shape interactive combat operations on the fly. That is, the new capabilities are enabling tactical decision-making at the edge and posing real challenges to traditional understandings of how information enables decision-making.

It is about learning how to fight effectively at the speed of the network to achieve combat dominance. This obviously requires rethinking considerably the nature of decision-making and the viability of the classic notion of the OODA loop. If the machines are fusing data or doing the Observe and Orient (OO) function, then the Decide and Act (DA) part of the equation becomes transformed, notably if done in terms of decision-making at the tactical edge. The decisions at the edge will drive a reshaping of the information about the battlespace because actors at the tactical edge are recreating the information environment itself. In effect, chaos theory becomes a key element of understanding of what C^2 at the tactical edge means in terms of the nature of the fleeting information in a distributed combat space itself.

The new C^2 and ISR infrastructure enables new warfighting approaches which need to be shaped, exercised, and executed, and in turn affect how the forces train for the high-end fight. How indeed do you train these skill sets? By focusing on the sanctuary concept, Averna explained that C^2 operating within a sanctuary or managing several operational sanctuaries is a core capability which needs to be built, trained for and evolved as well. According to Averna, "Who's going to be the battle commander and be able to have the confidence that they have the full picture of information. In some cases, the

F-35 may have better situational awareness than say on the E-2 or the Wedgetail. Who's going to make that call?"[21]

In an interview which Ed Timperlake and I did with LtCol (Retired) "Juice" Newton, a combat veteran, test pilot and airpower expert, he highlighted the nature of the impact of the kill web on skill sets for combat dominance. What is required is the capability to dominate an adversary through distributed engagement. Such a capability allows the blue side to multiply the effects which they can have for the time necessary to gain tactical and strategic advantage over the red side. And by gaining a key advantage, then leveraging that advantage for escalation control and dominance.

For example, by gaining control of spectrum through distributed kill-web engagements, a force may freeze the adversary's ability to detect and respond. In other words, that force can blind and dominate that force for critical periods of time.

Mission command guides a diversity of modular task forces which deploy into the areas of interest and provide engagement density. Sensor networks and C^2 enable the modular task force to execute its mission and to do assessments to ensure that the mission effect is being achieved. How do you train to shape such an outcome? How do you learn to use the evolving sensor networks, to make C^2 decisions rapidly enough to shape the desired combat effect and to have rapid battle damage assessment to ensure that they dynamics of the combat situation are working in your advantage?[22]

In short, the challenge of preparing and engaging in full-spectrum crisis management requires new skill sets and capabilities. The training challenge is to work effective ways to shape such skill sets and capabilities and interactively evolve with real world combat experiences.

21.　The quotes from Averna are taken from Robbin Laird, "Training Skill Sets and the High-End Fight," *Defense.info* (July 21, 2021), https://defense.info/re-shaping-defense-security/2021/07/training-skill-sets-and-the-high-end-fight/.

22.　Ed Timperlake and Robbin Laird, "Kill Webs, Engagement Density and Escalation Management," *Defense.info* (April 26, 2021), https://defense.info/re-shaping-defense-security/2021/04/kill-webs-engagement-density-and-escalation-management/.

The Pace of Conflict Piece

Underlying the strategic shift is a significant shift in the speed of combat and the core challenge of managing interactive disruption being delivered in that combat by both sides. Ed Timperlake has highlighted that the strategic shift indeed highlights the need to be able to fight at the speed of light. As Timperlake has put it: "After two decades of the land wars, we need to learn to fight again in higher intensity operations. We need to fight at the speed of light. This requires that a fighting force at all levels must take advantages of ever-increasing technological advances to make decisions using the speed of light.

"In other words, symbolically as the laws of theoretical physics are evolving, the test is the application phase or the success of the applied physics phase, so to speak. Nothing illustrates this more than E=MC squared to the atomic bombs that ended WWII. With advances in all forms of 'tron' war from directed energy, to cloud computing to artificial intelligence to robust encryption, many building block mathematical algorithms are now assisting the process of generating accurate and timely information in making the step from being theoretical to applied.

"At the moment battle begins, command and control are essential and has to have several attributes. First and foremost, accurate information has to flow through robust redundant systems at the speed of light in making everything come together to fight and win. The infantry platoon commander trusts the training and combat effectiveness of each Marine to do the right thing using initiative in following orders in the heat of battle while also trusting higher commands to provide supporting arms, including air, to get it right and at the right time. The communication and intelligence capability in this 21st Century evolution/revolution of global coms is the connective tissue for human decisions with how to conduct successful operations and to use payloads effectively at the speed of light."[23]

---

23.   Ed Timperlake, "Fighting at the Speed of Light: Making It All Work," *Second Line of Defense* (May 20, 2019), https://sldinfo.com/2019/05/ fighting-at-the-speed-of-light-making-it-all-work/.

The speed of the strike force is accelerating with the coming of systems like hypersonic cruise missiles. The response to the speed of an attacker is to shape an offensive–defensive enterprise which can deploy in a distributed manner but strike and defend (sword and shield) with an integrated effect. This means that correct information delivered to the right shooter at the right time with the right information is a key aspect of high-end warfighting.

The role of the digital warriors becomes a key part of the strategic shift because disruption of information flows, or information operations become a central part of the new warfighting paradigm. This includes cyber war, electronic warfare, digital spoofing and information dominance as key elements of the shift away from the relatively slo-mo war of the counterinsurgency campaigns.

Brigadier General Michael Winkler described one aspect of the challenge being faced: "We are working towards enhanced integratabilty in the force. A game changing capability is based on ensuring that every sensor out there is connected to a network, and that network shares information with everybody that we allow access to it. And we would want to make sure that all of our allies and partners have access to that network.

"Certainly, all the U.S. forces forward deployed would have access to that network, as well. We've got a lot of work to get from where we are today actually being able to build that capability, but that's one of the things that we need to redouble efforts on. Access to the right information is going to be the key to the next conflict. I also think that both parties in the next conflict will probably be trying to prevent the other country from being able to have an information advantage."[24]

The speed of combat is joined by the speed with which crises emerge and need to be managed. In part this is about the significant reduction in warning time with regard to crises or combat engagements. In an important 2021 paper by Australians Paul Dibb and Richard Brabin-Smith, the authors address the question of the impact of reduced warning time upon Australian

---

24.   "Shaping a Way Ahead for Pacific Defense."

Defence and security.[25] This comes from both the nature of the Chinese challenge and the changing nature of threats, such as cyberattacks. How best to defend Australia in an environment with reduced warning time?

Although obviously about Australia, the discussion in the report raises a broader set of questions of how to know when an event is setting in motion a chain of events which provide a direct threat to a liberal democratic nation and how to respond; it also raises the question of shaping capabilities which can be inserted into a crisis early enough to provide confidence in an ability to have effective escalation management tools available.

The question of an ability to move force rapidly to a crisis becomes increasingly significant as escalation control returns as a key element of constraining, managing and protecting one's interests in a crisis. This is why I have preferred to focus on full-spectrum crisis management as the challenge facing the liberal democracies in meeting the challenges of 21st century authoritarian powers, rather than simply preparing for the high-end fight.

They underscored that new digital technologies have altered the question of what warning time is all about. Notably, with regard to the cyber threats, when is there an attack, and what does it mean? As the authors note: "A campaign of cyberattack and intensified cyber-exploitation against Australia could be launched with little notice, given the right level of motivation, and would have the advantage of having at least a level of plausible deniability while imposing limits to what might be envisaged as a proportional response. Such response options available to Australia would include retaliation, such as a government-sanctioned cyberattack—a capability that the Australian Government has acknowledged that it has. (This capability has already been used against terrorists, but whether it's been used more widely isn't publicly known.)

"The warning time for the need to conduct such operations is potentially very short, meaning that there needs to be a high level of preparedness,

---

25.   Paul Dibb and Richard Brabin-Smith, "Deterrence through Denial: A Strategy for an Era of Reduced Warning Time" (ASPI, May 2021), https://s3-ap-south-east-2.amazonaws.com/ad-aspi/2021-05/Reduced%20warning%20time.pdf?I.oKvvZ9nT15GsOutK4qGWVLApGbC5s7.

including the ability quickly to expand the cyber workforce (with a concomitant need for expedited security clearances), and cyberattack campaigns that are thought out well in advance. There's a strong argument that such planning should include within its scope the possibility of causing high levels of damage to the adversary's infrastructure."

This is a long way from the world of the land wars in the Middle East and requires more than a mindset change. It is about a strategic redesign of how the force operates and the civilian leadership's comprehension of what needs to be done for escalation control and crisis management.

Shaping a Way Ahead

This new phase might be called shaping, exercising and building an integrated distributed force. This entails interactive technological, force structure and geographical deployment dynamic. This is a key part of the effort to shape a full-spectrum crisis management capability whose con-ops is shaped to deal with adversary operations within what some call the "gray zone" or within what has been labelled by some as the "hybrid warfare" engagement area.

For example, in my discussions with Brigadier General Michael Winkler in Hawaii in August 2021, he highlighted the importance of the USAF being able to contribute across the conflict spectrum, precisely because deterrence works only if demonstrated power is engaged from the lower to higher ends of conflict. He noted: "The more we build out our phase zero peacetime capabilities, the more we organize, train and equip our force right now to be able to have that information advantage. We need to continue to practice those tactics, techniques and procedures in phase zero, as we're doing normal training operations, or even normal real-world operations in phase zero. Every single HADR event is an opportunity to shape a mixed force that can then share that same type of data. I think that using those training reps as an opportunity to better build our joint interagency situational awareness is definitely a step in the right direction."[26]

---

26. "Shaping a Way Ahead for Pacific Defense."

Crisis Management Force Structure

From Presence to Conflict Dominance Force

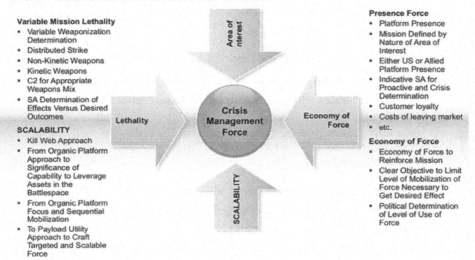

Variable Mission Lethality
- Variable Weaponization Determination
- Distributed Strike
- Non-Kinetic Weapons
- Kinetic Weapons
- C2 for Appropriate Weapons Mix
- SA Determination of Effects Versus Desired Outcomes

SCALABILITY
- Kill Web Approach
- From Organic Platform Approach to Significance of Capability to Leverage Assets in the Battlespace
- From Organic Platform Focus and Sequential Mobilization
- To Payload Utility Approach to Craft Targeted and Scalable Force

Presence Force
- Platform Presence
- Mission Defined by Nature of Area of Interest
- Either US or Allied Platform Presence
- Indicative SA for Proactive and Crisis Determination
- Customer loyalty
- Costs of leaving market
- etc.

Economy of Force
- Economy of Force to Reinforce Mission
- Clear Objective to Limit Level of Mobilization of Force Necessary to Get Desired Effect
- Political Determination of Level of Use of Force

Area of Interest

Lethality **Crisis Management Force** *Economy of Force*

SCALABILITY

This graphic conceptualizes the evolving nature of crafting a 21st century crisis management force able to operate across the spectrum of warfare. Credit: *Second Line of Defense*.

What is unfolding is that capabilities traditionally associated with high-end warfare are being drawn upon for lower threshold conflicts, ones that are designed to achieve political effect without firing a shot. Higher end capabilities being developed by China and Russia are becoming tools to achieve political-military objectives throughout the diplomatic engagement spectrum. This means that the liberal democracies not only need to shape more effective higher end capabilities, but they also need to learn how to use such force packages as part of overall crisis management.

What changes with the integrated distributed ops approach is what a presence force can now mean. Historically, the presence force has been about what organically can be included within that presence force; now we are looking at reach or scalability of a force operating in terms of its effects on an area of interest. Economy of force is a key attribute of a scalable force as well. The presence force, however small, needs to be well integrated but not just in terms of itself but also its ability to operate via C^2 or ISR connectors to an enhanced capability.

But that enhanced capability needs to be deployed in order to be tailorable to the presence force and to provide enhanced lethality and effectiveness appropriate to the political action needed to be taken. This rests really on a significant rework of network accessibility for C^2 in order for a distributed force to have the flexibility to operate not just within a limited geographical area but also to expand its ability to operate by reaching beyond the geographical boundaries of what the organic presence force is capable of doing by itself.

This requires multi-domain situational awareness -- this is not about the intelligence community running its precious space-based assets and hoarding material. This is about looking for the coming confrontation which could trigger a crisis and the SA capabilities airborne, at sea and on the ground would provide the most usable SA monitoring.

This is not "actionable intelligence." This is about shaping force domain knowledge to anticipate events. What is required is tailored force packaging and an ability to take advantage of what the new military technologies and platforms can provide in terms of multi-domain delivery by a smaller force rather than a large air–sea enterprise which can only fully function if unleashed in sequential waves.

It is clear that connectivity for a distributed force is a foundational element; it is also clear that such connectivity must be secure and able to operate in peer-to-peer conflict and is capable of being multi-domain and operated by air, sea and ground elements in an interactive and distributed combat environment.

But it is equally clear that we are not talking about traditional C^2 as understood in the world of legacy combat radios or as evidenced in the period of the land wars. We are talking about being able to operate at the speed of light and to make decisions at the tactical edge and to do so while engaged in operations and to generate responses while still engaged, rather than relying on reachback intelligence evaluators and decision makers.

CHAPTER TWO:

THE MARINE CORPS IN THE STRATEGIC SHIFT

The USMC has been preparing its transition away from the land wars significantly before the termination of the Afghan operation. It began with the Osprey transition coupled with the return to the sea in the Bold Alligator exercises. It continued with the F-35 transition, which, like the Osprey transition, is still going on, as the aircraft evolves and with them concepts of operation with the joint and coalition forces.

The next transition revolves around basing and projecting power more flexibly into the adversary's weapons engagement zone (WEZ). This entails adding new expeditionary basing capabilities to the tool kit for the USMC.

The Marines are working to shape a force of greater range and speed, able to operate flexibly across sea, mobile and expeditionary bases. And as the Marines are really at the vortex of U.S. Navy and USAF transitions, they interact with and feed into those transitions.

The Marines, unlike the U.S. Army, are not primarily a land force. They are not only the nation's crisis management force but are also built as a multi-domain force. As warfighting shifts towards more emphasis on multi-domain operations, the Marines have unique traditions and capabilities to fight as a multi-domain force. What is required is to draw up the transition started with the Osprey and Bold Alligator and build on those dynamics to prioritize what skill sets were highlighted and underscored by that pairing as a launch point in their Marines approach to the strategic shift.

In this chapter, I will address the core phases of transition and then consider their convergence on a transformation approach associated with the strategic shift. Throughout the rest of the book, the interviews I have done with Marines provide very specific examinations of the transition challenge and approach being worked within the Marine Corps itself at the operational levels.

The following graphic highlights the nature of the USMC transition within the strategic shift which I am focusing on in this chapter:

USMC Transformation, 2007-2021

Working Integratability with the Joint and Coaltion
Forces in the New Age of Multi-Domain Warfare

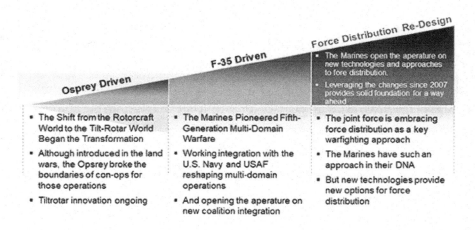

This graphic conceptualizes the transformation path of the USMC which began with the introduction of the Osprey in 2007. Credit: *Second Line of Defense.*

The Tiltrotor-Driven Transition

When the Osprey was introduced into combat in September 2007, the Marines could have simply replaced the CH-46 with another rotary aircraft for the land wars, but they did not. They went down a revolutionary path and introduced a completely new and unique warfighting capability, namely, the Osprey. With its speed and range, the Osprey could take Marines throughout the extended battlespace and to operate with an agility and flexibility no rotorcraft can deliver.

Or put another way, because the Marines fight on the land but are not primarily a land-based force, they put in play an asset which could take them rapidly and at distances that could allow them to fight from the sea, at land and throughout littorals and which broke the limitations of what rotorcraft possess. They were working the land wars but already shaped capabilities which were beyond the limitations of rotorcraft-limited operations.

During the first five years of its employment, the Osprey was introduced first into Iraq and then began operating in Afghanistan. Early deployments were challenging in terms of support and taking the steps to begin to learn the transition from a helo-enabled assault force to a tiltrotor assault force.

And at sea, this learning would take the USN-USMC team to rethink the deployment of the classic three-ship formation of the Amphibious Ready Group-Marine Expeditionary Unit (ARG-MEU) and to move the ships further away from one another, and to expand the operational engagement area of the ARG-MEU. It was used for assault operations from the beginning but over time, the role would expand as the support structure matured, readiness rates grew and airplane availability became increasingly robust.

The Osprey's speed and range meant that the very large number of forward operating bases, which rotorcraft require, were not needed, and this became crucial as the drawdown in Afghanistan occurred. And this would lead to the Osprey being tasked with the Army's medevac mission, as the golden hour could NOT be met by the Army with the drawdown of bases. The Marines were tasked to provide for this capability because of their ability to cover Afghanistan without numerous Forward Operating Bases (FOBs).

When Odyssey Dawn entered the picture in early 2011, the Osprey altered the performance of the ARG-MEU and provided a core capability ensuring that a downed pilot did not become a political pawn by Qaddafi. The ability to link seamlessly support services ashore with the deployed fleet via the Osprey allowed the Harriers aboard the USS *Kearsarge* to increase their sortie rates dramatically. By providing a whole new speed and range enablement of the strike fleet aboard a large deck amphibious ship, the future was being redefined by the Osprey.

The USN began to see a whole new way to look at COD, or carrier on-board delivery, and this would lead eventually to their decision to replace their C2s with CMV-22Bs.

And the five-year transition was marked by a further demonstration of transformation in the "return to the sea" associated with the initiation of the Bold Alligator exercises begun in 2011. It was clear as these exercises unfolded that the Osprey was redefining amphibious assault. It was no longer about being close to shore and launching amphibious vehicles; it was defining your assault vector and moving into the objective area from a much greater distance with Ospreys as a tip of the spear insertion force.

This photo shows the Osprey about the land onboard the UK warship HMS Illustrious in July 2007. The Marines trained onboard the UK warship with Harriers and with the Ospreys making their first landing onboard a foreign warship, something that would be expanded in the years ahead. This photo was shot by the author after his own landing onboard the HMS Illustrious via the Osprey. Credit: *Second Line of Defense*.

The battle testing which the Osprey underwent in the land wars has been a key part of taking transformation forward, for battle-tested Marines bring capabilities which no peer competitor who is not battle hardened, pacing threat or not, can bring to the fight. The engagements in the land wars and in Libya from the sea operations led to greater combat learning by the Marines in using and leveraging the Osprey. From 2012 on, we saw a maturing of the Marine Corps in their use of Ospreys to the point whereby the Marines, as the only tiltrotor-enabled assault force in the world, were redefining force insertion.

The redundancy of systems aboard the aircraft and the performance of the composite systems to take battle damage have been clearly combat proven. This has been recognized with the awarding of the first Distinguished Flying Crosses to Osprey pilots in 2013. The story of what two Marine aviators did to be the first V-22 Osprey pilots awarded Distinguished Flying Crosses is simple, elegant and tactically telling. The double-DFC incident underscores how the Marines used the unique tiltrotor aircraft—which can take off and land like a helicopter, then fly long distances at high speeds like an airplane—and its ability to perform in extreme battlefield conditions.

I interviewed the two pilots, Major Michael Hutchings and Captain David Haake, at New River Air Station in 2013. Here's what happened in Afghanistan in June 2012. Two Ospreys, operating with conventional helicopters Hueys and Cobras were supporting the insertion of a Marine reconnaissance battalion. The Ospreys, piloted by Maj Hutchings and Capt Haake, were flying in a two-ship formation and planning to put down Marines in two waves.

Major Hutchings after the Second Line of Defense 2013 interview at Marine Corps Air Station New River. Credit Photo: *Second Line of Defense*.

The first wave went well, and the Ospreys returned to insert the second group of Marines, to provide for enough armed manpower to perform the mission in Taliban-infested territory. As Hutching's V-22 came down, it took heavy fire, which so damaged the plane that the systems on board told the pilot to not fly the aircraft. Of course, not flying was to face certain death, so the task for the pilot and the crew was to find a way out. The plane was badly damaged, but because of the various redundant systems on board and the skill of the pilot and the crew, they were able to depart and to make it back to Camp Bastion in airplane mode. With a traditional rotorcraft, of course, you do not have the relative luxury of switching between two modes of travel.

As Capt Haake followed Maj Hutchings in, the Hueys and Cobras informed him that Taliban were occupying the area around the intended landing zone. Capt Haake took his plane up and took stock of his options. While he did, he learned that Maj Hutchings had landed and was under attack, which meant that Capt Haake had little choice but to insert Marines to reinforce the reconnaissance battalion. He did, also under heavy fire. His plane was badly damaged as well and also had on board a wounded Afghan soldier working with the Marines.

In addition to battle damage to the aircraft, the plane was leaking fuel very badly. This meant that the pilot and crew knew they could not make it back to Camp Bastion but would have to land at a Forward Operating Base, which also had medical support, about 20 miles away. Again, flying on helicopter mode, the plane and crew made it to the base.

But for Maj Hutchings, the day was not yet over. This was a night insertion, so the Marines needed to be extricated the next day. Maj Hutchings flew an Osprey the next morning as part of the effort to pick up the Marines and get them out. He landed the plane and took onboard the Marines, who were firing at the enemy as they boarded the plane. The Osprey took off to altitude with speed. "I asked the crew chief after about 10 minutes how the Marines in the back were doing. He said they were asleep," Hutchings added.[27]

A clear recognition of the Osprey driving con-ops innovation was the formation of the SP-MAGTF, or Special Purpose Marine Air-Ground Task Force. The first SP-MAGTF was formed in 2013 and combined the Osprey with the KC-130J to provide a force for supporting humanitarian or crisis interventions at the range and speed which was historically unprecedented.

---

27.   Robbin Laird, "Maturing of the Osprey; First V-22 Pilots Awarded DFCs," *Breaking Defense* (July 31, 2013), https://breakingdefense.com/2013/07/maturing-of-the-osprey-first-v-22-pilots-awarded-dfcs/.

The Operational Reach
of Special Purpose MAGTF-CR

- With a KC-130J and Osprey Tandem, the USMC Special Purpose MAGTF Crisis Response Force Can Operate Over a Significant Operational Area.

- This is a significant change for ground forces from a rotorcraft-enabled and airlift force structure.

The graphic highlights reach and range from the Moron Air Base in Spain, where the SP-MAGTF operated from. The graphic is credited to *Second Line of Defense*.

In a 2013 interview which I did with then Brigadier General James S. O'Meara, then serving as commander, U.S. Marine Forces Europe, we discussed his thinking about the Osprey and the creation of the SP-MAGTF. As he put it: "The SP-MAGTF is the basic Marine Corps air ground team or MAGTF approach but applied to a Special Purpose Mission. Special means it's uniquely tailored to a particular mission or a few mission sets. In this case, the focus is upon security embassy reinforcements or a noncombatant evacuation.

"Also, it is a rotational force, which provides a crisis response force able to deal with EUCOM and AFRICOM needs. General Dempsey provided strategic guidance, which was looking for a force, which operates with a small footprint, and is low-cost, and rotational. This is the answer to that guidance. The SP-MAGTF meets the need to respond rapidly to a developing situation either proactively or reactively with a small force with a small footprint and has its own organic air, which means that it has operational reach as well. The force is trained and operational and currently operating from a USAF base at Moran in Spain."

BGen O'Meara added: "We can operate over a significant combat radius and of course, refueled with our C-130Js can reach throughout the region and all while carrying equipment, and/or two-dozen Marines inside. It gives AFRICOM commander a unique tailored operational tactical level force with significant operational reach.

"The V-22 allows for a paradigm shift and enables a force like SP-MAGTF. The V-22 gives you that C-130-like distance and speed with the versatility to land in confined, limited area, with no runway or an expeditionary Landing Zone (LZ) like a helicopter. And when you add organic lift and tanking with our C-130Js, the reach is even greater and allows us to operate throughout Africa and the Mediterranean as needed.

"And the self-deploying capabilities of the V-22 means that we can plus up the Osprey component as well as needed or other sites throughout the operating area. And being Marines, it did not take long to go from formation of the capability to its use."

Innovations have continued to be driven by the Osprey capabilities and their own evolution over the next few years. Because of the range and speed of the Osprey, the Marines onboard an Osprey needed updated battle management information prior to landing in a combat area. Because of the length of time the sortie might take, compared to a rotorcraft, the Marines introduced Marine Air-Ground Tablet (MAGTAB) for the Ground Combat Element onboard the aircraft to regularly update information in flight. The coming of the F-35B was heavily anticipated as the Osprey engagement evolved, and with the coming of the new class of LHAs, the Osprey–F-35B combination would give a whole new capability to the USS America class, the impact of which is now clearly being seen in the Pacific.

New capabilities can be added through roll-on/roll-off systems, such as C^2. And in recent exercises, discussed later in interviews in the book, the Osprey can now play a C^2 role for a distributed force. And as the Corps looks to expand their basing flexibility, the ability of the Osprey to deliver new capabilities, such as new unmanned sensors and various payloads with the speed and range which only the MV-22 can deliver, will be a key part of ongoing USMC transformation in its role within full-spectrum crisis management.

I will conclude this section on the tiltrotor revolution by highlighting an interview I did in 2012 with then LtCol Boniface, who has recently retired as Col Boniface, with his last assignment being at Headquarters Marine Corps. This Osprey pilot and commander highlighted how he saw the future of the USMC driven by the introduction of the Osprey.

Col Christopher Boniface poses with LtCol Brandon Whitfield in front of a MV-22 Osprey at Marine Corps Air Station New River, North Carolina, July 2, 2019. Boniface participated in a final flight as the commanding officer of Marine Aircraft Group 26. July 2, 2019, and photo is credited to Cpl Paige Stade, 2nd Marine Air Wing.

This interview was conducted after the Osprey and the Harriers had done a historically unprecedented rapid extraction of a downed USAF pilot in Libya, which avoided what would have been a significant event if the Libyans had captured that pilot in the Odyssey Dawn operation. What is especially notable in this interview is that Boniface presaged what is only now happening in terms of Expeditionary Strike Group and Marine Expeditionary Brigade collaboration, a subject addressed in interviews later in the book with II MEF. He also anticipated its impact on reshaping USMC and U.S. Navy operations, which are now clearly underway and a key part of shaping Naval approaches to distributed maritime operations.

In that 2012 interview, we discussed the impact of the Osprey on the expeditionary strike group.

Shortly after the Bold Alligator 2012 exercise, Second Line of Defense *sat down with LtCol Boniface to discuss his experiences during Bold Alligator 2012. As the Osprey squadron commander involved in the exercise, he was in charge of the key toolset, the Osprey, which re-defined the ESG-MEB operationally.*

Two images defined how the Osprey had changed things since the last major amphibious exercise in 1996. In 1996, airborne forces were involved to do the raiding function. In 2012, a raiding force led by Ospreys from a SUPPLY ship performed the mission.

An assault raid was conducted from the sea base deep inland (180 miles) aboard the Ospreys with allied forces observing or participating. The Osprey was the key element operating in this exercise, which was not there during the last big "amphibious" exercise.

As the key coalition officer (Lt. Commander Pastoor) in the planning process, a Dutch naval officer underscored: "We had Dutch observers and they were very impressed with the game changing capabilities of the Osprey in terms of range and speed. Normally, in such an exercise we would take the beach and operate

30 miles inland. With this new capability we can operate throughout the entire battle space and move forces as if across a
chessboard."

Let us hover over this image. Instead of assaulting the beach,
the forces aboard the sea base are maneuvering within and over the
battle space inserting, moving and withdrawing forces. This is a far
cry from just looking at photos of the landing ships and assault
vehicles.

The second image was the Osprey landing on a SUPPLY ship
and then conducting the raid. The MV-22 landing on a T-AKE ship
means that the ability of this new aviation asset to connect the
supply ships with the combat ships can potentially allow a much
more efficient use of those combat ships. Supplies can be re-config-
ured off of the combat ships to the supply ships and with the MV-22's
delivery capabilities further enhancing the speed and agility of the
battle group.

What this in turn means is that by building more of these
new supply ships, the combat power of the fleet can be enhanced,
and the USN-USMC team gets its ship numbers up. This is not a
substitute for adding new amphibious ships to the fleet, it is not.
But with the new approach and new con-ops the combat capabilities
can become extended and more sustained. It is about sustainable
maneuver warfare from the sea. And the new VM-22 T-AKE combination is a potential war winner.[28]

In earlier conversations with the Osprey commander, we
discussed the use of the Osprey in the Libyan operations. Here the
Osprey went from a key base in Italy to the USS Kearsarge off of the
Libyan coast and this rapid resupply meant that the small number

---

28. "Re-thinking the Role of Supply Ships in Maneuver Warfare from the Sea,"
     Second Line of Defense, February 16, 2012, https://sldinfo.com/2012/02/
     re-thinking-the-role-of-supply-ships-in-maneuver-warfare-from-the-sea/.

of Harriers aboard of the Kearsarge could triple their sortie generation rates.

Second Line of Defense: *It has oft been repeated that Bold Alligator 2012 is the biggest exercise in more than 10 years. You would have to go back to 1996 to find that exercise. And one of the biggest differences between then and now is clearly the Osprey. How important is the V-22 in defining the con-ops of the ESG-MEB operation in Bold Alligator 2012?*

LtCol Boniface: I think that first of all, the comparison of the MV-22, to the CH-46 is a dead argument and we need to move on. The MV-22 is here to stay, it is bought and being paid for, and its sheer capabilities alone are causing us to rethink how we can and should perform expeditionary/amphibious operations from the sea.

The MV-22 and its capabilities are changing how we should be doing business.

Traditionally our MEU concept focuses on a radius of about 100 NM. With the speed and range of the Osprey, why can't we change this radius to, 500, 1,000, or even 1500 miles? We should be able to support a concept like this and we need to think in these terms.

I sort of think of it like a game of chess. I think of a traditional or legacy ARG-MEU as being able to move a pawn one space at a time towards the enemy. If you have ever played chess it sometimes takes a while to engage your opponent. We now have the ability to move a knight, bishop, or rook off of this same chessboard and attack 180 degrees towards the rear of our enemy. We can go directly after the king. Yes, it's not really fair, but I like that fact. The speed, range, and don't forget the reliability of the MV-22 allows me to do this.

We talk about staying ahead of the bow wave. Well there is a tsunami of change coming when we talk about the ability to fight an enemy and to support Marines ashore.

We can increase our area of operations (AOR) exponentially because we can spread out our ships; now we have an aviation connector that can move Marines a tremendous amount of distance and in a very short amount of time. We can also use this capability to leverage our other aviation assets like our AV8-Bs, CH-53's, AH-1Ws and UH-1Ys to support the MAGTF and ultimately damage the enemy's will to fight. Let's not just move 50-100 miles ashore, but let's move 200-500 miles ashore, and do it at an increased speed, range and lethality.

There are still a lot of naysayers who will cast doubt on this. How are you supporting those Marines ashore? How will the fire support piece work? Harriers and the F-35 concept along with a CSG can easily answer the fire support question for limited time until organic assets like artillery catches up. I think we need to challenge the autonomy of the CSG in regards to how it fits into a modern ESG concept....

From 1996 to the Bold Alligator are light years apart. And the big questions are how do we command and control it? And how do we integrate surface navy? And how do we integrate big aviation and big navy into that concept?

Second Line of Defense: *At the heart of the change is a shift in mindset. And in earlier pieces, we have discussed the cultural change rooted in understanding a plane called Osprey, which can land like a helicopter. But it is not a helicopter and we do not want the operational constructs inherited from the past to limit the innovation possible now and in the future.*

LtCol Boniface: *With legacy aviation assets we have had to think inside the ARG-MEU 100NM operational box. We have to get out of this mindset.*

And we are starting to do so by operating a more disaggregate ARG-MEU and relying on the MV-22 as an aviation connector. Now we can move from a few hundred miles away in our operational sphere to more than a 1,000-1500 in our area of influence (AOI). We need to adjust our operational mindset to align with this new capability, especially with the coming of the F-35B.

We also need to look at the Passengers, Mail, and Cargo (PMC) requirement amongst ARG shipping. Because of the increased capability of the MV-22 a lot of this requirement is being levied on the MV-22. This is both good and bad. While I can support not only the MAGTF (MEU/ESG), but I can also support the Navy as well. I can move Marines and sailors back in forth in bad weather, I can carry a lot of cargo, I can do it over long distances and very quickly.

However, as we expand this ESG concept we need to look at the aviation connector for the Navy. The SH-60 will struggle to keep up with these distances. While yes, I can do a lot of this for the ARG, I only have so many sorties allotted for this kind of mission. At some point I will not be able to support this mission when it will really count- I think the Navy needs to look at what we are doing here with the MV-22 and hopefully replicate our success.[29]

In short, the Osprey-enabled assault force has redefined ways to think about the insertion and withdrawal of force and new ways to engage, prevail and disengage. This is part of the next phase of the evolution of the Osprey when married with the F-35B, namely, to do some serious strategic rethinking on how to use newly crafted insertion forces.

The F-35-Driven Marine Corps Transformation

The Marines were on the ground floor for the development and launch of the F-35. They did not sign on to buying Super Hornets to replace their

---

29.   "The Impact of the Osprey on the Expeditionary Strike Group: 'There is a Tsunami of Change Coming,' *Second Line of Defense*, April 2, 2012, https://sldinfo.com/2012/04/the-impact-of-the-osprey-on-the-expeditionary-strike-group-there-is-a-tsunami-of-change-coming/.

Hornets but preferred to wait until they could acquire a fifth-generation multi-domain capability, namely, the F-35.

In addition to the capabilities which the aircraft brought to the force, the F-35 as a global enterprise has meant that the Marines are able to plug in worldwide to both joint and coalition common combat aircraft. This is already being demonstrated in the Pacific as the Marines operate their F-35s inside the first island chain and work closely with joint and coalition F-35 partners.

An example of what is now happening could be seen in the 2021 version of the BALTOPS exercise. In my interview with senior U.S. officers involved in BALTOPS 50, how the USMC general looked at working with allied F-35s from the standpoint of the Corps was highlighted. This is how I highlighted that in my interview with the senior officers:

"The Nordics are enhancing their defense capabilities, and one example is the Norwegians operating F-35s with the Danes now having received their first F-35. Brigadier General Annibale is an experienced Harrier and F-35B operator, and he noted that the F-35 participated for the first time in a BALTOPS exercise, and the F-35s in the exercise were Norwegian. He noted not only did they participate and provide the unique capabilities of fifth generation aircraft but are providing data into the operating force networks. "They were completely included in our link network. The fact that they were in our link architecture was almost as big a win as just having the airplane play."

"Col Anthony Henderson, Commanding General, 2d Marine Expeditionary Brigade, noted that a key focus of the exercise is "how do you maneuver effectively across the littorals in a maritime campaign? The U.S. Navy, US Marine Corps are looking at under the current Chief of Naval Operations (CNO) guidance at new ways to do so, such as expeditionary advanced based operations and littoral operations in a contested environment. The exercise also allows us to work on ways to optimize the engagement of different coalition members capabilities to achieve the overall coalition objectives."[30]

In the interviews later in this book, Marines discuss how the F-35 is being worked into the force, and how it is changing how the Marine Corp can operate as an insertion force. But a major part of that change has been seen already with regard to a further transformation of the ARG-MEU. With the Osprey, the ARG-MEU could operate over greater range and distance and be deployed in a more effectively distributed but integrated manner.

A visit by the author to Marine Corps Air Station Beaufort in 2015 shortly after the transfer of the F-35B squadron from Eglin AFB. Credit Photo: *Second Line of Defense*.

Now with the F-35 operating from the sea, the capabilities which the ARG-MEU can bring to the fight at sea, or extended littoral engagement

30.   Robbin Laird, "BALTOPS 50: Part of the Mosaic of Re-working North Atlantic Defense," *Second Line of Defense* (June 11, 2021), https://sldinfo. com/2021/06/baltops-50-part-of-the-mosaic-of-re-working-north-atlantic-de-fense/.

or ashore, are exponentially expanded. And of course, the F-35 provides the kind of U.S. Navy and USAF integration which is increasingly desired for the USMC working within the joint and coalition force for the full spectrum of conflict.

In books which I wrote in 2008 and then updated in 2013, I highlighted the impact of the Osprey/F-35B dyad as allowing the Marines to become "three dimensional warriors," or to use the latest jargon multi-domain warriors. This is how I highlighted the coming change in the preface to the 2008 book: "*Three-Dimensional Warriors* provides an overview of how United States Marine Corps (USMC) aviation shapes their capabilities and directs how they operate. Aviation allows the USMC to be 'three dimensional warriors' in fighting the 'three block war.' Not only does aviation provide for 360-degree situational awareness, but aviation leverages the ground warrior against the 'hybrid' enemies he faces today. As a former Commandant of the USMC characterized the challenge, the Marines have to be prepared to fight the 'three block war.' For then-Commandant General Krulak, Marines had to be prepared to operate over the spectrum of warfare within confined space. USMC aviation provides the essential glue for such a capability. The new elements being added to the USMC—the V-22 and the F-35B—provide a significant advancement in capability to support these concepts of operations. The role of the air element for the USMC is essential to its future. One can have a police force that wears military uniforms, or one can have a flexible military force enabled by full-spectrum capability.

"The choice depends upon the central role provided by an integrated air element for USMC operations and options. The air element enables diversified, decentralized, and flexible USMC operations. The aviation element within the USMC force structure plays a number of crucial functions. Because of the integrated nature of air and ground elements, it would be difficult to conceive of effective distributed operations without the air element."[31]

---

31.   https://www.amazon.com/Three-Dimensional-Warriors-Roles-Osprey-ebook/dp/B003ZDO6ZY/ref=sr_1_1?dchild=1&keywords=three+dimensional+warriors+laird&qid=1634114345&sr=8-1.

And in 2021, we have now seen the USS America–led amphibious task force work in the Pacific with the U.S. Navy, with HMS Queen Elizabeth, with USAF F-35 pilots flying onboard, with Japanese pilots flying onboard and with the Australians. With the South Koreans adding a larger amphibious ship, there will now be several nations operating F-35Bs in the Pacific, and as mobile basing is increasingly seen as a key enabler of operations in the peer fight, the Marines pioneering of the F-35 effort is now paying real dividends for the Marines and the joint and coalition force going forward.

And such change was already anticipated at the time of the initial launch of the USS America. In a 2014 article based on extensive interviews with the USS America staff, I focused on how amphibious assault was being redefined by the USS America.

The USMC is the only tiltrotor-enabled assault force in the world. The USS America has been built to facilitate this capability and will be augmented as the F-35B is added to the Ospreys, and helicopters already operating from the ship and as unmanned vehicles become a regular operational element as well.

To set the proper landscape to discuss the changes within aviation and the amphibious fleet, one can go back a decade ago and look at the aviation and ship pairings and their operational reach. The ARG-MEU a decade ahead operated within the LPD-17, without the T-AKE ship, without the Osprey and was primarily a rotorcraft, landing vehicle and mixture of Harrier fast jets force. And the three ship ARG-MEU would operate largely in a 200-mile box affecting the objective area where it was located.

The Osprey has obviously been a game changer, where today, the ARG-MEU can "disaggregate" and operate over a three-ship distributed 1,000-mile operational area. Having the communications and ISR to operate over a greater area, and to have sustainment for a disaggregated fleet is a major challenge facing the future of the USN-USMC team.

A major change in the ship can be seen below the flight deck, and these changes are what allow the assault force enabled by new USMC aviation capabilities to operate at greater range and ops tempo. The ship has three synergistic decks, which work together to support flight deck operations. Unlike a traditional large deck amphibious ship where maintenance has to be done topside, maintenance is done in a hangar deck below the flight deck. And below that deck is the intermediate area, where large workspaces exist to support operations with weapons, logistics and sustainment activities.

Captain Robert Hall with the USS America's ship sponsor Lynne Pace, the wife of Chairman of the Joint Chiefs of Staff General Peter Pace, at the christening of the USS America in 2012. The author was present for the ceremony and the photo is credited to *Second Line of Defense*.

In an interview with the ship's Captain Robert Hall, just prior to the departure in mid-July from the Ingalls Huntington shipyard in Pascagoula Mississippi, the CO highlighted some of the ship's capabilities: "The ship has several capabilities, which allow us to stay on station longer than a traditional LHA and to much better support the Ospreys and the F-35Bs which will be the hallmark of USMC aviation to enable long range amphibious assault. These aircraft are larger than their predecessors. They need more space for maintenance and this ship provides it. We have two high-hat areas to support the maintenance, one of them located behind the aft flight deck elevator to allow movement through the hangar. We have significantly greater capacity to store spare parts, ordnance and fuel as well. We can carry more than twice as much JP-5 than a traditional LHA."

The ship has three synergistic decks, which allow for a significant enhancement of the logistical or sustainment punch of the amphibious strike force. According to Captain Hall: "I like the synergistic description. The flight deck is about the size of a legacy LHA. But that is where the comparison ends. By removing the well deck, we have a hangar deck with significant capacity to both repair aircraft and to move them to the flight deck to enhance ops tempo. With the Ospreys, we will be able to get the Marines into an objective area rapidly and at significant distances. And when the F-35B comes the support to the amphibious strike force is significantly enhanced. And we will be able to operate at much greater range from the objective area. With the concern about littoral defenses, this ship allows us the option to operate offshore to affect events in the littoral."

This is a major advantage for a 21st century USN-USMC team in meeting the challenges of 21st century littoral operations. The USS America will provide a significant boost to the ability to both maintain and to provide operational tempo to support the force....

The USS America will make a significant contribution to the amphibious strike force, but no platform fights alone. It will be a key element or even flag ship of evolving approaches. When one marries the new Military Sealift Command (MSC) assets –T-AKE and USNS Montford Point assets – to the LPD-17 and the USS

America, the USN-USMC team will have a very flexible assault force, with significant vehicle space, berthing space for embarked Marines and shaping the future mix and match capabilities of the modular force.[32]

The Next Phase: The 2020s

The significant change in USMC aviation since the introduction of the Osprey has set in motion fundamental changes overall in USMC capabilities and concepts of operations. In the past decade, the Osprey has matured as a combat platform and fostered significant change in concepts of operations. No less than the virtual end of the ARG-MEU and the shaping of a new approach to amphibious warfare and shaping new concepts of operations for dealing with peer competitors is underway.

With the end of the primary focus upon the land wars, the Osprey and changes to the attack and support helicopter fleets have changed how the Marines can operate in a combat space. The revolution in tiltrotor technology, and the much more effective integration of the Yankee- and Zulu-class helicopters, has allowed the Marines to have a smaller logistical footprint in covering a wider combat space.

Enter the F-35B. With the coming of the F-35B and the impact of the template of change laid down by the Osprey, with its range and speed, together they are driving significant change in distributed operational combat capability. This capability has not only been reinforced but is also being taken to the next level. Now with Integrated Communications, Navigation and Identification or CNI-enabled aircraft with 360-degree situational awareness, a Marine Corps MAGTF can deploy with an integrated EW-ISR-C^2-weapons carrier and trigger which can form the backbone for enabling an insertion

---

32.   Robbin Laird, "The USS America: Redefining Amphibious Assault," *Second Line of Defense* (October 8, 2014), https://sldinfo.com/2014/10/the-uss-america-redefining-amphibious-assault/.

force. In other words, the 2010s have seen the maturing of the tiltrotor revolution being combined with the arrival of fifth-generation capabilities.[33]

And the Marines are the only combat force in the world with cutting-edge integration of these new capabilities within the overall combat force. The success of the 2010s has fostered change in how the USMC was able to operate as a crisis management force. Those successes provide the tip of the spear as well for the innovations of the 2020s.

Now the challenge is full-spectrum crisis management which requires a force capable in operating in contested air and sea space and with an ability to provide more effective engagement within a broader integrated distributed force. It is clear that USAF and U.S. Navy, as well as the U.S. Army, are shifting from their legacy forces which operated in the land wars of the 2010s to working on becoming an integrated distributed force in which multi-domain operations and tactical decision-making at the edge are a core focus of effort and attention.

Yet there is some confusion in the analytical literature over where the Marines are headed with regard to their next round of innovation. For many the focus is upon a more traditional approach to crisis management rather than realizing that the strategic shift is to full-spectrum crisis management. Some analysts have argued that the Commandant's New Guidance is really the end of the crisis-management Marines in favor of becoming part of the Navy's overall combat force.

Others see the U.S. Army moving in a direction to subsume Marine Corps' capabilities and to displace them. As the Army shifts to buying, deploying and adapting to a new generation of high-speed helicopters, some see this as the inevitable outcome.

But in fact, the world has changed. Doing crisis management against adversaries which possess significant strike and defense capabilities clearly requires shaping a more lethal and effective distributed force. And in such a

---

33. Robbin Laird, "The F-35, CNI Evolution, and Evolving the Combat Force," *Second Line of Defense* (December 4, 2019), https://sldinfo.com/2019/12/the-f-35-cni-evolution-and-evolving-the-combat-force/.

world, sea-basing integrated with an ability to use flexible land basing is a core capability from which the U.S. and its core allies can gain an operational advantage. It also provides enhanced capability to do offensive–defensive operations with a distributed yet integrated force.

Enter Force Design 2030

In the 2019 guidance of General Berger, the 38th Commandant of the USMC is clearly focused on the strategic shift. A few years ago, the Corps returned to the sea, as one Commandant put it. With General Berger, not only has the Corps returned to a focus on sea-based operations but also fully intends to craft more integrated operations with the U.S. Navy and the joint force to project power from the sea in contested environments, as a key foundational capability.

According to the Commandant's Guidance:

"Adversary advances in long-range precision fires make closer naval integration an imperative. The focal point of the future integrated naval force will shift from traditional power projection to meet the new challenges associated with maintaining persistent naval forward presence to enable sea control and denial operations. The Fleet Marine Force (FMF) will support the Joint Force Maritime Component Command (JFMCC) and fleet commander concept of operations, especially in close and confined seas, where enemy long-range precision fires threaten maneuver by traditional large-signature naval platforms.

"Future naval force development and employment will include new capabilities that will ensure that the Navy-Marine Corps team cannot be excluded from any region in advancing or protecting our national interests or those of our allies. Marines will focus on exploiting positional advantage and defending key maritime terrain that enables persistent sea control and denial operations forward. Together, the Navy-Marine Corps Team will enable the joint force to partner, persist and operate forward despite adversary employment of long-range precision fires."[34]

General Berger underscored that "We are a naval expeditionary force capable of deterring malign behavior and, when necessary, fighting inside our adversary's weapons-engagement-zone to facilitate sea denial in support of fleet operation and joint force horizontal escalation."[35]

And to do so with a force designed to operate from the ground up (quite literally) against peer competitors. "We will divest of legacy defense programs and force structure that support legacy capabilities. If provided the opportunity to secure additional modernization dollars in exchange for force structure, I am prepared to do so."[36]

The focal point of the future integrated naval force will shift from traditional power projection to meet the new challenges associated with maintaining persistent naval forward presence to enable sea control and denial operations.

"Future naval force development and employment will include new capabilities that will ensure that the Navy-Marine Corps team cannot be excluded from any region in advancing or protecting our national interests or those of our allies. Marines will focus on exploiting positional advantage and defending key maritime terrain that enables persistent sea control and denial operations forward. Together, the Navy-Marine Corps Team will enable the joint force to partner, persist and operate forward despite adversary employment of long-range precision fires."[37]

---

34. "Commandant's Planning Guidance: 38th Commandant of the Marine Corps" (2019), p. 2. https://www.marines.mil/Portals/1/Publications/Commandant's%20Planning%20Guidance_2019.pdf?ver=2019-07-17-090732-937.

35. "Commandant's Planning Guidance: 38th Commandant of the Marine Corps" (2019), p. 23.

36. "Commandant's Planning Guidance: 38th Commandant of the Marine Corps" (2019), p. 2.

37. "Commandant's Planning Guidance: 38th Commandant of the Marine Corps" (2019), p. 2.

General Berger has highlighted the evolution of the amphibious task force in a way which has a very wide lens on what can and should be included in Marine Corps operations with regard to that task force. And most notably, he is focused on mix-and-match building blocks which can be deployed in a variety of force packages, rather than defining the Marine Corps in terms of the MAGTF per se.

On the one hand, "Moving forward, the Marine Corps must maximize our inherent relationship with the Navy, along with our expertise coordinating elements of the MAGTF, to effectively coordinate across all warfighting domains to support the Joint Force."[38]

But on the other hand, "We are not defined by any particular organizing construct – the Marine Air-Ground Task Force (MAGTF) cannot be our only solution for all crises."[39]

General Berger has highlighted the importance of both bringing to shore or operating from islands or other land or sea bases, long-range fires to support crisis management maneuver forces. "Marine Corps integration into the Fleet via composite warfare will be a prerequisite to the successful execution of amphibious operations: Marines cannot be passive passengers en route to the amphibious objective area.

"As long-range precision stand-off weapons improve and diffuse along the world's littorals, Marines must contribute to the fight alongside our Navy shipmates from the moment we embark. Once ashore, Marine Forces operating within Composite Warfare (CW) will increase the Fleet's lethality and resiliency and will contribute to all domain access, deterrence, sea control, and power projection."[40]

And later in the document he adds: "Our investments in air-delivered long-range precision fires (LRPF) are known, suitable, and sufficient;

38. "Commandant's Planning Guidance: 38th Commandant of the Marine Corps" (2019), p. 5.

39. "Commandant's Planning Guidance: 38th Commandant of the Marine Corps" (2019), p. 2.

40. "Commandant's Planning Guidance: 38th Commandant of the Marine Corps" (2019), p. 10.

however, we remain woefully behind in the development of ground-based long-range precision-fires that can be fielded in the near term which have sufficient range and precision to deter malign activities or conflict. Our capability development focus has fixated on those capabilities with sufficient range and lethality to support infantry and ground maneuver.

"This singular focus is no longer appropriate or acceptable. Our ground-based fires must be relevant to the fleet and joint force commanders and provide overmatch against potential adversaries, or they risk irrelevance."[41]

A Navy Marine Expeditionary Ship Interdiction System launcher vehicle deploys into position aboard Pacific Missile Range Facility Barking Sands, Hawaii, Aug. 16, 2021. The NEMESIS and its Naval Strike Missiles participated in a live-fire exercise, here, part of Large-Scale Exercise 2021. August 16, 2021. Photo Credit: LCpl Luke Cohen. USMC Forces, Pacific.

General Berger has focused on shaping a distributed force which can be commanded in a denied and contested combat environment. In my various visits to 2nd Marine Air Wing and MAWTS-1, it is very clear that the Marines have been working very hard on leveraging their new

41.   "Commandant's Planning Guidance: 38th Commandant of the Marine Corps" (2019), p. 13.

capabilities, such as the F-35B, to deliver a 21st-century full-spectrum crisis management force.

"While others may wait for a clearer picture of the future operating environment, we will focus our efforts on driving change and influencing future operating environment outcomes. One way to drive the continued evolution of the future operating environment is Distributed Operations (DO). DO capable forces are a critically important component of Marine Corps modernization."[42]

He then underscores the nature of the challenge to be met: "Our lack of progress in implementing DO is in part due to an inadequate description of why we would distribute forces and why we would conduct distributed operations.

"In my judgment, we distribute for five reasons: We disperse to better accomplish the mission against a distant or distributed adversary. We disperse to improve maneuver options in order to gain a positional advantage to assault or engage more effectively with direct or indirect fires. We disperse to reduce the effects of enemy fires. We disperse to impose costs and induce uncertainty. We disperse to reduce our signature to avoid detection. In a precision strike regime, sensing first and shooting first are a tremendous advantage."[43]

To do so requires a significant focus on robust C^2, which means an ability to operate in a degraded and contested environment. In many ways, working this challenge is at the heart of the kind of force integration, which the Commandant seeks.

"Future force development must also contribute to an integrated operational architecture and enable information environment operations. Friendly forces must be able to disguise actions and intentions, as well as deceive the enemy, through the use of decoys, signature management, and

---

42. "Commandant's Planning Guidance: 38th Commandant of the Marine Corps" (2019), pp. 11–12.

43. "Commandant's Planning Guidance: 38th Commandant of the Marine Corps" (2019), p. 12.

signature reduction. Preserving the ability to command and control in a contested information network environment is paramount."[44]

The Commandant has focused his Force Design 2030 on building out the capabilities mentioned in his guidance, including envisaging changes in the amphibious fleet.[45] "The amphibious fleet and littoral maneuver craft also require significant future force development. The amphibious fleet must be diversified in composition and increased in capacity by developing smaller, specialized ships, as a complement to the existing family of large multipurpose ships.

"Doing so will improve resilience, dispersion, and the ability to operate in complex archipelagoes and contested littorals without incurring unacceptable risk. Initial options for examination include:

- A 'hybrid' amphibious ship to transport landing craft and enable the ability to fight in a contested littoral.

- An inexpensive, self-deploying 'connector' capable of delivering rolling stock on or near-shore in a contested littoral.

- Considering how a wider array of smaller 'black bottom' ships might supplement the maritime preposition and amphibious fleets."[46]

And the mix-and-match capability he has in mind for the evolving amphibious task force and tailored to a wide variety of force insertion settings is suggested in his treatment of sensors and remote systems. He has in mind that the so-called unmanned systems are integrated within the task force not so much to replace the current manned systems but to do what a remote can

---

44.   "Commandant's Planning Guidance: 38th Commandant of the Marine Corps" (2019), p. 12.

45.   *Force Design 2030: March 2020*: https://www.hqmc.marines.mil/Portals/142/ Docs/CMC38%20Force%20Design%202030%20Report%20Phase%20I%20 and%20II.pdf?ver=2020-03-26-121328-460.

46.   "Commandant's Planning Guidance: 38th Commandant of the Marine Corps" (2019), p. 12.

do— provide enhanced SA, assist in C², and to help in determining how best to guide and operate the insertion force operating in a crisis setting.

"Creating new capabilities that intentionally initiate stand-in engagements is a disruptive 'button hook' in force development that runs counter to the action that our adversaries anticipate. Rather than heavily investing in expensive and exquisite capabilities that regional aggressors have optimized their forces to target, naval forces will persist forward with many smaller, low signature, affordable platforms that can economically host a dense array of lethal and non-lethal payloads.

"By exploiting the technical revolution in autonomy, advanced manufacturing, and artificial intelligence, the naval forces can create many new risk-worthy unmanned and minimally-manned platforms that can be employed in stand-in engagements to create tactical dilemmas that adversaries will confront when attacking our allies and forces forward.

"Stand-in Forces will be supported from expeditionary advanced bases (EABs) and will complement the low signature of the Expeditionary Advanced Base Operations (EAB0s) with an equally low signature force structure comprised largely of unmanned platforms that operate ashore, afloat, submerged, and aloft in close concert to overwhelm enemy platforms."[47]

In his guidance, General Burger speaks of the growing importance of Expeditionary Advanced Base Operations or EABO: "… we are going to build a force that can do EABO opposed to building an EABO force."[48]

When you couple this with the opportunity to combine the use of the fleet (amphibious, surface, subsurface, Unmanned Surface Vessels (USVs) and Unmanned Underwater Vehicles (UUVs) with islands and allied territory, the challenge will be to find effective ways to integrate the operational force in the area of interest. Part of the challenge will be to be able to establish

---

47. "Commandant's Planning Guidance: 38th Commandant of the Marine Corps" (2019), p. 12.

48. "Commandant's Planning Guidance: 38th Commandant of the Marine Corps" (2019), p. 11.

Forward Arming and Refueling Points or FARPs and to fold those into the integrated distributed force. Also crucial is to shape C^2 mesh networks which can combine distributed forces into a coherent combat force and operate at the tactical edge.

A MARTAC MANTAS system participating in a 2015 USMC exercise whereby the MANTAS USV provided logistical support to the Marine Corps force during the exercise. The MARTAC family of USVs can deliver ISR, and other payloads to the force right now and such capability is clearly envisaged as part of the Force Design 2030 force. Credit Photo: MARTAC

The projected additions of USMC aviation assets in the decade ahead clearly can provide enhanced capabilities to enable greater logistical cross-support across a distributed domain enabled by a diversity of basing options and capabilities.

Three key additions are crucial to this evolution. The first is the addition of the CH-53K.

Without an effective heavy lift asset, the ability to operate from the sea base or to establish or support distributed FARPs would be undercut and with it, the efforts to enhance mobile and expeditionary basing. The CH-53K will provide a key element of being able to carry equipment and/or personnel to the objective area. And with its ability to carry three times the external load of the CH-53E and to be able to deliver the external load to different operating bases, the aircraft will contribute significantly to distributed operations.

But the digital nature of the aircraft, and the configuration of the cockpit, are key parts of its ability to contribute as well. The aircraft is a fly-by-wire system with digital interoperability built in. And with multiple screens in the cockpit able to manage data in a variety of ways, the aircraft can operate as a lead element, a supporting element or a distributed integrated support node to the insertion force.

A key change associated with the new digital aircraft, whether they are P-8s or Cyclone ASW helicopters, is a different kind of workflow. The screens in the aircraft can be configured to the task and data moved throughout the aircraft to facilitate a mission task-oriented work flow.

In the case of the CH-53K, the aircraft could operate as a Local Area Network for an insertion task force, or simply as a node pushing data back into the back where the Marines are operating MAGTABs.

Marines carrying MAGTABs onboard the CH-53K will be able to engage with the task force to understand their role at the point of insertion. The K as a digital aircraft, combined with the digital transformation of the Marines, creates a very different ground force insertion capability.

The second is the addition of new and more capable unmanned assets to empower the force, and to provide for the proactive ISR which the integrated distributed force needs to enhance their operational effectiveness.

The third is further progress in shaping the digital integration of the force so that distributed operations can be more effective in contested environments. For the Marines, working digital interoperability has been a high priority, as they prepared for the shift from the land wars to engaging in contested multi-domain operations.

According to the USMC 2019 Aviation Plan:

"Digital interoperability is the seamless integration of digital systems and exchange of data, across all domains and networks throughout the MAGTF, naval, joint, and coalition forces, to include communication in degraded or denied environments, to rapidly share accurate information, provide greater situational awareness, accelerate the kill chain, and enhance survivability in order to outmaneuver and defeat the threat across the Range of Military Operations (ROMO)....

"The Marine Corps executes mission threads primarily as an integrated MAGTF organized to support the Marine rifleman. The integration of the MAGTF and the successful execution of mission threads relies on the effective exchange of critical information; communication therefore, whether in the form of electronic data or voice, is critical to the exchange of mission essential information....

"We continue to pursue integration and data exchange throughout various arenas: situational awareness; aircraft survivability; intelligence, surveillance, and reconnaissance (ISR); fire support; and logistics by conducting continuous and iterative analysis of ever evolving information exchange requirements (IERs) and the technological tools needed to satisfy those requirements."[49]

In short, the progress in USMC aviation of the past decade is a prologue to the Commandant's 2019 guidance. Its progress in the 2020s will enable its realization. In the interviews throughout the rest of the book, Marines in the various commands interviewed highlight their efforts to continue the transformation process. The focus in these interviews is to highlight how the Marines are shaping a way ahead in practice. Because they have to fight tonight, they cannot shut down to be redesigned—they have to do it while engaged in operations. But then again, they already started in 2007.

---

49.   https://www.aviation.marines.mil/portals/11/2019%20avplan.pdf.

CHAPTER THREE:

THE VIEW FROM MAWTS-1

MAWTS-1 is the USMC center of excellence where the Marine Corps Aviation community works closely with the Ground Combat Element to shape real-world combat innovations for the force in transition. When new platforms are introduced, it is at MAWTS-1 and in its twice a year Weapons and Tactics Instructor courses are held which work the evolving Tactics, Techniques and Procedures (TTPs) for USMC integration.

As the USMC official publication on MAWTS-1 puts it:

"The WTI Course is a fully integrated course of instruction for highly experienced and fully qualified officers from all aviation communities. Officers from ground combat, combat support, and combat service support also attend the course to ensure appropriate air-ground interface. The WTI course academic syllabus allows the WTI candidate to put classroom lessons to work in the air. Briefing and debriefing techniques and airborne instructional skills are reviewed and tactics and weapons systems employment are evaluated. The course culminates in a fully integrated combined arms exercise encompassing all functions of Marine Corps aviation in support of a notional Marine Air Ground Task Force."[50]

In this chapter, my discussions and interviews with the MAWTS-1 staff during 2020 are presented.[51] These discussions include a visit to Marine

---

50. History of MAWTS-1, https://www.29palms.marines.mil/Units/Marine-Aviation-Weapons-and-Tactics-Squadron-One/History/.

51. For a summary of earlier discussions, see Robbin Laird, Edward Timperlake, and Richard Weitz, *Rebuilding American Military Power in the Pacific* (Praeger, 2013).

Corps Air Station Yuma in September 2020. The interviews highlight how the aviation community is working the next phase of USMC transformation, one which extends the reach of the Marines into the peer competitors Weapons Engagement Zone, expands flexible basing options, and focuses on ways to integrate more effectively with the joint force, notably in terms of contributing to naval missions, such as sea lines of communication (SLOC) defensive and offensive operations.

The chapter begins with the interview with the commanding officer of MAWTS-1, Col Gillette, an early user of the F-35 and who is perfectly placed to help shape the next phase of USMC transformation.

Col Gillette, CO of MAWTS-1

September 22, 2020

Prior to my visit in early September 2020, I conducted a series of teleconferences with MAWTS-1 officers in the late spring and early summer. The focus of those discussions was upon mobile and expeditionary basing and how the training for this key capability was being shaped going forward for the Marines.

During this visit, I had a chance to engage with a number of MAWTS-1 officers and with the CO of MAWTS-1, Colonel Gillette, with regard to the focus and training with regard to the USMC's emphasis on their contribution to naval warfare.

Question: How is the Marine Corps going to contribute most effectively to the Pacific mission in terms of Sea Control and Sea Denial? And how to best contribute to the defensive and offensive operations affecting the SLOCs? And I think both questions highlight the challenge of shaping a force with enough flexibility to have pieces on the chessboard and to move them effectively to shape combat success.

Col Gillette: Working through how the USMC can contribute effectively to sea control and sea denial for the joint force is a key challenge. The way I see it is the question being faced is how to insert force in the Pacific where a key combat capability is to bring assets to bear on the Pacific chessboard. How do you bring your chess pieces onto the board in a way that ensures or minimizes both the risk to the force and enhances the probability of a positive outcome for the mission? How do you move assets on the chessboard inside those red rings which allows us to bring capabilities to bear on whatever end state we are trying to achieve?

For the USMC, as the Commandant has highlighted, it is a question of how we can most effectively contribute to the air-maritime fight. For us, a core competence is mobile basing which clearly will play a key part in our contribution, whether projected from afloat or ashore. What assets need to be on the chessboard at the start of any type of escalation? What assets need to be brought to bear and how do you bring them there? I think mobile basing is part of the discussion of how you bring those forces to bear.

How do you bring forces afloat inside the red rings in a responsible way so that you can bring those pieces to the chessboard or have them contribute to the overall crisis management objectives? How do we escalate and de-escalate force to support our political objectives? How do we, either from afloat or ashore, enable the joint force to bring relevant assets to bear on the crisis and then once we establish that force presence, how do we manage it most effectively? How do we train to be able to do that? What integration in the training environment is required to be able to achieve such an outcome in an operational setting in a very timely manner?

Lieutenant Colonel Steve E. Gillette, the Commanding Officer of Marine Fighter Attack Squadron 121 based out of Marine Corps Air Station Yuma, Ariz., shows his squadron's F-35B hangar to MajGen Juan G. Ayala, the Commander of Marine Corps Installations Command, Tuesday. VMFA-121 is the first operational F-35 squadron in the Marine Corps and the Department of Defense. December 3, 2013. Marine Corps Air Station Yuma.

Question: Ever since the revival of the Bold Alligator exercises, I have focused on how the amphibious fleet can shift from its greyhound bus role to shaping a task force capable of operating in terms of sea denial and sea control. With the new America-class ships in the fleet, this clearly is the case. How do you view the revamping of the amphibious fleet in terms of supporting the U.S. Navy to deliver sea control and sea denial?

Col Gillette: The traditional approach for the amphibious force is to move force to an area of interest. Now we need to look at the entire maritime combat space, and ask how we can contribute to that combat space, and not simply move force from A to B.

I think the first leap is to think of the amphibious task force, as you call it, to become considered as pieces on the chessboard. As with any piece, they have strengths and weaknesses. Some of the weaknesses are clear, such as the need for a common operational picture, a command-and-control suite to where the assets that provide data feeds to a carrier strike group are also incorporated onto L-Class shipping. We're working on those things right now, in order to bring the situational awareness of those types of ships up to speed with the rest of the Naval fleet.

Question: A key opportunity facing the force is to reimagine how to use the assets the force has now but working them in new innovative integratable ways or, in other words, rethinking how to use assets that we already have but differently. How do you view this opportunity?

Col Gillette: We clearly need to focus on the critical gaps which are evident from working a more integrated force. I think that the first step is to reimagine what pieces can be moved around the board for functions that they typically in the past haven't been used for but can provide new options.

That's number one. Number two, once you say, "Okay, well I have all these LHA/LHD class shipping and all the LPDs, et cetera that go along with the traditional ARG-MEU, is there a ship that I need to either tether to that ARG-MEU to give it a critical capability that's autonomous? Or do I just need to have a way to send data so that they have the same sensing of the environment that they're operating in, using sensors already in the carrier strike group, national assets, Air Force assets, et cetera?"

In other words, the ship might not have to be tethered to a narrowly defined task force but you just need to be able to have the information that everybody else does so that you can make tactical or operational decisions to employ that ship to the max extent practical in terms of its capabilities.

There is a significant shift underway. The question we are now posing is: "What capability do I need, and can I get it from a sister service that already has something that provides the weapons, the C^2 or the ISR that I need? I need to know how to exploit information which benefits either my situational awareness, my offensive or defensive capability of my organic force. But you don't necessarily need to own it in order to benefit from it…

The key question becomes: "How do I get the most decisive information into an LHA/LHD? How do I get it into a marine unit so that they can benefit from that information and then act more efficiently or lethally when required?"

Question: We first met when you were at Eglin, where you were working the F-35 warfare system into the USMC. Now that the F-35s are becoming a fact of life for both the U.S. services and the allies in the Pacific, how can we best leverage that integratable capability?

Col Gillette: The development is a significant one. It is not only a question of interoperability among the F-35 fleet, it is the ability to have common logistical and support in the region with your allies, flying the same aircraft with the same parts. And the big opportunity comes with regard to the information point I made earlier. We are in the early stages of exploiting what the F-35 force can provide in terms of information dominance in the Pacific, but the foundation has been laid.

And when we highlight the F-35 as the 21st century version of what the World War II Navy called the big blue blanket with the redundancy and the amount of information that could be utilized, it's pretty astonishing if you think about it. The challenge is to work the best ways to sort through the information resident in the F-35 force and then how do you utilize it in an effective and efficient way for the joint force. But the foundation is clearly there.

Question: Clearly, the new focus on the maritime battle requires a shift in USMC training. How are you approaching that challenge?

Col Gillette: So long as I've been in the Marine Corps and the way that it still currently is today, marine aviation exists to support the ground combat. That's why we exist. The idea that we travel light and that the aviation element within the MAGTF provides or helps to provide the ground combat element with a significant capability is our legacy. We are now taking that legacy and adapting it. We are taking the traditional combat engagement where you have battalions maneuvering and aviation supporting that ground element and we are moving it towards Sea Control, and Sea Denial missions.

We are reimagining the potential of what the infantry does. That doesn't mean that they do that exclusively because, although I think that our focus in the Marine Corps, as the Commandant said, is shifting towards the Pacific that doesn't relegate or negate the requirement to be ready to respond to all of the other things that the Marine Corps does. It might be less of a focus, but I don't think that that negates our requirement to deal with a variety of core missions.

It's a question of working the balance in the training continuum. What does an infantry battalion train to? Do they train to a more traditional battalion in the attack or in the defense and then how do I use my aviation assets to support either one of those types of operations? As opposed to "I might have to take an island, a piece of territory that we're going to use a mobile base, secure it so that we can continue to push chess pieces forward in the Pacific, in the Sea Control, Sea Denial end-state."

Those are two very different kinds of skill sets. If there's one thing that the Marine Corps is very good at it's being very versatile and being able to switch from one to the other on relatively short order. But in order to do that, you have to have a very dedicated and well thought out training continuum so that people can do both well, because if you say that you can do it the expectation is that you can do it well.

We are shaping a new Marine Littoral Regiment, MLR, but we're still in the nascent stages of defining what are the critical tasks that something like that needs to be able to do and then how you train to it. How do we create not only the definition of the skill sets that we need to train large formations to, but then what venues must we have to train? How to best combine simulated environments with real world training out on a range?

We're working through all that right now and it'll be interesting to watch how that process unfolds. But it is a mind shift to rethink the context in which our Ground Combat forces will conduct offensive or defensive operations, and specifically, what tasks they are expected to be capable of in this environment.

What we've done in the past is very well-defined and we have a very defined training continuum for those large formations. In this new role in the Pacific, that's something that I think over the next few years we'll get our arms around and we will learn from doing. As we start to field these formations out to the Pacific we'll really start to figure out where are we good at training and where are gaps that we need to close and shape the venues and methods to fill those in those gaps.

We're constantly looking at new venues and new methods to start to do the things that we need to do with the new approach. For example, we are taking our TACAIR Community up to the Nellis range for large integrated strike missions. We do face-to-face planning with the Air Force and Navy so that our students can understand the capabilities and limitations of these different platforms. They rub elbows with the USAF and Navy operators and gain first-hand knowledge of the strengths and weaknesses of these different platforms.

Then we fly them all back home and then the next night we go out with this huge armada of joint assets. And it's, out of the assets that play on this, it's probably 50% Marines and the other 50% are Growlers, Air Force platforms, et cetera. And then we do a mass debrief.

And this starts to chip away at the legacy perspective: "Okay, I'm a master of my machine." They come to WTI and learn how to think in an integrated manner. But more importantly, they get exposed and actually go out and do the integration with joint service assets to see the strengths and weaknesses so that they understand the planning considerations required for the joint fight against peer competitors and how to work beyond what their Marine Corps platform can do.

Another example is when we do what we call our Offensive Anti-Air Warfare, OAAW Evolution. We fight peer versus peer against one another. We have real-time intelligent collections on what the other side is doing, so the plans change real-time, airborne and on the ground. There's deception; there's decoys. It's pretty amazing to watch and oh, by the way, they get to use their weapons systems, their command-and-control systems to the fullest extent of their capabilities on both sides. This allows us to engage a thinking, breathing enemy who is well-trained and has all the latest and greatest systems, but they do that with assets that not are resident just to the Marine Corps.

We are focused on operating, not just with the assets that you control, the ones that sit out on our flight line or sit in our command and control, but how these other things can contribute in the joint fight. And to shape effective methods to get the enabling information, digest it and then use it in near real-time.

It's pretty interesting to watch and the outcomes of this evolution are wildly different, based on the ability of the students to use these things that they're not used to working with, incorporate them in real-time into their plan and then execute. Which I think, if you were to look at any high-end conflict or contingency where you have similarly matched forces in terms of training and gear, that will make the difference between somebody who is wildly successful or wildly unsuccessful, with your ability to direct and use those things real-time being a crucial delineator to combat success....

Working Mobile Basing

May 31, 2020

The USMC has mobile basing in its DNA. For the Marines, this means an ability to operate an integratable force from sea bases, FOBs or FARPs. As the Marines look forward to the decade ahead, they are likely to enhance their capabilities to provide for mobile bases which can empower the joint and coalition force by functioning as a chess piece on the kill-web-enabled chessboard.

But what is required to do mobile basing? What are the baseline requirements to be successful?

A very good place to start to shape answers to these questions is the USMC's center of excellence on warfighting training, MAWTS-1 located at MCAS Yuma. In a discussion with LtColonel Barron, ADT&E Department Head at MAWTS-1. ADT&E we focused on the core task of fighting today with the current force but also looking forward to how to enhance that force's capabilities in the near to mid-term as well.

We had a wide-ranging discussion with regard to the flexible basing dynamic, and I will highlight a number of takeaways from that discussion. The first one is the crucial need for decision makers to determine why a mobile base is being generated and what the tactical or strategic purpose of doing is. It takes time and effort to create a mobile base, and the mobile base commander will need to operate with mission command with regard to his base to determine how best to operate and for what purpose.

The second one is the importance of determining the projected duration of the particular base. This will have a significant impact in shaping the question of logistics support. What is needed? How to get it there? And from what supply depot? Is it either afloat or ashore in adjacent areas?

The third one is clearly the question of inserting the force into the mobile base and ensuring its optimal capabilities for survivability. What needs to be at the base to provide for organic survivability? What cross-links via C^2 and ISR will provide for an extended kill web to support the base and its survivability?

A fourth one is to determine what the base needs to do to contribute to the wider joint or coalition force. With the evolution of technology, it is possible now to have processing power, and strike capabilities distributed and operated by a smaller logistics footprint force, but how best to configure that base to provide the desired combat effect for the joint or coalition force?

A fifth one is crucial for operating in a contested environment. Here the need is for signature control, or an ability to have as small a signature footprint as possible commensurate with achieving the desired combat effect. Signature management could be seen as a component of survivability.

However, the management of signatures down to the small unit level requires a disruptive shift in our mindset.

The sixth one is clearly having an exit strategy in mind. For how long should the force be at the mobile base? For what purposes? And what needs to be achieved to enable the decision to move from the mobile base? In effect, the discussion highlighted what one might refer to as the three Ss. An insertion force operating from a variety of mobile bases needs to be able to be sustainable, survivable and signature manageable.

With regard to current USMC capabilities, the MV-22, the C-130, the Viper, the Venom, the CH-53E and the F-35 are key platforms which allow the Marines to integrate and move a lethal combat force to a mobile base. But the C^2/ISR enablement is a key part of the requirement and the digital interoperability efforts are a key part of shaping a more effective way ahead. And in the relatively near term, the CH-53K replacing the E is a key enabler for an enhanced mobile basing strategy.

Moving Forward with Mobile Basing

June 3, 2020

As noted earlier, a key contribution which the USMC can provide for the joint and coalition force is mobile and expeditionary basing. As the joint and coalition force shapes greater capabilities through C^2/ISR innovations and integrability of the sensor-strike kill web, the capabilities will be enhanced to operate distributed expeditionary basing for the insertion forces.

But one fights with the force one has and builds forward from there. So where are the Marines currently with regard to mobile basing capabilities?

In the discussion with Major Brian Hansell, MAWTS-1 F-35 Division Head, it is clear that the coming of the F-35 to the USMC has expanded their ability to operate within a broader kill web and to both empower their expeditionary bases and contribute to the broader kill-web approach. The Marine's F-35s are part of the broader joint and coalition force of F-35s, and notably in the Pacific this extends the reach of the Marine's F-35s significantly and brings greater situational awareness as well as reach to other strike platforms to the force operating from an expeditionary base as well as enhancing the kill-web reach for the joint or coalition force. As Major Hansell put it: "By being an expeditionary, forward-based service, we're effectively extending the bounds of the kill web for the entire joint and coalition force."

The F-35 brings a unique capability to the Marine Corps, as it works mobile basing but reworking the assault force more generally is a work in progress. The digital interoperability initiative is a crucial one, as the assault assets will have integrability they do not currently have, such as the Viper attack helicopter getting Link-16 and full motion video.

And the heavy lift element, which is a bedrock capability for the insertion force, is older, not easily integratable and is in diminishing numbers. The CH-53K, which is to replace the CH-53E, will provide significant capabilities enhancements for an insertion force operating from afloat or ashore mobile bases but needs to be ramped up in numbers capable of raising the combat level of the current force.

In a discussion with Major James Everett, head of the Assault Support Department at MAWTS-1, we discussed the force that we have and some ways ahead for enhanced capability in the near to mid-term. The Assault Support Department includes a number of key divisions: CH-53, MV-22, KC-130, UH-1 and AH-1.

There a number of key takeaways from that conversation which are my conclusions, rather than directly quoting Major Everett. The first point is that indeed we need to focus on the force we have now because we will fight with the force we have now. The Marines, by being in the land wars for the past twenty years, have become part of the joint force, and have relied on elements from the joint force, that they would not necessarily have access to when doing force insertion in the Pacific. This means that the digital interoperability effort underway within Marine Corps innovation is not just an effort nice to have, but a crucial one to ensure that the insertion force package can work more effectively together and to leverage other key support assets which might be available from the joint or coalition force. After all, a mobile base is being put on the chessboard for a strategic or tactical objective and survivability is a key requirement.

The second point is about sustainability. And sustainability is a function of the lift assets which can bring the kit and supplies needed for the duration of the mission. For the Marines, this is defined by KC-130J, CH-53E, MV-22 and UH-1Y lift support. And it is also defined by air-refuellable assets to the assault force as well. The Marines have limited indigenous assets to provide aerial refueling, which, dependent on the mission and the time scale of the force insertion effort, might need to depend on the Navy or Air Force for this capability.

The third point is about C^2. With the shift from the land wars, where the Marines were embedded within CENTCOM forces, C^2 was very hierarchical. This clearly is not going to be practicable or efficacious with a distributed insertion force. Working mission command for a force operating in a degraded environment is a key challenge, but one which will have to be met to deliver the kind of distributed mobile-based force which the Marines can provide for the joint and coalition force, and not just in the Pacific, but would certainly provide a significant capability as well for the fourth battle of the Atlantic.

The fourth point is the clear importance of the coming of the CH-53K to the force. It is a question of not only a modern lift asset with significantly enhanced capabilities to provide for assault support but also that it is a digital aircraft which can fully participate in an integrated distributed mission.

The fifth point is that the digital interoperable initiative will not only provide for ways to better integrate assets but will also enhance what those assets can do. A key example is the nature of what a Viper assault asset can do afloat as well ashore when operating with Link-16 and full motion video.

The sixth point is that the coming of remotes, whether air or maritime, can expand the situational awareness of the insertion force, as long as signatures can be managed effectively. And for the insertion force, this can be about remotes transported to a base, operating from an afloat asset or tapping into various overhead assets, such as Triton.

Or put another way, as digital interoperability is worked, there will be expanded effort to find ways to support the insertion force operating from a mobile base. This will be an interactive process between what C²/ISR assets are available in the kill web and how the Marines ashore or afloat can best use those resources.

We have seen such a migration with the U.S. Navy as the Carrier Strike Group and naval fleet is adding MISR, or Maritime ISR officers, and this change actually was inspired by the operations of 3rd MEF in Afghanistan. What we might envisage is simply the next iteration of what was done ashore with now the afloat and insertion forces in the maritime environment.

The seventh point is the key emphasis on timeliness for a mobile basing option. It is about the insertion force operating within the adversary's decision cycle and operating to get the desired combat effect prior to that adversary being successful in getting his combat result, namely, eliminating or degrading the insertion force. This is another way to understand the key significance of how C²/ISR is worked between the insertion force and the wider air-maritime force.

In short, the Marines will fight with the force they have; and as the C²/ISR kill webs are built out and remotes folded into these kill webs, force insertion via mobile basing will clearly be enhanced as well.

The Role of Heavy Lift

September 21, 2020

The insertion of force into a flexible basing environment requires lift capabilities, and with rapid insertion, movement and withdrawal of force being a key enabler for being able to work an effective basing chessboard, heavy lift is a key enabler. And heavy lift really comes in two forms: fixed wing aircraft and rotorcraft. My guide in the discussion of the lift-basing dynamic earlier this year was Major James Everett, head of the Assault Support Department at MAWTS-1. In that discussion, we focused on the importance of the CH-53E and the new aircraft, the CH-53K in enabling mobile and expeditionary basing. In September 2020, we met at MAWTS-1 to continue our discussion.

But the focus of my visit was on addressing the challenges the Marines face in supporting the U.S. Navy in terms of the maritime fight. In particular, my discussions with Colonel Gillette, the CO of MAWTS-1, focused on two key questions: How is the Marine Corps going to contribute most effectively to the Pacific mission in terms of Sea Control and Sea Denial? And how to best contribute to the defensive and offensive operations affecting the SLOCs?

We addressed how to answer these questions from the standpoint of the assault support force. As Major Everett put it: "A key focus of effort for the assault support community is upon how we can best assist through expeditionary basing to provide for sea control. We're trying to get away from any permanent type of land basing in a maritime contested environment."

A key enabler for flexible basing inserts or operations from the maritime fleet, inclusive of the amphibious ships, are the capabilities which the Marine Corps has with its tiltrotor and rotorcraft community. This community provides an ability to insert a sizable force without the need for airstrips of the size which a KC-130J would need. Or put in another way, the Marines can look at basing options and sustainability via air either in terms of basing options where a fixed wing aircraft must operate, or, in a much wider set of cases, where vertical lift assets can operate.

The third is obviously by sea, which depends on support by a mother ship or a Military Sealift Command (MSC) ship, but the challenge for the Marines is that moving bases deeper into the maritime area of operations creates enhanced challenges for the MSC and raises questions about viable sustainable options. We have already seen this challenge with regard to the littoral combat ship fleet, where the MSC is not eager to move into the littorals to supply a smaller ship, but it is much more willing to take its ships into a task force environment with significant maritime strike capability to give it protection.

The most flexibility for the mobile or expeditionary basing options clearly comes from vertical lift support aircraft. The challenge is that the current CH-53E fleet has been heavily tasked by the more than a decade of significant engagement in the Middle East. The Marines unlike the U.S. Army did not bring back their heavy lift helicopters for deep maintenance but focused on remaining engaged in the fight by doing just enough maintenance to continue safe and effective flight operations in theater. As Major Everett put it: "The Army brought their helicopters back from Afghanistan and they'd strip them down to the frame and they'd rebuild them basically. We just didn't do that." This means that the heavy lift operational force inventory is low compared to the required capabilities.

And as the focus shifts to the Pacific, with its tyranny of distance and the brutal operating conditions often seen in the maritime domain, having a very robust airlift fleet becomes a foundational element. The replacement for the E, the CH-53K, will provide a significant enhancement to the lift capability, and sustainability in operations as well. It is also a question of being able to deliver combat support speed or CSS to the mobile or expeditionary base, and clearly the combination of tiltrotor and heavy lift can do that.

But the challenge will be having adequate numbers of such assets, notably because the nature of the environment is very challenging, and the operational demand will go up significantly if one wants to operate a distributed force but one which is sustained and protected by an integrated force. As Major Everett put it: "There's no way with the types of shipping and numbers of shipping we have, that we could possibly carry enough aircraft on that shipping to enable any type of land control without 53s."

An aspect that makes the upgraded heavy lift fleet a key enabler for expeditionary basing will be the installation of a mesh network manager into the digital cockpit of the CH-53K, and its build into the legacy aircraft as well. This makes it part of an integratable force, not just an island presence force. As Major Everett put it: "The core kind of skills that 53 pilots train to, are not going to change. But obviously the physicality of the new helicopter is very different. It can lift more relevant materials or assets and in larger numbers. It holds the 463L pallets that allow for rapid off and on-loads from the fixed wing aircraft which could provide distribution points for the heavy lift fleet. Additionally, the impact of the CH-53K's integrated digital interoperability and its integration into the kill web will be significant."

In short, the desire to have a Marine Corps–enhanced role in sea control and sea denial with an island strategy really enhances the importance of heavy lift helicopters.

Forward Arming and Refueling Points (FARPs)

June 8, 2020

When considering contributions which the USMC can make to the joint or coalition force in Pacific operations, an ability to put an air arming and refueling point on virtually any spot on the kill-web chessboard is clearly a key contribution. These are referred to as FARPs, or Forward Arming and Refueling Points.

In looking at a theater of operations, and certainly one with the tyranny of distance of the Pacific, one needs to be able to have a layer of fuel support for operations. For the Marines operating from the sea, this clearly includes combat ships, MSC tankers and related ships as well as airborne tanker assets. By deploying a relatively small logistics footprint FARP or ARP, one can provide a much wider of points to provide fuel for the combat force. And in Marine terms, the size of that footprint will depend on whether that FARP is enabled by KC-130J support or by CH-53E support, with both air assets requiring significantly different basing to work the FARP.

I recently had a chance to discuss FARP operations and ways to rework those operations going forward with Maj Steve Bancroft, Aviation Ground Support (AGS) Department Head, MAWTS-1, MCAS Yuma.

There were a number of takeaways from that conversation which provide an understanding of the Marines working their way ahead currently with regard to the FARP contribution to distributed operations. The first takeaway is that when one is referring to a FARP, it is about an ability to provide a node which can refuel and rearm aircraft. But it is more than that. It is about providing capability for crew rest, resupply and repair to some extent.

The second takeaway is that the concept remains the same but the tools to do the concept are changing. Clearly, one example is the nature of the fuel containers being used. In the land wars, the basic fuel supply was being carried by a fuel truck to the FARP location. Obviously, that is not a solution for Pacific operations.

What is being worked now at MAWTS-1 is a much more capable mobile solution set. Currently, they are working with a system whose provenance goes back to the 1950s and is a helicopter expeditionary refueling system, or HERS. This legacy kit limits mobility, as it is very heavy and requires the use of several hoses and fuel separators. Obviously, this solution is too limiting, so they are working a new solution set. They are testing a mobile refueling asset called TAGRS, or a Tactical Aviation Ground Refueling System.

U.S. Marines with Marine Wing Support Squadron (MWSS) 371, Marine Wing Support Group (MWSG) 37, 3rd Marine Aircraft Wing (MAW) and Marine Fighter Attack Squadron (VMFA) 122, Marine Aircraft Group (MAG) 13, 3rd MAW, work together to refuel an F-35B Lighting II during a forward area refueling point operation at Marine Corps Air Station Yuma, Feb. 4, 2020. Photo by LCpl Julian Elliott-Drouin, 3rd Marine Aircraft Wing.

The third takeaway is that even with a more mobile and agile pump-ing solution, there remains the basic challenge of the weight of fuel as a commodity. A gallon of gas is about 6.7 pounds, and when aggregating enough fuel at a FARP, the challenge is how to get adequate supplies to a FARP for its mission to be successful. To speed up the process, the Marines are experimenting with more disposable supply containers to provide for enhanced speed of movement among FARPs within an extended bat-tlespace. They have used helos and KC-130Js to drop pallets of fuel as one solution to this problem.

The effort to speed up the creation and withdrawal from FARPs is a task being worked by the Marines at MAWTS-1 as well. In effect, they are working a more disciplined cycle of arrival and departure from FARPs. And the Marines are exercising ways to bring in a FARP support team in a single aircraft to further the logistical footprint and to provide for more rapid engagement and disengagement as well….

MAWTS-1 and the F-35

May 29, 2020

Over the past few weeks, I have been discussing with USAF and U.S. Navy officers how the two services are training to shape greater synergy with regard to the integrated distributed force. The fusing of multiple sensors via a common interactive self-healing web enhances the ability of the entire force, including key partners and allies, to engage cooperatively enemy targets in a time of conflict.

From the USAF and U.S. Navy perspective, where does the USMC fit into the evolving integrated-distributed force? Clearly, one answer which has been given several times in my interviews can be expressed in terms of one of the Marines' key competences—bringing an integrated force to a mobile operational setting whether afloat or ashore.

It is important to consider a base afloat or ashore as part of the chess-board from a basing point of view. Too often when one mentions basing, the mind goes quickly to a fixed air or ground base, but in the evolving strategic environment, an ability to work across a wide variety of basing options is crucial. And no force in the world is more focused on how to do this than the USMC. With the arrival of the USS America–class LHA, the amphibious fleet moves out from its greyhound bus role to being able to contribute fully to sea control in transit or in operations, thereby relieving the U.S. Navy large-deck carriers from a primary protection role.

To be clear, when one is talking about a combat cloud, the processing power empowering webs comes from cloud processing power. With a focus on interactive kill webs, the processing power is distributed. The integration of the F-35 into the Marine Corps and its ability to work with joint and coalition F-35s provides significant reach to F-35-empowered mobile bases afloat or ashore.

Recently, I had a chance to talk with Major Brian "Flubes" Hansell, MAWTS-1 F-35 Division Head, with regard to how the Marines are working the F-35 into their approach or better yet approaches to expeditionary basing.

The first takeaway is that following a significant focus on the land wars in the past twenty years, combined with the return to the sea, the Marines are shaping new capabilities to operate at sea and in a way that can have significant combat effects on the expanded battlespace.

And they are doing so from expeditionary bases, afloat and ashore. According to Major Hansell: "The Marine Corps is a force committed to expeditionary operations. When it comes to F-35, we are focused on how best to operate the F-35 in the evolving expeditionary environment, and I think we are pushing the envelope more than other services and other partners in this regard. One of the reasons we are able to do this is because of our organizational culture. If you look at the history of the Marine Corps, that's what we do. We are an expeditionary, forward-leaning service that prides itself in flexibility and adaptability."

A second takeaway is how the concepts of operations empower a kill-web approach. The F-35 is not just another combat asset but also at the heart of empowering an expeditionary kill-web-enabled and enabling force. The

F-35 force operates as a wolfpack. This was a concept which Secretary Wynne highlighted when I worked for him in DoD. His perspective then is now reality and one which empowers an expeditionary force. As Major Hansell put it: "During every course, we are lucky to have one of the lead software design engineers for the F-35 come out as a guest lecturer to teach our students the intricacies of data fusion. During one of these lectures, a student asked the engineer to compare the design methodology of the F-35 Lightning II to that of the F-22 Raptor. I like this anecdote because it is really insightful into how the F-35 fights. To paraphrase, this engineer explained that the F-22 was designed to be the most lethal single-ship air dominance fighter ever designed. Period. The F-35, however, was able to leverage that experience to create a multi-role fighter designed from its very inception to hunt as a pack."

Simply put, the F-35 does not tactically operate as a single aircraft. It hunts as a network-enabled, cooperative four-ship fighting a fused picture, and was designed to do so from the very beginning. "We hunt as a pack. Future upgrades may look to expand the size of the pack."

The hunt concept and the configuration of the wolfpack is important not just in terms of understanding how the wolfpack can empower the ground insertion force with a mobile kill-web capability but also in terms of configuration of aircraft on the sea base working both sea control and support to what then becomes a land base insertion force.

Another takeaway focuses on the reach, not range point, about the F-35 global enterprise.

The F-35 wolfpack has reach through its unique C^2 and data fusion links into the joint and coalition force F-35s with which it can link and work. And given the global enterprise, the coalition and joint partners are working seamlessly because of common TTP or Tactics, Techniques, and Procedures. As Major Hansell put it: "From the very beginning we write a tactics manual that is distributed to every country that buys the F-35. This means that if I need to integrate with a coalition F-35 partner, I know they understand how to employ this aircraft, because they're studying and practicing and training in the same manner that we are. And because we know how to integrate so well, we can distribute well in the extended battlespace as well. I'm completely integrated with the allied force into one seamless kill web via the F-35 as a global force enabler."

The fifth takeaway is the evolving role of the amphibious task force in the sea control mission.

With the changing capabilities of strategic adversaries, sea control cannot be assumed but must be established. With the coming of the F-35 to the amphibious force, the role of that force in sea control is expanding and when worked with large deck carriers can expand the capabilities of the afloat force's ability to establish and exercise sea control.

With the coming of the USS America–Class LHA, the large-deck amphibious ship with its F-35s onboard is no longer just a greyhound bus but a significant contributor to sea control as well. As Major Hansell noted: "The LHA and LHD can plug and play into the sea control concept. It's absolutely something you would want if your mission is sea control. There is tremendous flexibility to either supplement the traditional Carrier Strike Group capability with that of an Expeditionary Strike Group, or even to combine an ESG alongside a CSG in order to mass combat capability into something like an expeditionary strike force. This provides the Navy-Marine Corps team with enhanced flexibility and lethality on the kill web chessboard."

The sixth takeaway is that MAWTS-1 overall and the F-35 part of MAWTS-1 are clearly focusing on the integrated distributed force and how the Marines can both leverage an overall joint and coalition force able to operate in such a manner as well as how the Marines can maximize their contribution to the integrated distributed force.

According to Major Hansell, "the CO of MAWTS-1, Colonel Gillette has put a priority on how to integrate as best as we can with the Navy, as well as the joint force. And for the F-35 period of instruction during all Weapons Schools, we focus a tremendous amount of effort on integrating with the joint force, more so than I ever did on a legacy platform. We really strive to make our graduates joint integrators, as well as naval integrators. And I give Colonel

Gillette (the current CO of MAWtS-1) all the credit in the world for moving us to that mindset and pushing us to learn how to operate in the evolving expeditionary environment."

Expeditionary Basing and C^2

June 14, 2020

A key element of the challenge for successful mobile or expeditionary basing which must be met is the command and control required to operate a distributed force which is integratable with the appropriate air-maritime force. This allows the expeditionary force both to make its maximal contribution to operations and to enhance its survivability.

I discussed the C^2 challenges associated with expeditionary basing with Maj Tywan Turner Sr., TACC Division Head, Marine Aviation Weapons and Tactics Squadron 1. The TACC serves as the operational command post for the commander of the aviation combat element and their staff and at WTI plays a key role in integrating aviation assets from the West Coast, East Coast and overseas.

The Aviation Command and Control System is referred to as "common" because all Marine Air Command and Control System (MACCS) agencies either have or are planning to adopt the software and equipment suite. Prior to the hard shift towards Naval Integration, it was a major step towards digital interoperability. But the baseline Common Aviation Command and Control System (CAC2S) during the land wars has operated from a Humvee frame, which obviously is not the best way to work the ship to shore concepts of operations which expeditionary C^2 will require.

Moving forward, combing enhanced digital interoperability with much smaller footprint server capabilities to manage C^2 data will provide a way ahead for working to deploy more efficacious expeditionary deployable C^2 As Major Turner put it: "We need a smaller mousetrap to do C^2 in the expeditionary basing environment."

The Marines are working with a CAC2S smaller form factor to meet the evolving needs for force insertion. They are experimenting with decreasing the footprint of the server–software configuration to make it more deployable and overcome mobility and sustainment limitation (lift required, power requirements and fuel, cooling). According to Major Turner: "CAC2S small-form factor SFF, also has also shown early promise in being incorporated aboard naval vessels." It could provide enhanced digital interoperability between expeditionary bases and Naval strike groups as well. With regard to working the CAC2S deployable system, a correlated effort is working new ways to handle the wave forms which the ashore force would need in a variety of expeditionary environments. And along with this effort, clearly signature management is a key consideration as well.

A key part of the C^2 effort is to enable the wave forms needed to be deployed with an expeditionary basing force, for those wave forms will determine with which force elements the Marines can integrate with both to achieve their mission and to support the broader integrated distributable force. Clearly, a major challenge facing USMC–USN integrability revolves precisely around how best to ensure integratable C^2.

Are the Marine decision makers operating from expeditionary bases or are they nodes in a fire control network? With the new computational technologies, which allow for the enablement of the internet of things at the tactical edge, the capability for the Marines to play the decision-making role with an extended kill web can be emphasized and enhanced going forward.

For the Marines to play a decision-making role from mobile basing, there is a key challenge as well associated with the evolution of the wave forms enabling deployed integrability. There needs to be management of the various wave forms to deliver what one might call a 360-degree waveform delivery system to the deployed Marines, to have both the situational awareness and the decision space to support the proper scheme of maneuver from the mobile base.

By 360 degrees, I am referring to an ability to manage wave forms which provide management of the ship to shore to airborne platform space to deliver the kill-web effect. Such a 360-degree solution should also support all-domain access (specifically the space and cyberspace domains) to information that is normally held at the operational level. If the Marines are deploying strike teams to expeditionary basing, how best to ensure that they have the 360-degree waveform capability to achieve mission success?

The Evolving Amphibious Task Force

June 4, 2020

With the return to the sea on which the USMC has been working with the U.S. Navy over the past few years, the role of "amphibiosity" has been in evolution as well. The Bold Alligator Exercises started in 2011 and refocused on the importance of the return to the sea. The *Second Line of Defense* team attended Bold Alligator exercises and we have written several articles about those exercises. In effect, the evolution was crafted around the coming of the Osprey and under the influence of the coming of the F-35.

Put in blunt terms, it was about the Marines moving from a significant focus on the land wars to a "return to the sea." It is one in which the force would change from a primary role of providing a greyhound bus to insert force to an engagement force able to operate from sea. It has involved shaping and understanding what an air-mobile force could do when able to operate at greater reach into littoral regions with a rapid insertion force. And one empowered by the Ospreys coupled with fifth-generation capability.

Under the twin influence of these two assets, the new LHA class, the USS America ships, was introduced and with it, significantly different capabilities for the amphibious force itself. As the U.S. Navy reworks how it is operating as a distributed maritime force, which is being reshaped around the capability to operate a kill-web force, the question of how best to leverage and evolve the amphibious force is a key part of that transition itself.

This is a work in progress, and one in which a determination of various paths to the future are in evolution and will be subject to debate as well. Part of that evolution are changes in other elements of the amphibious task force which can over time play roles different from how various "legacy" platforms can be reworked to provide for new or expanded capabilities for the U.S. Navy overall. A case in point is how the Viper attack aircraft can evolve its roles AT SEA with the addition of key elements being generated by the digital interoperability effort, as well as adding a new weapons capability to the Viper, namely, the replacement for the Hellfire missile by the Joint Air-to-Ground Missile (JAGM).

Four U.S. Marine Corps AH-1Z Vipers with Marine Light Attack Helicopter Squadron (HMLA) 469, Marine Aircraft Group (MAG) 39, 3rd Marine Aircraft Wing (MAW), take flight to participate in exercise Viper Storm at Marine Corps Air Station Camp Pendleton, Calif., Dec. 11, 2019. December 11, 2019. Photo by Pfc. Victor Mackson. 3rd Marine Aircraft Wing.

What this means is that the Viper can be a key part of the defense of the fleet while embarked on a variety of ships operating either independently or as part of an amphibious task force. Because the Viper can land on and operate from of a wide range of ships, thus enabling operational and logistical flexibility, and with integration of Link 16 and full motion wave forms as part of digital interoperability improvements, the Viper can become a key member of the kill-web force at sea.

In discussions with Major Thomas Duff and Mr. Michael Manifor, HQMC Aviation, APW-53, Attack and Utility Helicopter Coordinators, I learned of the evolving mission sets which Viper was capable of performing with the digital interoperability upgrades. According to Duff and Manifor: "With the upgrades coming soon via the digital interoperability initiative, the Viper through its Link 16 upgrade along with its Full-Motion video access upgrade, can have access to a much wider situational awareness capability which obviously enhances both its organic targeting capability and its ability to work with a larger swath of integrated combat space. This means that the Viper can broaden its ability to support other air platforms for an air-to-air mission set, or the ground combat commander, or in the maritime space. Because it is fully marinized, it can land and refuel with virtually any ship operating in the fleet, which means it can contribute to sea control, which in my view, is a mission which the amphibious task force will engage in with the expanded reach of adversarial navies."[52]

Recently, I had a chance to discuss with Major "IKE" White, the AH-1Z Division Head at MAWTS-1, the evolution of Viper enabled by upgrades for fleet operations as well as its well-established role in supporting the ground maneuver force. In that conversation, there were a number of takeaways which highlighted potential ways ahead.

The first takeaway is that the Marine Corps' utility and attack helicopters have been part of integrated operations and escort tasks throughout the land wars and can bring that experience to bear in the return to the sea. The Viper and the Venom have provided airborne escorts for numerous Amphibious Ready Groups over the last decade, partnering with destroyers, MH-60 Sierra and MH-60 Romeo helicopters have been used to protect amphibious warships as they transited contested waterways.

The second takeaway is the coming of the Joint Air-to-Ground Missile (JAGM), which will provide a significant strike capability for the maritime force in providing for both sea control and sea denial. This missile provides increased lethality through a dedicated maritime mode, enhanced moving

---

52.   Robbin Laird, "Digital Interoperability and Kill Web Perspective for Platform Modernization: The Case of the Viper Attack Helicopter," *Second Line of Defense* (Jun 16, 2020), https://sldinfo.com/2020/06/digital-interoperability-and-kill-web-perspective-for-platform-modernization-the-case-of-the-viper-attack-helicopter/.

target capability and selectable fusing, providing capability against both fast attack craft and small surface combatants. Millimeter wave (MMW) guidance increases survivability by providing a true fire-and-forget capability, removing the requirement for a terminal laser.

Coupled with the AIM-9 sidewinder, the Viper will be able to engage most threats to naval vessels. The Viper's flexibility will provide even the most lightly defended vessels with a complete air and surface defense capability.

The third takeaway is that by working integration of the MH-60 Romeo helicopter with Viper, the fleet would gain a significant defense at sea capability. Integration of the two helicopters within the amphibious task force would allow them to provide an integrated capability to screen and defend the flanks of the afloat force.

The MH-60 crews are optimized to integrate into the Navy's command and control architecture, and with onboard sensors can help detect potential targets and direct Vipers to engage threats. The integration of Link-16 will make this effort even more seamless.

My interviews with NAWDC in 2020 have underscored how the Navy is working through the question of how the integratable air wing will change when the MQ-25 joins the fleet and working ways for the Romeo to work with MQ-25 and Advanced Hawkeye as part of its fleet defense function.

Clearly, integrating Romeos which fly onboard the amphibious-class ships with the Viper would provide a significant enhancement of the flank defense capabilities for the amphibious task force. Working a Romeo/Viper package would affect the evolution of the Romeos that would fly off of the L-class ships as well. And all of this frees up other surface elements to support other missions at sea rather than having to focus on defending the amphibs as greyhound buses.

The fourth takeaway is that clearly this new role would have to be accepted and trained for, but I would argue that in general, the U.S. Navy needs to rethink how amphibious ships can operate in sea control and sea denial functions in any case. I would also argue that the enhanced efforts at digital interoperability within the USMC aviation force need to be accompanied by upgrades of the elements of the amphibious task force with regard to C^2/ISR capabilities as well. We are seeing MISR or Maritime ISR officers placed within the Carrier Strike Groups, but they could be proliferated more broadly within the fleet.

In short, the evolution of the Viper with digital interoperability and with a new weapons package can clearly contribute to the evolution of the amphibious task force, as it embraces sea control and sea denial missions, and these missions will be crucial to supporting insertion forces moving to ashore expeditionary bases as well.

The Ground Combat Element in the Pacific Reset

September 24, 2020

As the USMC works its relationship with the U.S. Navy, a core focus is upon how the Marine Corps can provide for enhanced sea control and sea denial. A means to this end is an ability to move combat pieces on the chessboard of the extended battlespace. But where does the ground combat element (GCE) fit into this scheme for maneuver?

The key is to ensure that the USMC is combat-capable today as it transitions to a new GCE that incorporates new capabilities, such as the Marine Littoral Regiment. I had a chance to talk with Major Fitzsimmons, the Ground Combat Department Head at MAWTS-1, about the transition challenge during my September 2020 visit to MAWTS-1. As Major Fitzsimmons put the re-orientation from the land wars: "we are focused on a more amphibious distributed force operation. And in my view, this is a very big shift."

Major Fitzsimmons provided a very helpful entry point into this discussion by recalling the earlier work which the Marines had done with the Company Landing Teams. As Major Fitzsimmons put it: "The Company Landing Team (CLT) was an experiment at how we lighten the footprint of the force while still giving them the capabilities of what we see in larger forces today. To do that, we would leverage digital interoperability, connectivity, and reach back to weapon systems, to information, to targeting, to any of those capabilities that you generally see at some of the higher echelons that were not organic to an infantry company at that time. The challenge then is to ensure that the infantry company has access to those types of capabilities and mature the force."

What Major Fitzsimmons meant by maturing the force was discussed later in the conversation.

He highlighted the importance of having Marines earlier in their career able to work with various elements of the joint force because they would need to leverage those capabilities as part of the more distributed GCE.

The Company Landing Team experiment also raised questions about equipment and personnel: These were key questions which flowed from the discussion with regard to the USMC operating the CLT: "How do we reinforce the CLT and how do we augment it with enablers? How do we augment it or enhance it with more proficient and more experienced fires personnel? How do we augment it with small, unmanned air system capabilities? How do we augment and enhance it with digital interoperability? How do they communicate with their organic radios across multiple waveforms? Whom are they talking to? What is their left and right for decisions? Do they have fires approval? Would the company commander have fires approval, or would he have to do what we were having to do in Afghanistan and Iraq, where I've got to call my boss and then the boss's boss, in order to get fires employed?"

With the introduction of the new Marine Corps Littoral Regiment, it is clear that these aspects of the CLT experiment are relevant to the way ahead. Major Fitzsimmons is an infantry officer with fires experience at the company and battalion level, and clearly is focused on the key aspect of how you enable smaller and less organically capable forces in the extended battlespace and ensure that they have adequate fires to execute its missions. And in dealing with peer competitors, clearly the ability to link the GCE with fires requires the right kinds of communication capabilities. As Major Fitzsimmons put it: "We are going to have to be significantly more distributed and quieter with respect to our emissions signatures than we have in the past."

A major challenge facing the GCE is the range of adaptability that they will have to be able to deliver and operate with in the future. As Major Fitzsimmons put it: "I think the biggest shock to my community is going to be the level of adaptability that we're going to have to be able to achieve. We are going to have to train smaller forces to operate more autonomously and to possess the ability to achieve effects on the battlefield previously created at higher echelons."

He focused as well on the tailorable aspect envisaged as well. "We will need to be tactically tailored to achieve whatever effect we need. It should be akin to a menu; based on the mission and the effects needed to shape the environment towards mission accomplishment, we will need this capability or that capability which may require each element to be manned and equipped differently."

Then there is the challenge of the sustainability of the tailored force. How best to ensure the logistics support for the distributed maritime focused USMC GCE? In short, fighting with the force you have while you transition to a new one is a major challenge for the USMC going forward.

Blue Water Expeditionary Operations

September 27, 2020

As the USMC focuses on how it can best help the U.S. Navy in the maritime fight, two key questions can be posed: How is the Marine Corps going to contribute most effectively to the Pacific mission in terms of sea control and sea denial? And how to best contribute to the defensive and offensive operations affecting the SLOCs? A key element for an evolving combat architecture clearly is an ability to shape rapidly insertable infrastructure to support Marine air as it provides cover and support to the Marine Corps ground combat element. This clearly can be seen in the reworking of the approach of the Aviation Ground Support element within MAWTS-1 to training for the execution of the Forward Air Refueling Point mission.

During my visit to MAWTS-1 in early September 2020, I had a chance to continue an earlier discussion with Maj Steve Bancroft, Aviation Ground

Support (AGS) Department Head, MAWTS-1, MCAS Yuma. In this discussion it was very clear that the rethinking of how to do FARPs was part of a much broader shift in combat architecture designed to enable the USMC to contribute more effectively to blue water expeditionary operations. The focus is not just on establishing FARPs but also on doing them more rapidly and moving them around the chessboard of a blue water expeditionary space more rapidly. FARPs become not simply mobile assets but also chess pieces on a dynamic air–sea–ground expeditionary battlespace in the maritime environment.

Given this shift, Major Bancroft made the case that the AGS capability should become the seventh key function of USMC Aviation. He argued that the Marine Corps capability to provide for expeditionary basing was a core competence which the Marines brought to the joint force and that its value was going up as the other services recognized the importance of basing flexibility.

But even though a key contribution, AGS was still too much of a pickup effort. AGS consists of seventy-eight MOSs or military operational specialties, which means that when these Marines come to MAWTS-1 for a WTI, they come together to work how to deliver the FARP capability. As Major Bancroft highlighted: "The Marine Wing Support Squadron is the broadest unit in the Marine Corps. When the students come to WTI, they will know a portion of aviation ground support, so the vast majority are coming and learning brand new skill sets, which they did not know that the Marine Corps has. They come to learn new functions and new skill sets."

His point was rather clear: if the Marines are going to emphasize mobile and expeditionary basing, and to do so in new ways, it would be important to change this approach. "I think aviation ground support, specifically FARP-ing, is one of the most unique functions the Marine Corps can provide to the broader military." He underscored how he thought this skill set was becoming more important as well. "With regard to expeditionary basing, we need to have speed, accuracy and professionalism to deliver the kind of basing in support for the Naval task force afloat or ashore."

With the USMC developing the combat architecture for expeditionary base operations, distributed maritime operations, littoral operations in a contested environment and distributed takeoff-vertical landing operations, reworking how to execute FARP operations is a key aspect in shaping the way ahead. FARPs in the evolving combat architecture need to be rapidly deployable and highly mobile and need to maintain a small footprint and emit at a low signature.

While being able to operate independently, they need to be capable of responding to dynamic tasking within a naval campaign. In my language, they need to be configured and operate within an integrated distributed force, which means that the C^2 side of all of this is a major challenge to ensure it can operate in a low-signature environment but reach back to capabilities which the FARP can support and be enabled by.

This means that one is shaping a spectrum of FARP capability as well, ranging from light to medium to heavy in terms of capability to support and be supported. At the low end or light end of the scale one would create an air point, which is an expeditionary base expected to operate for up to 72 hours at that air point. If the decision is made to keep that FARP there longer, an augmentation force would be provided and that would then become an air site.

Underlying the entire capability to provide for a FARP clearly is airlift, which means that the Ospreys, the Venoms, the CH-53s and the KC130Js provide a key thread through delivering FARPs to enable expeditionary basing. This is why the question of airlift becomes a key one for the new combat architecture as well. And reimagining how to use the amphibious fleet as lily pads in blue water operations is a key part of this effort as well. In effect, an ability to project FARPs throughout the blue water and littoral combat space supporting the integrated distributed force is a keyway ahead.

The F-35 and USMC–U.S. Navy Integration

September 29, 2020

During my visit to MAWTS-1 and NAWDC, one clear instrument of their enhanced integration in the contested battlespace was rather obvious:

the F-35 and its evolution as a global enterprise. With the F-35 coming to the large-deck carrier, the strike syllabus has changed. With the F-35 pioneered by the USMC, with its naval aviators leading the way, new capabilities have been brought to the force in terms of integratability, mobile basing and combat power from the sea on a wider variety afloat asset than simply the large-deck carrier.

With MAWTS-1 this year, I have discussed two sets of related questions: What is the way ahead with regard to mobile and expeditionary basing? And how can the USMC provide greater support for the maritime battle? Specifically, during my visit to MAWTS-1 in September 2020, we focused on two core questions: How is the Marine Corps going to contribute most effectively to the Pacific mission in terms of sea control and sea denial? And how to best contribute to the defensive and offensive operations affecting the SLOCs?

Prior to my visit, I discussed the mobile basing piece with Major Brian "Flubes" Hansell, MAWTS-1 F-35 Division Head. A key aspect of what we discussed was the capability of the F-35 to both empower their expeditionary bases and contribute to the wider integration in the fleet approach being worked. As Major Hansell put it: "By being an expeditionary, forward-based service, we're effectively extending the bounds of the kill web for the entire joint and coalition force."

Taking off from the USS Wasp in May 2015 during F-35 sea trials. The author shot this picture while part of a media visit to the ship to witness the sea trials. Credit: *Second Line of Defense.*

During my September 2020 visit to MAWTS-1, I met with Major Shockley, an F-35 instructor pilot at MAWTS-1, whose most recent F-35 experience has been in the Pacific with the squadron in Japan. He reinforced Col Gillette's point in terms of the ability of USMC F-35s to work with allied, USAF and US Navy F-35s as well to shape a situational awareness and strike force which expanded the reach of the joint or coalition force.

Indeed, Major Shockley highlighted the impact of F35-B thinking on base mobility. The F-35As and F-35Cs have some advantages in terms of fuel, and range and loitering time in comparison to the F-35B, notably with regard to the F-35C. Because the force is so inherently integratable, how best to work the chessboard of conflict with regard to where the various F-35 pieces move on the chessboard? From this standpoint, he argued for the importance of shaping a "rolodex of basing locations" where F-35s could land and operate in a crisis.

He had in mind not only what the very basing flexible F-35B could provide but also thinking through deployment of "expeditionary landing gear" to allow the F-35As and F-35Cs to operate over a wider range of temporary air bases. Here he was referring to preparing locations with the gear to enable landing on shorter run "airfields" as well as the kind of modifications the Norwegians have done with their F-35s enabling them to land in winter conditions in the High North.

With the F-35B, a much wider range of afloat assets are being used to enable the F-35 as a "flying combat system" to operate and enable ISR, C^2 and strike capabilities for the joint and coalition force. This is being demonstrated throughout the amphibious fleet, a fleet which can be refocused on sea control and sea denial rather than simply transporting force to the littorals.

A key consideration when highlighting what the F-35 as a wolfpack can bring to the force is deploying in the force multiples that makes sense for the force. This rests upon how the combat systems are configured on that force. In simple terms, the integrated communications, navigation and identification systems operate through a multiple-layer security system, allowing a four-ship F-35 force to operate as one. With the Block IV software coming into the fleet, now an eight-ship F-35 force can operate similarly. This allows for wolfpack operations, and with the ability of the reach of the F-35 into other joint or coalition F-35 force packages, the data flowing into the F-35 and the C^2 going out has a very significant reach and combat impact.

This is not widely known or understood but provides a significant driver of change to being able to operate and prevail in denied combat environments. Leveraging this capability is critical for combat success for the U.S. and allied forces in the Pacific. And my visits to NAWDC and MAWTs-1 certainly underscore that these warfighters get that.

Unmanned Air Systems and the USMC

October 22, 2020

In 2018, I published a chapter on the USMC's recent experience with unmanned air systems in the book edited by John Jackson, entitled *One*

Nation Under Drones.[53] I focused on the substantial experience they have accumulated with Scan Eagle and then with the Blackjack system. The primary use has been in terms of ISR in the land wars, but with the return to the sea and now the focus on how the Marines can best help the U.S. Navy in the maritime fight, the focus has shifted to how to best use UASs in the maritime domain.

With the recent decision to cancel its MUX ship-based UAS to pursue a family of systems, the focus will be upon both land- and sea-based UASs but not to combine these capabilities into a single air vehicle.

As the then Deputy Commandant of Aviation, LtGen Rudder, put it:

"In the next 10 years, the quickest way – the commandant wants to go quick on this – this quickest way will be some sort of land-based high-endurance that can be based and still be able to provide the surface force, the amphibious force the capabilities that we would call 'quarterback,' or some sort of node that can provide 24 hours on station time, it will have all the networking and early warning and electronic warfare capabilities that they require for that type of thing,"[54]

But the path to do this is not an easy one. And it is a path which is not just about the technology but also about having the skill sets to use whatever system is developed, the connectivity so that the combat effect can be connected to the maneuver force, and to have communication links which have low latency, notably in the maritime fight.

During my visit to MAWTS-1 in early September 2020, I had a chance to talk with Captain Dean, an experienced UAS officer who is a UAS instructor pilot at MAWTS-1. We discussed a wide range of issues with regard to UAS within the USMC, but one comment he made really gets at the heart of

---

53.   John E. Jackson, editor, *One Nation Under Drones: Legality, Morality, and Utility of Unmanned Combat Systems*, (USNI Press, 2018).

54.   Megan Eckstein, "Marines Ditch MUX Ship-Based Drone to Pursue Large Land-Based UAS, Smaller Shipboard Vehicle," *USNI News* (March 10, 2020), https://news.usni.org/2020/03/10/marines-ditch-mux-ship-based-drone-to-pursue-large-land-based-uas-smaller-shipboard-vehicle.

the transition challenge: "What capabilities do we need to continue to bring to the future fight that we currently bring to the fight?"

What this question highlights it there is no combat pause for the Marines—they need to be successful in the current range of combat situations, and to reshape those capabilities for the combat architecture redesign underway.

But what if this is not as significant and overlapping as one might wish? This is notably true with regard to UAS systems. In general terms, the UAS systems which have been dominant in the Middle East land wars have required significant manning, lift capability to move them around in the battlespace and are not low-latency communications systems. Although referred to as unmanned, they certainly are not so in terms of support, movement of exploitation systems or how that data gets exploited.

There clearly is a UAS potential for the blue water and littoral engagement force, but crafting very low-demand support assets with low-latency communications is not here as of yet.

And in the current fights ashore, UASs like Blackjack provide important ISR enablement to the Ground Combat Element. And as the Marines have done so, they have gained very useful combat experience and shaping of relevant skill sets to the way ahead for the UAS within the future force.

The goal is to have more flexible payloads for the UAS force going forward, but that means bringing into the UAS world experienced operators in fields broader than ISR, such as electronic warfare. But there is clearly a tension between funding and fielding of larger UASs for the amphibious task force, and between shaping new systems useable by combat teams. And the challenge here clearly is to manage information and to distribute by communications system. Although the phrase about distributing information at the right time and at the right place sounds good, this is very difficult to do if the data links expose the combat force to adversary target identification.

This is yet another key area where contested combat space has not much to do with how UASs can operate in uncontested air space. Captain Dean underscored that since 2015, "we have been able to normalize unmanned aviation with the USMC. We have been able to bring in a lot of experience into the VMUs and with the sundowning of the Prowlers, have brought in Marines experienced with electronic warfare as well. We continue to prioritize our training on the Blackjacks going to the MEUs."

This photo was taken during the author's visit in 2015 to VMU-2 at Cherry Point. The Marines are working to prepare a launch of the Shadow UAV. Credit: *Second Line of Defense.*

He highlighted that this posed a challenge for transition. To get full value out of the Blackjacks operating off the amphibious force, changes need to be made on those ships to get full value from operating these UASs. But if the Blackjack is a short- or mid-term solution, the kind of investment which needs to be made is not likely to happen.

What he highlighted was the crucial importance of the infrastructure afloat to make best use of the UASs which the USMC and U.S. Navy will operate. And given the challenge of managing space onboard the ship, sorting out the nature of the infrastructure and how to manage it is a key aspect of the way ahead for UASs.

Another challenge is who wants what within the combat force. If we are looking at the fleet as a whole, the desire is to have fleet-wide ISR capabilities. If one is focused on the battalion, they are focused on having capabilities organic to the battalion itself.

Again, this is a development and investment challenge which also raises questions of what kind of infrastructure can be developed to deal with each of these different operational-level requirements. "What does the MAGTF want? What does the battalion want? These are not the same things."

In short, a key question facing the Marines with regard to UASs is what capabilities do they need now and in the future?[55]

---

55. The Marines are operating Predators as an interim solution but interestingly the USAF itself is shifting from Predators to a family of systems solution set. Valerie Insinna, "Get Ready for another fight over the future of the MQ-9 Predator," *Defense News* (May 26, 2021), https://www.defensenews.com/air/2021/05/26/get-ready-for-another-fight-over-the-future-of-the-mq-9-reaper/.

CHAPTER FOUR:

THE VIEW FROM II MEF AND NORFOLK

The way ahead for reshaping the USMC as a full-spectrum crisis management force in the North Atlantic is being worked around enhanced integration with the U.S. Navy and focusing on the skill sets needed for operations in the High North and the Nordic region. As we argued in our book on the return of direct defense in Europe, a defense arc from Poland through the Baltic Republics to the Nordics to the High North is a key element of the challenge facing direct defense in the North Atlantic.

With the launching of the new version of Second Fleet in 2018, Admiral Richardson, the CNO, set in motion the process of working maritime force transformation for the 4th Battle of the Atlantic. As that reworking unfolded, the only NATO operational command on U.S. soil has been set up in Norfolk, Allied Joint Forces Command, and both commands were then placed under VADM Lewis.

In addition, the Nordics—two members of NATO and two not—have focused on enhanced integration and defense transformation in the wake of Russian actions in the seizure of Crimea. As I wrote in my book with Murielle Delaporte:

"Nordic defense and security cooperation are part of a broader global trend in which clusters of states are working together to enhance their ability to enhance their defense and security against the return of Russia and the rise of China. 'Clusterization' is the next phase whereby liberal democracies do more for themselves in their joint defense rather than simply relying on diplomatic globalization initiatives through organizations like the EU or NATO to do that for them.

"Clusterization is key to generating enhanced capabilities that can work interdependently with key allies outside of a regional cluster to reinforce the capabilities in a realistic and effective way to deter core adversaries. In the case of the Nordics, clearly the United States is the key outside power, with Brexit Britain and those states within continental Europe which have capabilities which can show up effectively to bolster the underbelly of the Nordic region are the key players that can reinforce Nordic defense.

"But at its heart, the Nordics need to bolster their own capabilities as well to work more effectively with their offshore allies and their continental European partners. But to be blunt: this requires looking more realistically at what the defense of the Nordic region means against the evolution of Russian policies, strategies, and capabilities rather than simply to assume that NATO as a multimember alliance will simply show up.

"The Trident Juncture 2018 exercise in Norway is a good example of how a leading Nordic nation is rethinking its policies. On the one hand, Norway is working their national mobilization approach, and on the other hand, they hosted several allies within Norway, and in part, it is a question of what capabilities can be brought in a timely manner that would really make a difference in a crisis.

"It is not simply a question of showing up; it is about blending those domestic and allied capabilities into an effective crisis management force against specific and targeted Russian threats. But providing for enhanced Nordic capability within a broader transatlantic framework remains a work in progress, notably when measured against Russian activities, behavior, and evolving capabilities.

"To the point about the blending of what the Nordics are doing and shaping in terms of defense capabilities, the question on the U.S. side is what capabilities we are bringing to bear into 'an effective crisis management force against specific and targeted Russian threats.'"[56]

The Perspective of VADM Lewis

May 26, 2021

VADM Lewis highlighted his thinking about the way ahead for the U.S. Navy with regard to North Atlantic defense as well as his working relationship with the USMC in shaping that way ahead in a May 2021 interview which I did with Ed Timperlake, and the excerpts where he focused on the USMC are highlighted.

Question: The template which you and your team have put in place, shaping an integrated distributed force, is well positioned to encompass a number of the new technologies, such as maritime autonomous systems. How do you see the relationship between reworking concepts of operations and technologies?

VADM Lewis: I've become somewhat jaded with technology because technology is just a means to an end. Said another way, it's just a tool. You have to ask what are we trying to get out of it? What's the objective? And then, how are we going to use that technology? The key point is that our processes need to be agile enough to absorb new technology without missing a beat. That's where I think we need to focus our efforts.

Later in the conversation, VADM Lewis brought together in a very clear way the importance of getting the C^2 piece right and leveraging technologies approach to that effort to do so.

According to VADM Lewis: "An operational headquarters or a high-end tactical headquarters is a weapon system. Normally, when warfighters discuss weapon systems, they refer to their platforms. But the operational or tactical headquarters should be looked at as being a key weapons system, the glue that pulls a multitude of different weapons systems together in a coherent

---

56. Robbin Laird and Murielle Delaporte, *The Return of Direct Defense in Europe: Meeting the 21st Century Authoritarian Challenge* (2020).

manner – both kinetic and non-kinetic. They can mass fires, mass effects, and maneuver in a coordinated fashion at the fleet level. That's what operational and tactical headquarters do.

"But we need to get better at being able to craft, shape and leverage operational or tactical headquarters as a weapon system. We have to get a lot better at doing so, and new technologies can be helpful here, which is one of my objectives for working with the Mid-Atlantic Tech Bridge."

Vice Adm. Andrew Lewis, Commander, U.S. 2nd Fleet, speaks with a group of Sailors he intends to present a challenge coin to during a visit to the U.S. 2nd Fleet's Expeditionary Maritime Operations Center (ExMOC) Joint Expeditionary Base Little Creek-Fort Story Aug. 11, in support of Large-Scale Exercise (LSE) 2021. August 11, 2021. U.S. Navy photo by Mass Communication Specialist Seaman Juhlena Royer.

Question: There are other command challenges, such as the division between Second and Sixth fleets in the Atlantic or how C2F will work going forward with II MEF, for example. How do you see the way ahead?

VADM Lewis: We are working hard on this challenge. My main effort as the Commander of two NATO commands and a U.S. Fleet command is to ensure there are no seams in the Atlantic – seams that our adversaries can exploit. By communicating and working closely with our counterparts on the other side of the Atlantic, we can ensure we are working to close any perceived gaps. As an example, we recently conducted staff talks with Second Fleet, Sixth Fleet and II MEF. We are making progress thanks to the relationships we have spent time developing.

In terms of C^2, we can always be better about how we talk about and exercise command and control. My focus has been on the principles of mission command in which you emphasize trust with your commanders to lead distributed forces. You have to first understand the environment, and then you have to give clear intent. Once you have given this guidance, you let the distributed forces operate in a way that allows them to self-organize in order to meet the mission. This doesn't involve a whole lot of detailed control from various headquarters, rather it only provides enabling guidance that allows them to take initiative at the right level and to manage risk at the right level.

I believe my role with regard to my subordinate commands it to mentor the commanders below me. My goal is to give them the right guidance and then let them command.

I have two discussions each week with the operational strike group commanders that work for me – the first is focused on man, train and equip issues, and the second is focused on mission command and operational issues. It's an opportunity for me to hear about various issues and spend time listening. At other times, we'll bring in a guest speaker and discuss operational dilemmas others have faced to use as case studies for the group. It is truly time well spent with the strike group commanders who make up our waterfront leadership.

Question: How do you view the way ahead with integration with the USMC?

VADM Lewis: We have a fantastic relationship with our USMC counterparts, and because of that relationship we have made great progress with integration. We have a few Marine staff officers working at 2nd Fleet, but I think we would also benefit from an exchange of sorts at the Flag level. I think we could make additional progress if we integrate a Marine as the deputy commander of C2F, and vice versa, a Navy commander as the deputy commander at II MEF. I have such an approach with my NATO JFCNF command, and it works well as we shape very concrete ways ahead to build more effective fleet operations with our NATO counterparts.[57]

In this interview, VADM Lewis highlighted the importance of shaping a distributed integrated force into which allies, and American forces can work closely together and are able to do so with the right kind of mission command structures enabling the distributed force to operate effectively at the combat edge.

A key element which needs to be worked for sure is how American and allied airpower integrates effectively with the distributed maritime force to deliver the desired combat and crisis management effects. With the recent exercises involving U.S. bombers operating from Norwegian bases, and providing fighter escort from the Nordics, one part of the equation is in play. Another part of the equation is the role of fifth-generation aircraft, which the joint force will provide, in the case of the USAF operating in the future from RAF Lakenheath, the UK F-35s operating from sea or the Norwegian and Danish F-35s from their national territory or forward deployed to Iceland, or other locations in the areas of interest. But what is the role of the USMC? Or better yet, what could be the role of the USMC in such effort with regard to North Atlantic defense?

---

57.   Robbin Laird and Ed Timperlake, "Shaping a Way Ahead for North Atlantic Defense: The Perspective of VADM Lewis," *Second Line of Defense* (May 26, 2021), https://sldinfo.com/2021/05/shaping-a-way-ahead-for-north-atlantic-defense-the-perspective-of-vadm-lewis/.

The Perspective of the Commanding General of II MEF

June 7, 2021

During visits to Camp Lejeune in April and June 2021, I had a chance to talk with the Commander of II MEF, Lieutenant General Brian D. Beaudreault. This command is a key part of the overall effort to reshape the working relationship between the operational Navy and the USMC to enable integrated operations. The entire effort encompassed by Second Fleet, Allied Joint Force Command, 2nd Marine Air Wing and II MEF constitutes a significant reshaping of how to fight the 4th Battle of the Atlantic.

For II MEF, such an effort provides both significant challenges and significant opportunities for transformation. The significant challenge can be put simply: the U.S. Navy is in the throes of significant change as it refocuses on blue water operations and fighting as a fleet. This is a work in progress.

The USMC under the current Commandant is focused on enhancing the USMC capability to work with Navy more effectively in integrated operations but doing so when the fleet itself is changing is particularly challenging. And the strategic shift from the land wars to blue water expeditionary operations is very challenging as an entire generation of Naval and Marine Corps sailors and Marines and their officers have worked in support of COIN operations and not upon high-end warfare.

At the same time, for II MEF there are significant opportunities as well. The redesign of North Atlantic defense is coming at a time when the Nordic allies are committed to direct defense and to enhancing their own integration to deal with the Russian challenges. Although II MEF is not the epicenter for receiving new Marine Corps equipment, with the exception of the CH-53K (it does not yet have F-35Bs as part of its organic fighting force, for example), it must find ways to innovate with the equipment it has and must find new ways to work with an evolving U.S. Navy to sort through how to deliver combat effects from ashore and at sea in support of the maritime fight.

U.S. Marine Corps LtGen Brian Beaudreault, center, the commanding general of II Marine Expeditionary Force, speaks with MajGen David Furness, left, the commanding general of 2nd Marine Division, Col Michael McWilliams, right, commanding officer of Combat Logistics Regiment 2 and LtCol Kate Murray, commanding officer of Combat Logistics Battalion 252, at a forward combat service support area at Marine Corps Air Ground Combat Center Twentynine Palms, California, Oct. 25, 2019. Photo by Cpl Scott Jenkins. 2nd Marine Logistics Group.

During the April 2021 visit, we started by the CG highlighting the command guidance he has received from the USMC Commandant. As LtGen Beaudreault put it: "Paraphrasing the guidance: tighten your lifelines with second and sixth fleet. As the Navy shapes itself to do distributed maritime operations, how do we help, and how do we reconfigure?"

One of the challenges clearly is working both with Second and Sixth Fleets, with C2F as the new kid on the block and Sixth Fleet reworking its efforts in Atlantic defense. There is a clear command issue which needs to be sorted out going forward, which is important in helping the Marines to better integrate with the evolution of the Navy, as it works distributed maritime operations. Second Fleet command authorities end with Greenland with the 6th Fleet having command authorities after that point. But Vice Admiral

Lewis is the commander as well of Allied Joint Force Command whose forces obviously extend beyond Greenland into the continent.

In my discussions with the command during my visit, this issue was raised several times and clearly the command authorities is a work in progress. For the Marines, a key Cold War mission for the Marines was to get to Norway as rapidly as possible to reinforce NATO's efforts against the Soviets. In those days, the Warsaw Pact geography gave the Russians key advantages in a conflict which they do not have in the new geography for European defense. The Soviets planned in case of full-scale conflict, a World War II German style operation against Norway and Denmark. This is off the table as the political geography has changed along with the forces arrayed against the Russians as opposed to the Soviet empire.

For the Marines, a key contribution to the maritime fight in the region is clearly to be able to operate afloat and ashore, and interactively between the two in providing key reconnaissance, key choke point capabilities and fires in support of the maritime maneuver force. And at the outset, the new capabilities which the Marines are developing will be viewed by the Navy as complimentary to their capabilities and will need to demonstrate to the fleet that some of their sea denial and sea control functions can be ceded to the Marines in time of conflict.

In effect, a chessboard is being shaped where the fleet interacts with air and land assets to create a 360-degree operational area from Florida to Finnmark. And the goal as seen by LtGen Beaudreault is to "leave no operational seams the Russians can exploit in times of conflict."

A key toolset important to the reworking is clearly training and exercises. LtGen Beaudreault emphasized that what is occurring is a "refocus on scale" where the focus is upon the expeditionary strike force level, not at the MEB level. The C^2 redesign efforts prioritized by VADM Lewis are a key part of how II MEF is addressing how to shape the kind of distributed force capability which can deliver a more effective integrated force able to deliver the kind of crisis management and combat effects needed in the North Atlantic.

As LtGen Beaudreault put the challenge: "What command and control arrangements do we need for a naval distributed force to be effective?" And as this is being crafted, how will the MEF be reshaped as a key partner in the maritime fight?"

The April 2021 testimony of the head of the Defense Intelligence Agency highlighted the central nature of the Russian challenge to the United States and its allies. For the United States, in many ways the most direct threat to our country comes from the forces operating from the Kola Peninsula. This means that although China may be the pacing threat, warfighting and deterrence of the Russians is crucial. What this means is that experimentation to shape the integrated distributed force needs to reinforce combat capability and not have open-ended disruption which reduces the ability to engage the adversary at his time and choosing.

What this means in turn is that there is a clear need to work with the capabilities that II MEF has now and not a decade from now. Part of this is re-imaging what the amphibious forces can bring to the maritime fight. Part of this is focusing on how legacy assets like Hueys and Cobras (now Yankees and Vipers) can be retrofitted with anti-surface weapons and sensors. Part of this is relaying on the central role which Ospreys can play in moving forces and support across the chessboard. In other words, modernization accounts need to keep abreast of how the Marines can support the kind of innovation underway with the fleet and the allies in the Atlantic.

In the Commandant's focus on the Pacific, III MEF is prioritized. This leaves II MEF in the position to ensure that it can work more effectively with allies in support of the reshaping of the Marines role in the maritime fight. As LtGen Beaudreault put it: "One of our lines of effort in the campaign plan is to deepen our ties with our alliance partners, and not just from an interoperability point of view but focusing on interdependent operational capabilities."

And this clearly is happening with what Rear Admiral Betton, Deputy Commander of Allied JFC refers to as the "relevant nations." In our 2021 interview with Betton in Norfolk (I first interviewed him in Portsmouth when he as the first commander of HMS Queen Elizabeth), he underscored how the allied and U.S. efforts were blending and how that blending was central to the strategic redesign.

As Betton put it: "The U.S. is by far the dominant figure of NATO, but it's not the only piece. And it's not always just the heavy metal that is relevant. It's the connectivity, it's the infrastructure and the architecture that enables the 30 nations of NATO to get so much more than the sum of the parts out of their combined effort. But it's particularly the relevant nations in the operational area and their ability to work together which is an important consideration."[58]

This perspective is certainly shared by LtGen Beaudreault and is part of the focus on the redesign of II MEF. He highlighted in our discussion their working relationships in recent exercises with the UK Royal Marines, with the French 6th Light Armored Brigade, operational working relationships in Norway, with the Canadians, with the Dutch, etc. This is not just about exercising, it is about shaping an integratable force, and doing so is a key part of ensuring that Atlantic defense capabilities can be enhanced even while China is being focused on as the "pacing threat."

We discussed some of the innovations being pursued by II MEF. One innovation is working a way ahead to be able to deploy fires ashore in support of a maritime maneuver force. Currently, II MEF is working with the High Mobility Artillery Rocket System (HIMRS) artillery systems and anticipate working in the near term with the naval strike missile, which of course was developed by the Norwegians but is managed on the U.S. side by Raytheon.

A second innovation is working new ways to shape and leverage C^2 and firing solutions, and II MEF's work with 18th Airborne Corps at Fort Bragg is an important part of this effort. He noted that later in 2021, II MEF

---

58.   Robbin Laird and Ed Timperlake, "The Role of Allied Joint Force Command Norfolk in Atlantic Defense: The Perspective of its Deputy Commander," *Second Line of Defense* (March 24, 2021), https://sldinfo.com/2021/03/the-role-of-allied-joint-force-command-norfolk-in-atlantic-defense-the-perspective-of-its-deputy-commander/.

will be working with 18th Airborne Corps in support of a Navy large-scale exercise to work C^2 enabled third-party firing solutions.

LtGen Beaudreault argued that going forward, with a new generation of amphibs he would like to see them have organic fire power to operate more independently. This is how he put it: "We need more air defense systems, and we need more offensive striking capability out of an amphib with less reliance on cruisers, destroyers, in the future."

In terms of next steps in working integration, he highlighted the importance of the role which the Marines can make to the maritime fight in terms of sensing. He argued that a key effort will be to "refashion Marine Corps reconnaissance. What can we put on manned aircraft and unmanned systems to help extend the eyes and ears of the Navy?"

Expeditionary basing is being worked as well to "help unlock naval maneuver from support of forces ashore. How can we best help support naval maneuver from our distributed forces ashore? And crucial to all of this will be our ability to change the C^2 arrangements we have to be able for our forces to be either the supported or supporting capability in a blue water maneuver force."

Such an approach which can be labelled as Naval–Marine Corps integration obviously involves integratability with air forces as well. Notably, if the Marines do not have organic F-35s, they are relying then on Nordic air power, which in the case of Norway and Denmark are F-35s.

With the refocus as well on the High North and the progress in Nordic integration, there clearly is a rethinking of what the USMC's role in supporting a maneuver force in the region. This is a major challenge and one driving the force design which II MEF is undergoing in interaction with the changes occurring in Norfolk and the Nordics as well.

When I visited in June 2021, LtGen Beaudreault was two weeks from relinquishing command and then retiring from the USMC. In that discussion, we discussed on further developments in USMC–Naval integration involving II MEF. LtGen Beaudreault underscored that an agreement was being coordinated with 6th and 2nd Fleets whereby 2d MEB would stand up an integrated headquarters, potentially based at Camp Lejeune that would work integrated operations between the fleet and the MEB.

Although details will need to be worked with regard to the standing up of an integrated naval headquarters, the strategic direction was clear. LtGen Beaudreault noted: "Conceptually, this force would be ESG 2 integrating with 2d MEB to form an integrated naval headquarters that supports NAVEUR. When ESG 2 and Second MEB came together and went to a BALTOPS, they went to the Mount Whitney to train and then were disestablished and went back to their respective locations. But we are interested in creating a permanent structure which stays together. Whether it's for exercises, we see it as an opportunity to command rotational forces in the high north. When we send battalions or squadrons or a fighter squadron to Finland, all of those kinds of organizations could be underneath the integrated headquarters. The goal is to create permanent structure, with full-time personnel."

He added that it would function in some ways like Task Force 51/5, which was established under CENTCOM in 2018. And as Vice Adm. Jim Malloy, commander of U.S. Naval Forces Central Command/U.S. 5th Fleet/ Combined Maritime Forces, noted concerning the integrated Task Force 51/5 command: "Task Force 51/5 is an integrated force that demands a combination of agility and forethought from its leaders, in part because it's a unique command model that is innovative and new. This Task Force remains vital and irreplaceable in this region – a catalyst for tailored combat effects and an accelerant for Amphibious Forces from the sea. Their tactical strength and ability to be 'where it matters, when it matters' protects American and partner lives and assets."[59]

The command could work flexibly with the "relevant nations" in a crisis response as well. And there is a clear interest to work with allies as they

---

59.   Paul Williams, "Task Force 51/5 Holds Second Ever Change of Command Ceremony in Bahrain," (July 6, 2020), https://www.tf515.marines.mil/News/ News-Article-Display/Article/2261588/task-force-515-holds-second-ever- change-of-command-ceremony-in-bahrain/.

transform their force insertion capabilities from the sea as well. An example would be the UK's Littoral Response Group North.

As Johnathan Bentham noted in his article on this new UK force:

"The LRG is part of a broader initiative to adapt the UK's amphibious forces to operate in a more dispersed and agile way in response to the increasingly challenging environments that they are now facing. These adaptations include a new Future Commando Force, as reforms to the Royal Marines are being dubbed, with greater focus on technology and raiding missions from the sea. The LRG idea could form part of that, including within a larger UK or multinational force, and the latest deployment has involved exercises with NATO allies and other partners, including this year's BALTOPS exercise in the Baltic Sea.

"As part of this, the LRG is being used as a testbed for a range of innovative capabilities including uninhabited systems. These changes are also meant to provide force packages able to undertake a range of maritime security tasks, potentially including counter-terrorism, limited interventions and evacuation operations, as well as humanitarian assistance and disaster-relief missions. Another priority for the LRG concept is to maintain forward presence and undertake capacity building and defence diplomacy, a key component of a wider effort to increase the Royal Navy's global presence and improve its responsiveness."[60]

LtGen Beaudreault added: "The new integrated command would give the NAVEUR commander a third operational arm. He's got Second Fleet, he has Sixth Fleet, and now he would have this Task Force to provide him more C^2 options to support distributed maritime operations. And this focuses on a key question: What do we want an integrated naval headquarters to do in support of NAVEUR? The answer is more effective crisis management and escalation control. This organization could be a key part of escalation management and help to create both pressure and potential off ramps in a crisis. Amphibious forces

---

60.   Jonathan Bentham, "UK Littoral Response Group: The Shape of Things to Come?" *IISS* (June 25, 2021), https://www.iiss.org/blogs/military-balance/2021/06/uk-littoral-response-group.

forward deployed in international waters are able to deter, assure, ratchet up or dial down until policy makers can get some kind of resolution to the crisis."

The Perspective from II MEB

May 7, 2021

The Russian seizure of Crimea set in motion the return of direct defense for both Europe and the United States. With Putin's Russia reshaping its defense capabilities and concepts of operations, there is a significant reset in terms of how the United States and the allies are working force integration in the North Atlantic. With the Nordics leading the way in terms of European responses to the Northern Flank, the reestablishment of Second Fleet and the standup of a NATO command on U.S. soil, Allied Joint Forces Command have set in motion a Norfolk-led effort for reworking how the United States Navy works with allies in shaping the way ahead in what has been called the "Fourth Battle of the Atlantic."

With the shift from the land wars to full-spectrum crisis management, and with a new focus by the U.S. Navy on fleet combat operations, a new phase in working Marines with the evolving approach to Naval integration is underway. This clearly affects the North Carolina–based Marines, and no force more so than the 2nd Marine Expeditionary Brigade within II MEF.

During my visit to II MEF during the last week of April, I had a chance to meet with the acting commander of 2nd MEB, Colonel David Everly, 2nd Marine Expeditionary Brigade.

As their website highlights: "The MEB Command Element (CE) provides a Marine Air Ground Task Force /Joint Task Force (MAGTF/JTF)-capable headquarters that can rapidly deploy and when directed composites with naval and / or land-based forward-deployed and/or rapidly deployable forces to form a MAGTF or the core element of a JTF headquarters in order to fulfill Geographic Combatant Commander (GCC) operational requirements."[61]

---

61. "2nd Marine Expeditionary Brigade," https://www.2ndmeb.marines.mil/.

But that force construct faces significant challenges as the effort to shape new approaches to naval integration unfolds. As Colonel Everly put it in our discussion: "We're changing our culture. We're shifting our culture back to align with the naval character of our force." He added that "understanding the Navy's warfare concept is not something culturally ingrained in how the USMC has been trained and operates."

But there is a cultural challenge on the Navy side as well. "Our expertise as a MEB is in composite warfare. How well does the U.S. Navy fighting as a fleet, understand that expertise and how best to leverage that and shape new approaches to integration." In other words, a core challenge is co-evolution of the U.S. Navy and the USMC to create new integrated combat capabilities. On the one hand, as the Navy reworks fleet operations, how best to leverage what the USMC can contribute? Conversely, how should the USMC reshape to better support fleet operations and reshape its approach to composite operations?

A key challenge for the USMC is working two key elements: How to contribute as a task force element and how to be able to deploy as a self-sufficient force in a crisis? On the one hand, what is being worked are new ways to shape modular task forces within which the Marines bring core competencies and capabilities. On the other hand, how to ensure that the Marines are a survivable force when they deploy as a unit?

For Colonel Everly, a key way ahead is for the USMC and U.S. Navy to train and exercise together and to reshape interactively the kind of co-evolution which will lead to mission success. The MEB is clearly pursuing such an approach as seen in the recently completed Dynamic Cape 21 exercise. In this exercise, working how to shape expeditionary logistics as a key part of support to force projection in the North Atlantic was a key part of the effort. Logistics is crucial as well as shaping the kind of distributed C^2 which can be leveraged to craft flexible force integration as well.

The C^2 piece and the expeditionary logistics pieces are two key parts of adapting 2 MEB's composite warfare capabilities to the new focus on integrated operations with the U.S. Navy, but they are a work in progress.

A couple of examples of what the MEB can bring in the future to the maritime fight are ashore fires, such as HIMARS or the Naval Strike Missile. Another example is working signature management so that Marines operating in expeditionary base locations can provide ISR and other capabilities to the fleet.

Both face challenges. Col Everly was part of the team that brought HIMARS to the land wars. When the HIMARS was introduced into the land wars, the focus was not on shaping them for a dynamic employment concept. I have seen at MAWTS-1, the Marines working integration of HIMARS with F-35s, which is the kind of dynamic employment concept which makes sense for the way ahead for Marine Corps integration for the maritime fight.[62]

The signature management piece is part of the larger challenge of working information warfare as part of force insertion and engagement which would enhance integratability as well. As Col Everly put it: "The information domain is still something that both the MEB and the MEF are working to put their arms around."

Another piece to the Marines working to enhance their ability to contribute to the 4th Battle of the Atlantic is enhanced integratability with the relevant nations in the areas of interest and operations. Col Everly underscored that exercising and training in the region is a key part of enhanced integrability which enables the Marines working with allies can bring to the fight. "Our interoperability with the Nordics, the French and the British is a key part of our effort as well. And this is part of the co-evolution which we are experiencing as they are evolving as we are ourselves...."

---

62.   Robbin Laird, "Working F-35 HIMARS Integration: Shaping a Way Ahead for a 21st Century Distributed Shooter-Sensor Capability," *Second Line of Defense* (June 19, 2018), https://sldinfo.com/2018/06/working-f-35-himars-integration-shaping-a-way-head-for-a-21st-century-distributed-shooter-sensor-capability/.

Working II MEF Operations in Transition

May 16, 2021

While reshaping how it will operate in the future, II MEF has to be ready to fight now. And to do so for 2nd and 6th Fleets as well as United States European Command (EUCOM). This means reshaping what it can do but to rework how it is integrated with the NAVY and the evolving joint force.

During my visit to II MEF at Camp Lejeune, I had a chance to discuss with the leadership at the MEF the challenges of so doing and shaping a way ahead. I have also had the chance with my colleague Ed Timperlake in visiting Second Fleet, to discuss with C2F leadership the challenges of working a co-evolution with the USMC, and with the Nordics on what they view as the kind of force engagement by the Navy and Marines which dovetails most effectively into their own force transformation and reworking of European defense. These are three trajectories in motion and the challenge is effectively to work ways to ensure convergence on effective approaches.

During my visit to Camp Lejeune, I had a chance to discuss the challenges of shaping the way ahead with Col David S. Owen, the Assistant Chief of Staff for Operations (G-3), and LtCol Jon Erskine. For an enhanced focus on working with the U.S. Navy, both officers have significant relevant experience. Col Owen has several years of experience at sea with MEUs and on aircraft carriers. With regard to LtCol Erskine, he was a Navy surface warfare officer who later became a Marine.

The current USMC Commandant has highlighted the importance of integration with the U.S. Navy as it focuses on the high-end fight. And to do so by finding ways for the Marines to operate in the WEZ. Another way to put this is to shape the ability of the Marines to operate as an "inside" force to support the "outside" force.

As Col Owen put it quite clearly in our discussion, "Above all, even if we are focused on enhanced naval integration, what we are really focused on is warfighting and how best to do it."

It is clear that figuring out how the Marines can fight, survive and best deliver a desired combat effect while operating in the WEZ is challenging. As Col Owen put it: "We need to figure out how best to operate within the WEZ. We have operated as MAGTFs, and MEUs and that entails bringing a force that is wholly capable. A MEU is a little suitcase of MEF-wide capabilities that can deliver scalable effects. It is a Swiss Army Knife. With a focus on the inside force approach, we are acting as an enabler for the joint or coalition force. How best to do so?"

One way to look at the force re-configuration is for a Marine Corps formation to operate, as Col Owens noted, "to facilitate decisions in a larger kill web. For example, a Marine Corps Reconnaissance force could be part of a larger formation with tentacles which it extends to enable the force either through its own resources or tapping into other capabilities, such as the P-8."

For LtCol Erskine, as a former Surface Warfare Officer (SWO), he has very relevant domain expertise to work the problem of how Marines can contribute to a distributed kill-web firing solution. He underscored the importance of working the sensor/shooter "mesh." As he noted: "How do you connect any sensors on the battlefield to provide targeting quality data into a system and route it to the right decision-maker who has the authorities to either employ that weapon or coordinate it with other fire-decision authorities?"

If one is putting Marines inside the WEZ with strike weapons, those weapons clearly need to be integrated with the other services, to ensure that combat effectiveness is the outcome, rather than fratricide, negative impacts on the tactical situation or impacting negatively on the strategic crisis management decisions which need to be made as well in a conflict situation.

Marines operating as an inside force might be aides to the process of finding targets and then passing those targets to the right shooter and use an asset they do not even own. As LtCol Erskine highlighted: "You could reach out to a Joint Strike Fighter (JSF) that's in your engagement area, or you could reach out to a ship at sea or any aircraft flying through your airspace to pass the appropriate data for a firing solution. It may not even work for you as a Marine Corps unit."

In effect, the goal is for the Marines to work with the joint and coalition force to shape a "fires network of things." For enhanced Navy and Marine Corps integration, clearly one challenge to be met is how to shape an integrated maritime campaign. How do you coordinate fires on land with fires at sea? As LtCol Erskine underscored the challenge: "How do I provide those fires in support of the fleet from land-based capabilities and vice versa?"

In our discussions with Second Fleet, VADM Lewis put this challenge as one of enabling the fleet and the joint and coalition force to be able to operate either as supporting or supported elements dependent on the combat situation. Shaping such a flexible combat capability is clearly a work in progress, and II MEF and C2F are key innovators in shaping such a way ahead.

The C² Piece

June 4, 2021

As II MEF transforms, a key challenge will be to ensure force cohesion and force aggregation. For example, with the current Marine Expeditionary Unit, the MEU has a well-defined organic capability which allows it to operate effectively and to scale up with force integration with other force units.

But going forward, how will the MEF forces be organized? What will the force packages look like? How much organic ISR and fire power? How much reliance on externally supplied ISR and fire power? And how to build a viable distributed but integratable force?

The only way such questions will be answered effectively is with the evolution of C² capabilities and systems which can shape integratable modular task forces, which can either be the supported or supporting building block for a scalable force. But working C² to achieve the kind of force flexibility which could lead to significant reworking of the mosaic of a joint or coalition force is a major challenge.

During my visit to II MEF in April 2021, I had a chance to focus specifically on the C² piece with II MEF's G-6 command, which is the communications element. I had a chance to discuss C² issues with the assistant chief of staff of G-6, Colonel Hyla, and the chief of II MEF Defense Information Network, Master Gunnery Sergeant Stephens.

We discussed a number of aspects of the C² challenges and transition. The first takeaway was that the goal of greater Navy and Marine Corps integration faces a major challenge of ensuring that the two forces can work over compatible ISR and C² systems. This simply is not the case currently. If there is an end goal of empowering Marines to be able to provide ISR to the fleet to enable fire solutions, or ashore Marines to leverage Navy ISR and provide for firing solutions either from afloat or ashore assets, the C² needs to be adequate and effective to do so.

Data from various Navy systems must be usable by afloat or ashore Marines. USMC aviation assets afloat or ashore can provide for firing solutions organically or in terms of current USMC C², but if third-party targeting in support of the fleet is desired, then C² needs to be integratable across the fleet into the Marine Corps force.

The second is that meeting the challenge of what the Aussies refer to as transient software advantage is a major challenge.[63] An ability to rewrite software code ahead of adversary capability to disrupt ISR/C² systems is crucial. During a visit to Jax Navy in 2020, I saw the P-8 team working such an approach with regard to rewriting code. In an interview with Lt. Sean Lavelle, he described the approach as follows:

"They are focusing on ways to execute in-house software development under PMA-290, the Program Office for the P-8. Within PMA-290 is an office called the Software Support Activity, which Lt. Lavelle and his team works with. There they are focused on building a system on the P-8 where mission system data, including data links, and information generated by the sensor

---

63.   Robbin Laird, "Shaping Force Integration: The Aussies Work a Way Ahead," *Second Line of Defense* (June 15, 2017), https://sldinfo.com/2017/06/shaping-force-integration-the-aussies-work-a-way-ahead/.

networks goes to the 'sandbox' which is a secure computing environment that can take data, process it, and generate decision-making recommendations for the operator or alert them to tactical problems. It does not directly push data to the aircraft, so it is divorced from safety of flight software considerations."

According to Lt. Lavelle: "This allows us to push updates to the sandbox on timescales measured in days or weeks, rather than years. The Weapons School is building the software for the sandbox based on operators' experiences, while the traditional acquisitions enterprise builds the infrastructure to allow that development. The process is that we observe the fleet's problems, we write code to solve those problems, we send the finished application to PMA-290, they do a security analysis, and then they push it back to be integrated onto the aircraft. We are funding this process operationally rather than on a project basis. We have four to six people at the weapons school at any one time who are trained to write software for the sandbox."[64]

The Marines are focused on a similar effort. As Col Hyle put it: "The Marine Corps has recognized the need to code ourselves, and we have our first cohort of what is now 0673s is the new Military Occupational Specialty (MOS)."

The third is working new ways to integrate with core allies in terms of C² capabilities This rests not simply on sorting through ways to work more traditional security arrangements but new, innovative ways of leveraging commercial networks in secure manners as well. II MEF has been hard at work in this area, notably in working with Canadians, Norwegians, the British and French forces in Europe, to be able to shape shared C² capabilities in new and innovative ways.

The fourth is the force aggregation and disaggregation issue which is at the heart of the flexibility in being able to operate as a distributed but integratable force. Colonel Hyla put it this way: "How do we fit into the transformation of composite warfare? For example, I may be working under potentially the MEF today, but we may for a couple days move over to work for the carrier

---

64.   Robbin Laird, *Training for the High-End Fight*, (2021), Chapter Three.

strike commander, or we may transfer a couple aircraft to work for the anti-sub warfare commander for a couple days, depending on the availability of assets in the battlespace. But we're not used to cutting away a platoon or a battery from a battalion or a company from a battalion to work for the Navy for a day or two and then come back to us. We've got to make sure, once they decide how we do that, that all our C^4 systems align and work with them and we can talk with them, whoever our direct combat boss is in the battlespace."

Much easier to do with briefing slides than with operational forces. And being able to fight tonight remains an imperative as II MEF serves many masters, including, EUCOM, Second and Sixth Fleets.

The ISR Piece

May 10, 2021

The terms C^2, ISR and training are changing significantly in the shift from the land wars to the high-end fight. C^2 is migrating from hierarchical direction to mission command and distributed operations; ISR is moving from intelligence, surveillance, reconnaissance to INFORMATION to decision-making for an integrated distributed force; and training is an open-ended learning process of how to shape modular task forces that can work together to deliver the desired crisis management and combat effects.[65]

But as the Marines work with the Navy towards more effective integration for the high-end fight, both sides face significant challenges to work with one another. On the one hand, the U.S. Navy has new added ISR capabilities in the form of P-8s and Tritons which have not been designed in any way to support the kind of maneuver operations which the Marines are built to do. On the other hand, the excellent C^2 which the Marines have built to operate ashore are not built to work with the at-sea maneuver force.

There is no technological magic wand which can be waved over the two forces to create integratability. This must be worked from the ground up on each side, and the ultimate purpose of doing so needs to be shaped in very

---

65.   Robbin Laird, *Training for the High-End Fight: The Strategic Shift of the 2020s* (2021).

concrete ways and in very clear mission areas. Why are they integrating? For which crisis management or combat effect? Against which adversaries and for what demonstrated positive outcome?

During my visit to II MEF, I had the chance to discuss the way ahead on the Marine Corps side with a very experienced Signals Intelligence (SIGINT) officer, who is the head of II MEF G-2 and the senior intelligence officer for the MEF, Col William McClane. He joined the Marines towards the end of the Cold War, and as I have seen in both Marine Corps and Navy interviews, there are a smattering of such officers towards the end of the careers who bridge the end of the Cold War and the beginning of the new phase of peer competition.

Obviously, the bulk of their careers has been through the land wars period, but these officers understand how very different those wars are from facing an adversary with full-spectrum forces able to conduct contested operations across the battlespace, up to and including the threat and ability to use nuclear weapons.

I have referred to this as the strategic shift, but in many ways, this is more of a strategic shock than a strategic shift. The Navy is shifting from support to land operations to blue water maneuver warfare; the Marines are shifting from being best mates of the U.S. Army to reworking into a maneuver force for full-spectrum crisis management. As the Navy shifts from a primary focus on supporting the the land wars to blue water expeditionary operations, the Marine Corps is reworking how it can assist in such a shift.

I had a chance to talk with Col McClane on several issues but will highlight three major ones. The first one is the return of Russia as a definer of North Atlantic defense. The second is the intelligence to information transmutation of ISR. And the third is the challenge of working more convergence between Navy and Marine Corps ISR systems.

But the overview point made by Col McClane was clearly articulated by him: "We are in a campaign of learning to shift from COIN operations to great power competition." Part of that learning is refocusing on the Russians. When I went to Columbia University for my PhD in the late 1960s and early

1970s, the universities were committed to Russian studies. They certainly are not now. If there is a refocus on dealing with the Russians, generating new analysts with Russian knowledge, language and substantive expertise is a major requirement.

This is certainly reflected in refocusing a force like the USMC. What Col McClane noted was that our Nordic allies certainly have not taken a vacation from dealing with Russians, and that their domain knowledge is a key part of shaping a rethink of how to understand Russian behavior, training and operations. And clearly, it is the Russian military we are dealing with, not the Soviet Union.

This means that there is a double knowledge challenge. The first is that much of the residual U.S. knowledge remains under a Soviet hangover. And second that fresh knowledge of how the Russians operate under President Putin militarily needs to be built out.

The second is the intelligence to information shift in ISR. As Col McClane put it: "We tend to get too fixated on the cyber piece to the determinant of working the information piece about how Russian decision makers operate and will operate in a crisis. That is a craft which we need to master."

The information piece is about shortening the cycle from knowing to acting, as well as working information war. Col McClane noted that "it is crucial we master the process whereby information can be tailored for messaging that affects the adversaries' cognitive decision making. The messaging is key."

The third key challenge we discussed is aligning USMC and U.S. Navy intelligence, surveillance and reconnaissance systems. A key example is that the P-8, which is being operated by the U.S. Navy and our allies in the North Atlantic, is not generating data easily usable by the USMC. In fact, in the recent Dynamic Cape 21 exercise, the Marines were able to work much more effectively with USAF unmanned aerial systems than Navy assets in terms of ISR missions.

For Col McClane, this means: "We need naval capability development not just U.S. Navy, and USMC separate acquisitions in the ISR area. If we are truly going to fight a naval campaign, the Marines will need to be able to tap into U.S. Navy systems useful to a Marine air-ground task force. Fixing and resourcing the Naval ISR enterprise is a key part of shaping the way ahead."

II MEF Information Group

July 8, 2021

During my April 2021 visit to II MEF, LtGen Beaudreault underscored: "I think it would be hugely valuable to just rifle a bunch of questions, because there's a lot going on in the information space that we're also coordinating and collaborating with Second Fleet, Sixth Fleet but primarily Sixth Fleet. Whether it's BALTOPS, Sea Breeze, and the other exercises that are going on, or real-world operations, we are in the competitive information space every day against our competitors. Col Brian Russell is front and center on leading that effort. In many ways, I think he's the best I've ever met in working in that space. And he's very well connected, and he's not shy about reaching out to organizations like the 16th Air Force and other joint partners, on how all of us are working collaboratively in the information domain."

Needless to say, I did follow up, and the CG's assessment of his information group certainly was on the mark. The MIGs or Marine Information Groups were first stood up in 2018. Colonel Russell noted that "the MIG was borne out of the MEF Headquarters Group here. We had some of the components already, but they were reorganized under a different construct with some different capabilities, like the communication, strategy and operations company. Psychological operations capabilities, defensive cyber capabilities, were packaged in this MEF Information Group. I think the key for the MEF Information Group is taking all those capabilities and making them work together rather than having operational silos such as just coms and just intel; we need to work information operations as a whole."

Col Russell then underscored: "Marines are the original hackers, in my sense. You give them a piece of technology and a piece of equipment, and you give them a different mission, they will absolutely reconfigure that kit or gear to meet that mission. We've done that throughout our entire history. I think of my cyberspace marines, my coders, my application developers, really as cyberspace engineers. They can modify that terrain to our operational advantage and make it go faster, better. Or they can modify that terrain to make it harder for the adversary to disrupt our operations.

U.S. Marine Corps Col Brian E. Russell, commanding officer of II Marine Expeditionary Force Information Group (MIG) is interviewed by a representative of the Information Professionals Organization for The Cognitive Crucible Podcast at Camp Lejeune, N.C., Sept. 28, 2020. Photo by Cpl Tanner Seims, II MEF Information Group.

"We need to realize that in the information space everybody fights. Whether you recognize it or not, whether you like it or not, you are in the information environment. All of our marines on their computer systems every day are in that environment, you need to be careful about it, but we can maximize some opportunities as well."

He argued that for a MIG to be successful they need to pursue a campaign approach. It is about working in a joint warfighting context and being embedded with the joint force as well. In the case of II MEF, there is a concerted effort to work with 6th Fleet, for example, and to shape Naval–Marine Corps integration in the information space.

The allied piece is certainly of increasing importance as working a distributed force able to operate over an extended battlespace requires effective communication in the information space. For example, in the recent BALTOPS 50 exercise, "we had a team with the 30-commando information exploitation group supporting 45-commando, also operating with second MEB." These two groups are part of the UK Royal Marines.

A key task for the MIG in the operations information environment is providing information environment battlespace awareness. According to Col Russell: "We scope our efforts to the need at hand, what is the commander interested in his particular area of operation? We could support US EUCOM in the high north, working with our Norwegian partners, or we support MEF forces in the exercise Sea Breeze right now with division forces on the ground in the Ukraine. There is a complicated information environment in Sea Breeze, so what do we need to do to provide that commander on the ground with an awareness of what is going on around him, not only from the threat perspective, but the opportunities in the information space.[66]

"What does the commander of 1/6 want to think about the COMMSTRAT photo of his marine and the Ukrainian navel entry brigade soldier working together, that really helps with the narrative that we're trying to attain there, that's the level of thinking the commanders need to take nowadays.

"We help provide that to elements of the MEF, and it gets back to a basic ground truth in the information domain: humans are in fact more important than hardware. We get very technical focused sometimes in this information warfare fight. There's a human adversary behind that trying to influence whatever we're doing; we need to understand what that is.

"But this true from the standpoint of the individual marine in terms of his training and education: how do we make that marine resilient to the

---

66. The interview was done during my April 2021 visit. Sea Breeze 2021 turned into information war at sea, more akin to warfighting than an exercise.

message he's going to get from a Russian on his cellphone while he's overseas during an exercise? I think that's the aspect we have to take as commanders, prepare for the environment, understand the adversary approach to it, and then make our marines resilient to adversary information in the operational environment as well."

Clearly, operating effectively in the information environment is a key part of crisis management and escalation control. By gaining significant battlespace awareness, one is better positioned to be proactive and to act with the most relevant means without generating undue escalatory pressures.

The Logistics Piece

July 11, 2021

Logistics is often viewed as the enabler of operations. But if one is designing the force to operate throughout an extended area of operations, logistics capabilities are part of the definition of the art of the possible for crisis management. In a crisis, the goal is to be able to put force up against the critical choke point in the crisis seen as a process.

Getting to that choke point or decision point with the right force with enough sustainability to achieve the desired effect is the goal. The duration of the crisis and the scope and nature of escalation then define what other pieces on the chessboard one brings to bear and with enough sustainability and lethality to get the job done. This is a function of how sustainable the crisis management force is at the point of influence.

For the USMC, the nation's crisis management force—certainly at the initial stages—to be able to play their desired role they have built significant organic support to their force insertion capabilities. But those core assets— the Osprey, the C-130J, the CH-53E and the Yankee—have been taxed significantly in the land wars and need replenishment and augmentation to play their base line role.

This is significantly true as in the redesign of what II MEF is to do in support of Second Fleet (C2F) and Sixth Fleet (C6F) is to engage in operations from the High North to the Western Mediterranean. II MEF is receiving the new CH-53K soon, but in limited quantities. The Ospreys are being cut back in the North Atlantic region, and the Viper/Yankee family is being reduced in the region as well. The venerable C-130J has seen significant engagements in the Middle East and needs upgrades and enhanced numbers as well.

This is even before we get to the duration challenge. For how long, and with what combat effect, does want the initial USMC insertion force to integrate with joint and coalition forces to have the duration necessary to get the desired escalation control and crisis management effect?

The first question—initial insertion—can be answered by a focus on organic assets. The second can only be answered with regard to how robust the logistics combat enterprise is in terms of supporting the desired joint or coalition operations in the crisis area.

During my April 2021 visit to II MEF, I had a chance to speak with LtCol Smith, the senior strategic mobility officer. He and his team focus on the end-to-end supply to the force, through air, sea and ground movements to deploying or deployed forces. As he noted, the Marines work end-to-end transportation, which means that "the embarkers at the units actually do all the preparation for their own equipment, do all the certifications, do all the load planning, and move their units out."

When I visited II MEF in June, LtCol Smith was on terminal leave from the USMC but was kind enough to come into II MEF to continue our discussion. And in this discussion, we focused on this second question: How can we build out a more sustainable force through longer duration crises?

For the Marines, who are working deeper integration with the U.S. Navy, part of the answer is enhanced integrability with the fleet. This means that there needs to be a combat logistics management system which encompasses both the Marines and the fleet in their entirety to provide the kind of supportability which sustained combat engagement requires.

Clearly, such a system is not yet in place, but the new approach to joint task force management between Expeditionary Strike Group 2 (ESG-2) and

Second Marine Expeditionary Brigade (2dMEB) will certainly require such capabilities and could shape building blocks going forward.

By purposing distributed maritime operations with an overall integrated distributed force, the Navy and the Marines clearly need to focus on sustainability across a distributed chessboard. How to get the supplies from industry to depots or prepositioned locations? How to move those supplies to the afloat Marine Corps forces, the fleet or ashore? How to do it with the speed and effectiveness required?

What we focused on in the discussion was ways to build out such capacity to sustain forces throughout the distributed battlespace. On one level, the fleet and afloat combat force simply need more supplies afloat to get the job done. This requires enhanced MSC capabilities, and one way to do so might be building out the very effective T-AKE ships. On another level, the challenge is to move supplies throughout the battlespace to the point of need. Here the challenge would be met by the tiltrotor and rotary force in terms of ship-to-ship and ship-to-shore movement or movement from pre-positioned locations to combat locations.

There are new systems in train, which their numbers are increased can play this role. The CMV-22B and the CH-53K each with different but complimentary capabilities could provide a very significant combat sustainability capacity. But a key point which he underscored throughout the discussion was the following: "You need a fleet logistics management system that is integrated into not only every naval platform but also with regard to Marine Corps platforms if you're going to truly do integration between the Navy and the USMC."

Another key element to shaping a re-invigorated logistics backbone is the question of tanking the fleet, both in terms of getting the new fleet tankers into the fleet and tanking for the lift force. There is a tanking shortfall, and when I worked for Secretary Wynne, we certainly saw that and tried to get the job done. But now the demand side on the USAF and on the USMC already exceeds demand and will be a key delimiter of the ability to sustain the combat force for the duration required for full-spectrum crisis management.

How might we deal with this issue? The MQ-25 is coming to the carrier to deal with carrier requirements, but can autonomous systems be developed to support the tiltrotor and rotary fleet working to support the distributed force? The challenge is to shape a sustainable combat force at the point of interest and to be able to do so through the duration of a crisis. You need to have a robust launch capability and then to build up capacity throughout the duration of the crisis.

And he underscored that the integration with the deployable supply chain was crucial as well. "If you look at the defense of the North Atlantic, you still have several nodes that you have to create to make sure supply is moving." He underscored the importance of building in redundancy to such an effort as well.

In short, logistics is not simply what you think about down the list of what you need; it defines what one can accomplish in a crisis management setting. As the Marines work with the U.S. Navy to reshape capabilities for the maritime fight, two key elements for successfully doing so are the right kind of C^2 for distributed integrated operations and logistical capabilities to support such a force. The logistics piece is not an afterthought but a key enabler or disrupter for mission success. With a sea-based force, the force afloat has significant capability built in for initial operations, but the challenge is with air and sea systems to be able to provide the right kind of support at the right time and at the right place.

The Challenge of Preparing for Future Operations

May 22, 2021

II Marine Expeditionary Force supports service and Combatant Commander's initiative as required. At the same time, II MEF is in transition and must focus on preparing for future operations and shape new ways to do so while being able to operate now. This is hardly an easy challenge, but one which II MEF must meet head-on.

At the command, the head of G-35, Future Operations is Colonel Ryan Hoyle. He noted in our discussion that for the command, a look ahead in an 18-to-24-month period is the focus of future operations. But as we discussed, the focus on change was coming through exercises but also working ways to rework the Marines' ability to integrate with the Navy and with allies to shape evolving capabilities for the future fight.

His background is diverse, and very impressive. I mention this because if you want someone to work through how to work a way ahead with the force in being, it is clearly an advantage to have someone with wide-ranging experience with the current force and enough experience in working with non-Marine joint and allied forces focused on change.

Among other experiences, he has been aide to camp to the Deputy Chairman of the NATO Military Committee, Amphibious Staff Officer and exercise planner at NATO's Special Operations Headquarters. And he has a Master of Science in Political Science from the Israel National Defense College. There is probably no force in the world which has work joint integration in a more challenging political and military environment than the Israeli Defense Force (IDF).

He brings this experience to the current challenging task of transitioning and preparing for the future fight while reshaping the force in being. How do you do this? And how is II MEF approaching this challenge? In the discussion, there are a number of takeaways which provide answers to these difficult questions.

The Israelis provide an interesting case because post–Abraham Accords, they are focusing on their ability to have a strategic reach to be able to deal with threats on their periphery. It is no surprise than that the IDF is operating a core USMC capability, the F-35, and are adding the latest capability, namely, the CH-53K. The IDF is increasingly focused on becoming more mobile and expeditionary, which brings them closer to the USMC trajectory of change as well.

Col Hoyle noted that they work within an 18-month and two-and-a-half-year planning cycle and work "to align resources to achieve the objectives that the CG or higher headquarters have given us. This is in terms of exercise preparation and providing forces of operations." He reminded that as well as the Atlantic operations, II MEF provides forces deployed to Okinawa.

He has the naval integration portfolio in his shop as well, which encompasses amphibious training and deck and well deck certification for those ships. According to Col Hoyle: "We coordinate the entire MEU program from the formation of the force to the integration with the Navy and their deployments with both NAVEUR and MARFOREUR in terms of their tasks in support of those commands."

The refocus on Naval integration is a major challenge. If one looks at the North Atlantic as a chessboard, how do the Navy, the Marine Corps (and the USAF) and allies work the pieces on the chessboard? How do the Marines use their afloat resources differently with the fleet? How does the fleet fight differently with those afloat assets integrated into the fight? How do mobile or expeditionary bases play into the effort? What pieces are placed on the chessboard which the Marines can or might be able to provide? How do the Marines work force integration with allies afloat or ashore to provide for more integrated warfighting solutions?

With the current amphibious fleet in the Atlantic region not likely to get new ships any time soon, how can the Marines work more effectively with allies afloat? Clearly, the integration of Marines onboard HMS Queen Elizabeth or USMC Ospreys (or for that matter the new CMV-22Bs for the Navy) operating off allied ships in an area of interest provide ways to enhance the contribution which Marines can make to the direct defense of Europe. As the Navy and the Marines work with allies in the North Atlantic Defense, the challenge will be to shape flexible or modular task forces which can demonstrate interactive interoperability to expand what Marines can contribute, rather than deploying them in isolated force fragments.

An MV-22B Osprey with the 24th Marine Expeditionary Unit, Iwo Jima Amphibious Ready Group, lands on Her Majesties Ship Queen Elizabeth, at sea on May 10, 2021. The 24th MEU transported Marines and equipment assigned to Marine Fighter Attack Squadron 211, United Kingdom (UK) Carrier Strike Group 21. May 19, 2021. Photo by 1st Lt. Zachary Bodner, 3rd Marine Air Wing.

Col Hoyle put the goal of the transformation effort in the following terms: "How do we provide operational flexibility to the fleet commander, to the combatant commander, to cause the decision calculus of the adversary to change? To do so, you need capabilities with which to project that force, whether it's afloat capabilities or whether it's basing rights somewhere and having the proper airframes in order to project that force."

In short, the focus needs to be not simply on new ways to do Naval integration. The focus has to be on effective forces that an adversary sees as viable and capable of shaping effective crisis management or combat effects. As Col Hoyle put it: "You have to have your high-end capabilities demonstrated to be effective in order to ensue deterrence, because if you are not demonstrating that you have the capabilities, then no—one is really deterred."

Shaping a Way Ahead

June 1, 2021

The Navy and the Marines are reworking ways to enhance their warfighting and deterrence capabilities in the North Atlantic. This effort has been referred to as preparing for the "Fourth Battle of the Atlantic" by Adm. James Foggo III when he was commander of U.S. Naval Forces Europe/Africa.

As CNO Admiral Richardson established 2nd Fleet, he highlighted a new role of the High North as a key area of interest in dealing with the Russian challenge, one which for the direct interest of the United States is focused on what Admiral Gortney highlighted as the 10:00 o'clock and 2:00 o'clock threats to the continental United States (CONUS). In an interview we did with the then head of Northcom and NORAD, Admiral Gortney, this is how he put the challenge:

"With the emergence of the new Russia, they are developing a qualitatively better military than the quantitative military that they had in the Soviet Union. They have a doctrine to support that wholly government doctrine. And you're seeing that doctrine in military capability being employed in the Ukraine and in Syria.

"For example, the Russians are evolving their long-range aviation and at sea capabilities. They are fielding and employing precision-guided cruise missiles from the air, from ships and from submarines. Their new cruise missiles can be launched from Bears and Blackjacks, and they went from development to testing by use in Syria.[67]

---

67. If ever there was a good student of Andy Marshall's approach to the Revolution in Military Affairs it is clearly Vladimir Putin.

"It achieved initial operating capability based on a shot from a deployed force. The Kh-101 and 102 were in development, not testing, so they used combat shots as 'tests,' which means that their capability for technological 'surprise' is significant as well, as their force evolves. The air and sea-launched cruise missiles can carry conventional or nuclear warheads, and what this means is that a 'tactical' weapon can have strategic effect with regard to North America.

"Today, they can launch from their air bases over Russia and reach into North American territory. The challenge is that, when launched, we are catching arrows, but we are not going after the archers. The archers do not have to leave Russia to reach our homeland. And with the augmentation of the firepower of their submarine force, the question of the state of our anti-submarine warfare capabilities is clearly raised by in the North Atlantic and the Northern Pacific waters.

"We need to shape a more integrated air and maritime force that can operate to defend the maritime and air approaches to North America as well as North America itself. We can look at the evolving threat as a ten o'clock and a two o'clock fight, because they originate from the ten and two. And the ten o'clock fight is primarily right now an aviation fight."[68]

68.   Robbin Laird and Ed Timperlake, "North American Defense and the Evolving Strategic Environment: Admiral Gortney Focuses on the Need to Defend North America at the Ten and Two O'clock Positions," *Second Line of Defense* (May 8, 2016), https://sldinfo.com/2016/05/north-american-defense-and-the-evolving-strategic-environment-admiral-gortney-focuses-on-the-need-to-defend-north-america-at-the-ten-and-two-oclock-positions/.

This is a notional rendering of the 10 and 2 o'clock challenge. It is credited to *Second Line of Defense* and not in any way an official rendering by any agency of the U.S. government. It is meant for illustration purposes only.

But how does meeting this challenge look from the standpoint of North Carolina–based Marines?

And with the enhanced focus on integration with Naval forces, how will the Marines reshape their forces and approach to operate in the 2:00 o'clock area of operations?

During my visit to Camp Lejeune in April 2021, I had a chance to discuss the challenge of shaping an effective way ahead with three members of the II MEF team who have taken the longer term perspective on meeting these challenges. At my meeting with Dr. Nick Woods, the Center for Naval Analyses II MEF Field Representative; Dan Kelly, a retired Marine Colonel who works within the G-5; and Major Ronald Bess, who works plans as well at the command, the three together provided a very helpful perspective in understanding how enhancing integration with the Navy looks like from a II MEF lens.

There are four key takeaways from that conversation which I would like to highlight. The first is that this is in the early phases of navigating the way ahead. As one participant highlighted, it is extremely important that both the Navy and Marine Corps work through what each side brings to the key warfighting functions in the North Atlantic.

And with the clear focus of Second Fleet working with the only operational NATO command on U.S. territory, how best to work with Allied Joint Forces Command? For example, if there is a shift from engaging the Marines built around the large-deck amphibious ship, what then is the role of frigates or destroyers in supporting Marine Corps operations?

The second is to understand what warfighting gaps exist as such integration unfolds, and how best to fill those gaps? And this needs to be realistic. What capabilities do we have now? What would we like to have? And what is a realistic acquisition strategy to fill those gaps? As one participant put it: "The joint force as well as those of our allies and partners all are going through change and we need to crosswalk this so we identify Marine Corps contributions and do we have any gaps."

The third is the impact of potential disconnect between what the Combatant Commands want from Marine Corps forces and potential new paths for future Marine Corps development. The demand side clearly needs to change to provide for room for transformations that might well attenuate Marine Corps' capability in the near to middle term but provide for prospects for new capabilities down the road.

The fourth is the general challenge of reworking how the fourth battle of the Atlantic would be fought. How will the joint and maritime forces work together most effectively with allies to deliver the desired combat and crisis management effects?

This ties back to the first point, namely, ensuring that the Navy and the Marine Corps work through most effectively how to deliver with regard to the key warfighting functions in a correlated and where possible integrated manner. As one participant put it: "We need to go to the White Board and work through each of the key functions to ensure that we can deliver an integrated capability before we let go of any current capabilities which we have." And as another participant concluded: "There is a strong argument to be made for divesting of legacy capabilities now in favor of future capabilities that would provide a greater contribution to European defense in the future."

Looking Back and Looking Forward for the USMC

July 15, 2021

I first met LtGen Beaudreault during my visit to II MEF, in April 2021. I returned on June 29, 2021, prior to the General's retirement in July. We discussed the evolution of the II MEF with the U.S. Navy and a recent agreement to shape a joint task force between 2nd ESG and 2nd MEB, and that is discussed in a separate article.

At the end of the meeting, I asked him to look back on the evolution of the USMC during his time of service and to provide some thoughts about the challenges going forward. As his career spanned the end of the Cold War and the global competition with a peer competitor, through the long period of the priority on the Middle Eastern land wars, and now with the return of global competition, but this time with peer competitors, his thoughts are especially helpful as we refocus on the new strategic context.

LtGen Beaudreault: "As I reflect on my time with the USMC, the most capable USMC during my time of service was the force in being we had in the 1988 through 1991 period. I should be clear at the outset I am not suggesting the Marines of today are not as capable as those in that period. I am referring to the size and capabilities we had available to us at the end of the Cold War.

"We were very lethal, agile, and combat flexible. In terms of naval integration, we had MEB elements which Saddam had to consider to be a serious threat of amphibious invasion. We could do either deception or forcible entry. We had a much more robust amphibious capability than today.

"We had a significant Force Reconnaissance capacity organic to the USMC. They embarked as part of the force and relationships are important in this business. There was nothing like having them eat in the wardroom or on the mess decks and interact with those that they supported. They were trained in *in–extremis* hostage rescue, ship take-downs, gas-oil platform seizures and in combination with the embarked SEALS were a tremendously capable force. Some of those skills have migrated to special operations forces which are not always co-located or physically present for integrated crisis planning.

"That was a very, very capable Marine Corps. For example, Force Reconnaissance had an ability to conduct insertion operations out of submarines, that might come in handy in the future. We need to recover some of that capability."

With the coming of 9/11 and the focus on counterinsurgency and counter-terrorism, the mission focus changed significantly. The Marines, out of necessity, supplemented what the U.S. Army and the nation required to be successful in those wars. But as the Marines now refocus on the challenge of dealing with peer competitors, how best to do so?

LtGen Beaudreault: "The Commandant is dealing with the challenge of making hard choices about the way ahead. But the nation needs to realize that we need a larger USMC to do our job more effectively. We need a bigger Marine Corps. We need a bigger amphibious fleet. We need a bigger Navy.

"We are a maritime nation, but with the force we have, we have limited shock absorption capability. Where's the shock absorption capacity? If we have to replace the number of combat losses we might experience in a peer-to-peer conflict, how are we going to do so? How do you sustain the fight? That gets into the industrial base and all other areas. We don't have enough shock absorption capacity in the department right now, in my view.

"We have just enough to meet requirements and get to a one to three deployment to dwell ratio under the current steady state environment. We've got enough to generate combat replacements. But creating whole cloth units is going to be challenging. And I'm very concerned about if we take losses, the ability to rapidly replace those losses. And the affordability and time factors that go with our modernization and fielding in having to replace our damaged equipment. What I worry about, it's insufficient capacity. And after your initial salvos, what's the buy look like?

"I do like the conceptual pieces of where the Commandant's going under his Force Design 2030 initiatives. I think you can complicate the adversary's targeting with some discreet units that are out there. But not everybody can be like MARSOC with small teams that are going to have this effect. I do share some of the concerns on how you sustain distributed forces.

"I think the strength of the Corps, as compared to the Army, is our relationship with the Navy and the organic mobility we get out of our sea lift. We are facing a declining amphibious fleet with potential decommissioning of the LSDs, that's a concern. What impact will this have on the nation and the nation's ability to have the Marine Corps-Navy team deploy to the crisis with sufficient shock absorption capability in the event we take some losses due to adversary action?"

The air power transformation the Marines have gone through over the past twenty years—with the coming of the Osprey, then the F-35B and now the CH-53K—transforms what an integrated Marine Corps–Navy team can bring to crisis management, but II MEF does not yet have F-35s in its force and is currently relying on allied F-35s to play their role.

LtGen Beaudreault: "By 2024, we start replacing our fighters at 2nd MAW with F-35s and should be full up by 2030. USMC F-35s have been prioritized for the Pacific, but this creates some challenges for us. The Harriers and the F-35s are not the same at all, and our deployments in the Atlantic region without F-35s creates a gap. But we are getting the CH-53Ks into our force as the initial operating force which will clearly augment our ability to provide greater capability to operate in the air-sea-ground domain as well."

In short, LtGen Beaudreault has lived through the last peer fight and led the II MEF in its initial process of adapting to the new strategic context. As he underscored: "We're all watching China, but you know what? There's another actor out there who merits watching."

LtGen Beaudreault retired from the USMC on July 9, 2021.

CHAPTER FIVE:

THE VIEW FROM 2ND MARINE AIRWING

I first visited 2nd Marine Air Wing (MAW) in 2007, at the beginning of the Osprey era. There I saw a small number of the aircraft on the tarmac and met with pilots and maintainers at the beginning of a long period of disruptive change, a period of change which delivered new capabilities and new approaches for the USMC in global operations.

Now with the rise of 21st-century authoritarian powers working skill sets for full-spectrum warfare, for 2nd MAW, it is about the challenge of being able to fight now and prepare for the future by leveraging current operations and shaping new approaches.

During a December 2020 visit to 2nd MAW, I talked with Major General Cederholm, the CG of 2nd MAW. The CG has flown almost every aircraft in the 2nd MAW inventory, the most recent being the F-35. We discussed how he viewed the challenges facing his command and key priorities moving forward.

He started by underscoring that in his view, 2nd MAW was 'America's Air Wing'. "We operate all over the globe. Right now, we have forces all the way from Europe into the Far East, and everywhere in between. The sun never sets on 2nd Marine Aircraft Wing. We have to have a ready force and generate combat power today as we face the challenges of transformation tomorrow. We can never lose our readiness trait, or our ability to respond immediately when called upon.

"We're looking at efforts right now to increase our readiness and our availability across fully mission capable aircraft, which is basically our no-go criteria when it comes to combat operations. The metric that matters to me is the availability of fully mission capable aircraft, not simply availability of an aircraft. When we send aircraft into harm's way, we owe the aircrew and the Marine Riflemen, a fully mission capable aircraft. In this context, we are focused on increased reliability of parts and weapons systems. I have been focused significantly in my career on training; now I am laser focused on the logistics side as well.

"We are examining reliability across the parts for every type, model, and series of aircraft at 2nd MAW, and working with various institutions to improve reliability. Even if there are higher upfront costs to get reliability enhanced, it will be cheaper in the long run for the operation of a more resilient force, which is clearly what one needs when the demand is to fight right now, when the phone rings."

With regard to the training side, the focus is upon transformation as well. The shift on the demand side to deal with the pacing threat means that the force needs to be more capable of operating as a distributed but integrated force. This means as well that the Marines operating the various units in 2nd MAW need to be prepared to work the shift between being a force supporting a command or becoming the lead element in an operation.

This is especially true of assault support innovations. The MV-22B was birthed at 2nd MAW, and the disruptive change which Osprey introduced is still driving changes with the force. The CH-53K is now at VMX-1 as the Marines prepare for it to generate similar processes of change. According to Major General Cederholm: "Changes, great changes, in Marine Corps assault support have always originated in 2nd MAW – today is no different."

The Marines are reworking the maintaining side of the business. "We are revising our table of organization and manpower for logistics. We are looking for new balances of working relationships as well between contracted maintenance and uniformed maintainers to free up capability for front line squadrons. Our biggest project associated with transformation is in this manpower area."

With regard to transformation, 2nd MAW as a ready-to-fight-now force works with what they have but are opening the aperture to rethinking about how to use the force elements they have and to operate them in new ways. These changes include new ways to operate the AH-1Zs and UH-1Y with the Ground Combat Element. New training approaches are underway to provide new engagement approaches by operating 2nd MAW with 2nd MEF to deliver new combat approaches to deploying the force.

A 2020 Deep Water exercise highlighted new ways to leverage assault support and to operate in an extended battlespace. Romeos are starting to train with Vipers to give the fleet better self-defense capabilities. There is a new focus on how Marine Air works with the fleet to contribute to surface and sub-surface missions as well. "We don't need to wait for force design initiatives to come to fruition to increase our lethality and transform our operating concept. We're doing that through training inside our own formations, our own platforms and focusing on better ways to deal with the pacing threat."

Major General Cederholm highlighted a key way the Marines working with the Navy can enhance combat flexibility within the fleet. The way the CG put it was as follows: "We are changing our mindset. We can swap out the composition on an amphibious deck within two hours to tailor the force to the mission or the threat. We can configure for Humanitarian Assistance and Disaster Relief (HADR) operations and swap out with a ship like the USS America into a full up lethal strike asset with F-35s and Ospreys onboard. Mix and match and swapping out assets is a part of working the chess board for 21st century combat operations."

Another example of the mindset change being worked on the training side can be seen in 2nd MEF/2nd MAW cooperation. "With the pacing threat, we may not conduct mass regimental lifts. I am excited to be working with Second Marine Division with regard to battlefield planning and training on the correlation of what forces they will insert and what assault support is most appropriate to that effort. You are taking a smaller element of the Ground Combat Element (GCE), combining it with a smaller element of the ACE, and operating in a chain saw like fashion. This means that every seat on the assault aircraft, every pallet being lifted, has to have a design purpose for force inserts. We are changing the way that we think about resupply for the insertion force."

In short, the challenge is to operate now but generate change. As Major General Cederholm put it: "We are generating combat power and transitioning at the same time."

When I returned to 2nd MAW in July 2021, we continued our discussion and the CG highlighted their work over the previous six months since I was last at the Wing. According to Cederholm, "We are in the process of approaching readiness levels that have not been seen in decades. On some days, our readiness rate has approached 73% of all our assets being flown. Marines at all levels have contributed to this success, one which is critical to enable us to meet our mission of being able to fight today."

He then indicated that this was one of four key priorities being pursued by the Wing going forward. "Our first priority is to continue increasing our readiness rates by adding more combat depth through our formations. The second is to drive more lethality into our training and readiness (T&R) manuals. The third one is a combination of force preservation and force development, ensuring that we are training Marines, protecting Marines, and understanding risk, both organizational and institutional risk. The fourth is alignment to the future, or alignment to the 2030 force design effort."

2nd MAW is clearly focused on the training piece as a key part of the way ahead. Major General Cederholm highlighted the need to train to fight today but to find ways in reshaping training and the T&R manuals to better position the Wing for the future fight. What he argued is that even though the Marine Corps continues to clearly have capabilities to engage with peer competitors, the T&R manuals over the years of engagement in the Middle East appropriately focused largely on the operations in support of CENTCOM.

This clearly needs to change going forward. The Wing leadership is focused on finding ways to do this more effectively going into the future. "What types of missions do we need to do for the evolving peer fight? How can we write T&R manuals that train to those missions, and not just what we have done over the past twenty years?"

Col Michael McCarthy, commanding officer, Marine Air Control Group MACG 28, explains MACG 28's lineage to MajGen Michael Cederholm, commanding general, 2d Marine Aircraft Wing, at Cherry Point, North Carolina, July 23, 2020. Photo by Staff Sgt Andrew Ochoa, 2nd

He argued that there is a clear need to shape an understanding of predictive readiness to be able to do the evolving missions which are required for the peer fight, something the Commandant of the Marine Corps and Chief of Staff of the Air Force have written about. "If we take our target as 2030, and we plan back from that, we can better inform our force design and development efforts. 2nd MAW currently has planners in the EUCOM AOR who are looking to smooth out any inhibitors or barriers that would hinder our ability to operate in and around the European continent, but they're also eyeballing the future to fall in alignment with our priorities, which is alignment to force design in the future.

"How do we plug into the 2030 operating concept, what tools do they need, and what missions do they need to train to? How do they integrate more effectively with the Joint Force and our alliances? How do they integrate into the kill web? We are working on that roadmap right now, and it will require a significant shift in how we educate and train our formations. We are retooling for the future fight. At the same time, we're prepared to answer the phone, time now, takeoff, and beat any and all potential adversaries out there."

Although F-35s are in 2nd MAW, they are there as part of the training effort. 2nd MAW will be receiving its F-35s over the next five years and will see the CH-53K as the latest USMC aircraft come to 2nd MAW prior to the rest of the USMC. Given that the VMX-1 detachment working the operational testing is actually at New River, this makes a great deal of sense.

But given the approach which MajGen Cederholm outlined, he clearly thinks the Marines need to look at their new platforms in a specific way. That way was highlighted in a quote he cited from an individual he described as an "incredible defense leader," who asked him several years ago: "Why do we stuff the F-35 into our current operating concepts? Why don't we take our current operating concepts and revise them based on the capabilities which the F-35 brings?"

But the Wing is receiving a new aircraft soon into the operational force, namely, the CH-53K, and the CG had recently flown on the aircraft. He underscored: "I was amazed at the automation that's built into the aircraft. To be honest with you, I can't stop thinking about what the different possibilities are of how we can make this platform support our operating concept on the battlefield of today; but not just today, but on the battlefield of the future."

And that is the real advantage of the reset which MajGen Cederholm is highlighting and working with his team at 2nd MAW: focusing on evolving missions, leveraging new capabilities to expand their capabilities to execute those missions and building out the Marines so they continue to be able to be a highly effective and lethal contributor to the defense wherever and whenever our nation may need.

Multiple Basing, Kill Webs and C²: Shaping a Way Ahead

January 7, 2021

As the United States and core allies build out the way ahead for an integrated distributed force, a key challenge is shaping C² systems which fully enable such a force. C² and ISR have been historically treated as separate terms, but increasingly the sensor networks are integrable with C² systems, and with the focus on a distributed force, how best to connect the distributed force with joint or allied forces which provide the critical combat mass to prevail in a crisis?

In my view, the kill-web approach recognizes the reality of current C² systems, which are that a combat cluster needs to take its C² capabilities with it for that force to integrate in operations. The reach back to a larger force depends on networks—both ISR and C²—which it does not directly control and may be denied in a crisis. The force package needs to have its own integratability built in; the broader reach to other force elements will shape how a particular force package can affect the wider battlespace.

With the challenges facing U.S. and allied forces with the forces being built by core adversaries, the importance of flexible basing is being highlighted. Sea basing is a core advantage along with an ability to operate multi-domain forces from a variety of bases which can intersect and operate with the sea bases.

For the Marines, this means that the reworking of the amphibious forces along with new approaches to basing are key elements of the force mix being worked. At the heart of the challenge for force effectiveness is how C² can be shaped to enable more effective force capabilities to be built and operate in a contested combat environment.

During my visit to 2nd Marine Aircraft Wing in early December 2020, I had a chance to discuss these challenges with the C² professionals in Marine

Air Control Group 28. We had a wide-ranging conversation on the intersection between the evolving tactical environment and C^2, and I will highlight a number of takeaways from that conversation.

The first point draws upon my discussions with Col Gillette at Marine Aviation Weapons and Tactics Squadron 1. We discussed during my visit in September, and in earlier conversations, the challenge of shaping more effective Marine Corps integration with the Navy, and he highlighted the key questions: How can the Marines most effectively assist in sea denial and sea control missions, and how can the Marines help in controlling sea lines of communication?

These questions highlighted the key challenge of defining the tactical missions of the Marines in providing support for a strategic maritime campaign. What they highlighted was that the focus was on operations short of total war, and the importance of escalation management and control.

We discussed this during our session and the importance of shaping C^2 approaches, which would allow for the command of such missions posed as a key challenge. How will different types of crisis situations be managed in which the force is distributed? How best to ensure that the force can be integrated to the extent necessary to deliver the right kind of crisis management effect or deterrence?

The second challenge is simply moving from where we are to where the force needs to be.

This certainly can be seen with regard to the amphibious force. The amphibious force has not been built with the most advanced C^2 available to the U.S. Navy, and the insertion of force from amphibious ships ashore has not been built around the construct of the sea base managing the force ashore.

This means that two immediate challenges in the shift to flexible basing is the need to have more robust and flexible—from an expeditionary point of view—C^2 onboard the ships, making up an amphibious task force and new capabilities to connect the expeditionary force ashore with the expeditionary force afloat.

The third challenge is associated with forces inserted into expeditionary bases in ensuring they have the C^2 capabilities needed to achieve their missions with the integrated force, and that they do not become combat orphans. This challenge was highlighted with regard to building a web of C^2 nodes or node basing, in the words of one participant in the conversation.

To be blunt, distributed C^2 is hard to do in the first place. There clearly is growing effort to find ways to have rapidly stood up distributed C^2 in an expeditionary basing sense which can reach to wider networks, but this is an aspiration more than a reality. That is why in my view, working ways to integrate the amphibious task force is the preliminary challenge to be met, prior to being able to push small combat teams ashore and expecting them with the current technologies to be able to manage C^2 complexities putting them in the broader fleet wide firing solution sets.

The fourth challenge is the question of the decision-making authorities. If the focus is upon operating from a variety of bases, who makes the decisions at the tactical edge? And how to do so, notably with regard to fires solutions? Mission command is clearly involved but that will not be enough when it comes to shaping integrated fires solutions with a mixture of launch points, including from expeditionary bases involved.

The fifth challenge is the reset of C^2 and ISR acquisition itself. With the historical focus on platform dominance over "seamless" C^2 and ISR data flows, how indeed will the kind of C^2 be built into the force that allows a distributed force to achieve the levels of integratability needed?

One of the participants raised a key question about the combat geography and force structuring. The question is, how do you visualize taking expeditionary basing and applying it to across the Atlantic as opposed to the Pacific?

This is a great question on many grounds. The first is that the Russians, in my view, pose the most direct threat to the United States, given Putin's actions, his nuclear build-up and the key role which the forces projected from the Kola Peninsula play in directly threatening U.S. forces and territory. There is nothing abstract here; this is a direct and current challenge.

This is why the 2nd Fleet was re-established in 2018, and it is why the U.S. NATO relationship is deepening with what we called the UK–Nordic–Polish arc of defense in my 2020 co-authored book, *The Return of Direct Defense in Europe.*

It also poses a very practical question of the relationship of 2nd MAW to 2nd Fleet going forward. In my own view, there are significant opportunities to reshape that relationship and adopt some of the force restructuring options on the table for the USMC. Again, I would underscore that in my view the Russians are the most pressing direct threat, so ramping up capabilities for greater integration of 2nd MAW with 2nd Fleet makes a great deal of sense to me.

If one shapes an arc from North Carolina, to Norfolk, to Halifax and Newfoundland, to Iceland, to Greenland, to Norway and the Nordics, how best to deploy Marines in support of the naval integration missions being highlighted? That is the question, and the answers clearly could be multifold. Force packages of Marines highlighting strike, ASW and anti-surface warfare missions, C^2 and ISR support missions, could be shaped and deployed across the territory of the arc from Canada to the Nordics. How best to use the air capabilities of the Marines centered on 2nd MAW would be a key part of a reshaping function as well. The lessons learned from this effort could be applied to the Pacific as well and would indeed be different from island-hopping approaches, but perhaps even more significant as well. And the C^2 side of this is crucial to shaping an effective integrable force.

And the way ahead would be paved by training, training, training as Admiral Nimitz ordered in World War II. Or, to put in the terms discussed with the Marine Corps C^2 experts, exercises, exercises, exercises, to determine how best to shape a more effective distributed force which could be survivable, sustainable and effective to an overall maritime campaign. As one participant put it: "We need to increase our C^2 communication dynamics in our exercises. We need to exercise our vulnerabilities and to find ways to enhance our strengths."

Further Thoughts on the C² Piece

August 2, 2021

During my July 2021 visit to 2nd Marine Air Wing (2d MAW), I had a chance to visit again with Marine Air Control Group 28, the Marines who provide command and control and air defense for the distributed force. I met with Commanding Officer Col McCarthy, Operations Officer LtCol Mui, Operations Chief Master Gunnery Sgt Braxton and Assistant Operations Officer Capt Megliorino. MACG-28 deploys personnel around the world as part of II MEF.

MACG-28 consists of around 2,000 Marines who collectively enable 2d MAW to fight as a cohesive and highly lethal force via the establishment and employment of the MACCS. The MACCS, a collection of C² agencies supporting the six functions of Marine Aviation, is often referred to as the Commanding General's weapon system because it provides him with the sensors, communications, and situational awareness necessary to employ aviation in support of II MEF in a decisive manner.

Col McCarthy elaborated on this by stating, "This is an incredibly exciting time to be a C² professional, more than any other time in my career I'm seeing an appreciation across the Service for the capabilities MACCS Marines provide to the Marine Corps. When you look at the kill webs we are trying to establish, how we need to integrate long range fires, and how we are going to C² in a degraded environment; these are the challenges we are currently getting after with a group of incredibly talented and innovative Marines."

Marine Corps C² has historically been focused on the concept of centralized command and decentralized control; this philosophy nests perfectly with how the Marine Corps plans to fight in the future via distributed operations integrated around mission command. They have a core template which they are building from as the Marines shift from the Middle East land wars to shaping a crisis management force which can fight as a globally deployable Naval Expeditionary Force in readiness against potential adversaries.

With regard to Naval integration, connecting Navy and Marine Corps C^2 systems has historically been a challenge but that is being worked. As one participant put it: "One of the key things that's happening right now is that all the L-class ships are being outfitted with the same C^2 system that we use to do air command and control ashore. Our primary system for C^2 is a system called CAC2S, the Common Aviation Command & Control System." Integrated operating concepts, capabilities and training will ensure the Naval team cannot be excluded from any region in a contested environment.

"Now the Navy is putting it on their L-class ships, and the program is called CAC2S Afloat. It's our program, but it's integrated with the ship. It's the blue side of the comm architecture and it's going into all the L-class ships. That's a big win for us in terms of Naval integration. We're excited to see that thing come online, and it's going to help us in the future."

And the Marines are working innovative new ways to work with the U.S. Navy. One example is an upcoming exercise off of the Atlantic Coast. The Marines are working a number of vignettes with the Navy to explore ways to integrate more effectively to deliver meaningful combat effects.

A key example is taking the core USMC sensors and deploying it to an expeditionary base within contested maritime terrain in support of fleet operations to disrupt, deny and deter aggressor actions. As one participant underscored: "We're going establish a sensor expeditionary advanced base. And we're going to control intercepts. We'll provide an air defense function in support of the fleet during this exercise. It's a good chance for us to work with the Navy in an integrated air missile defense role."

One of the participants I had met earlier during a visit to MAWTS-1 in 2018. And during that visit, what was addressed in that earlier visit was how to deal with the challenge of working C^2 in a degraded and disrupted environment. As I wrote in a piece based on that 2018 visit: "The shift from counter-insurgency habits, equipment and operations is a significant one and is clearly a work in progress. It is about shedding some past learned behavior as well in terms of shaping more appropriate ways to operate as a force in a contested electronic warfare environment. The cracking of the

Enigma code in World War II by the allies involved in part German soldiers and sailors using techniques which exposed the enigma system to intrusive learning from the British and the other allies working to break the Enigma Code.

"In today's situation, the Marines are facing a similar situation in which a combination of technology and appropriate combat techniques in handling data in a combat environment is a key element of the combat learning cycle as well. And disruptive technologies, which the adversary might use against the Marines, were being fielded to test the USMC approach."[69]

Since that time, the Marines are working TTPs to deal with the reality of operating in the contested communications space. As one participant put it: "I was at WTI when we started to focus on contested communications. Since then, we have been working our TTPs and our understanding to deal with jamming and radio interference. And the Marine Information Groups are clearly helping in our learning process."

A final issue we discussed is how technology is shaping new capabilities to operate at the tactical edge and for C^2 to shape force capabilities. The miniaturization of C^2 technologies allows small groups of Marines to deploy in support of a distributed force and bring C^2 capability that historically required large operational basing to deliver. With an increasingly small footprint, how best to leverage this capability to support an integrated distributed force? And as the Navy and Marine Corps find ways to integrate more effectively how can force distribution enable dynamic strike and targeting?

The question then remains: How best to operate the force to work organically or integrated with joint or coalition forces to deliver the desired crisis management or combat effect? Answering this question will define the evolution of the USMC over the decades ahead.

---

69. Robbin Laird, "Prevailing in a Disrupted and Degraded Combat Environment: MAWTS-1 Works the Challenge," *Second Line of Defense* (July 15, 2018), https://sldinfo.com/2018/07/prevailing-in-a-disrupted-and-degraded-combat-environment-mawts-1-works-the-challenge/.

Working the Distributed Operations Piece

December 31, 2020

In July 2020, North Carolina–based Marines organized an exercise which they called Deep Water. In a press release from November 5, 2020, this is how II Marine Expeditionary Force described the exercise: "Marines with 2nd Marine Division, 2nd Marine Logistics Group, and 2nd Marine Aircraft Wing are conducting Exercise Deep Water at Marine Corps Base Camp Lejeune, N.C., 29 July 2020. II MEF conducts these training events on a consistent basis. This year, Exercise Deep Water will see two battalions conduct an air assault in order to command and control many of the various capabilities organic to II MEF in preparation for major combat operations.

"Exercise Deep Water 20 is a great opportunity for the Division to work with aviation units from Marine Corps Air Station New River and the Logistics Combat Element, as well. 2nd Marine Regiment will be the provide command and control over the 2nd battalion, 2nd regiment, and 3rd battalion, 6th regiment, the logistics and aviation units."[70]

Additionally, 2nd Marine Division provided further details about the exercise in a press release dated November 5, 2020:

"A Regimental Combat Team (RCT) commanded by 2d Marine Division's 2d Marine Regiment undertook a two-battalion air assault to commence Exercise Deep Water today on Camp Lejeune (CLNC). At nearly double the size of last year's Exercise Steel Pike, Exercise Deep Water is the largest exercise of its type conducted on Camp Lejeune in decades.

"Exercise Deep Water is a 2d Marine Regiment-planned and led event that incorporates elements from across the II Marine Expeditionary Force Marine Air Ground Task Force (MAGTF). The participating Marines and Sailors will be engaged in a dynamic force-on-force scenario against a 'peer-level adversary,' as simulated by 2d Marine Division's Adversary Force

---

70. "II MEF Conducts Regimental Air Assault during Exercise Deep Water 20," (November 5, 2020), https://www.2ndmardiv.marines.mil/News/Press-Releases/Article/2406055/ii-mef-conducts-regimental-air-assault-during-exercise-deep-water-20/.

Company. 'Exercise Deep Water, a regimental air assault that utilizes the whole of CLNC and the outlying training areas, will allow us to sharpen our spear and help make us more lethal,' said Col Brian P. Coyne, commanding officer, 2d Marine Regiment.

"'With Marine air (2d Marine Aircraft Wing) serving as part of a robust team that incorporates every element of the MAGTF, this exercise provides an opportunity to display the unparalleled lethality of a well-orchestrated Marine fighting force. As 'RCT-2' takes on an independent-thinking adversary, the ability of our squads to shoot, move, communicate, evacuate and employ effective combined arms with excellence will be put to the test.'

"In addition to the air assault, 2d Marine Regiment will be conducting offensive, defensive, and stability operations in multiple urban training settings where both conventional and hybrid adversary forces will be acting against them.

"Exercise Deep Water continues to build upon 2d Marine Division's priority to build readiness against peer threats, in accordance with both the National Defense Strategy and the Commandant's Planning Guidance.

"Accepting and embracing the challenge of such a highly-complex event in these trying times is a reflection of our unit's commitment to remaining prepared for major combat operations or unexpected contingency operations,' Coyne said, adding, 'Along with the rest of the world, our adversaries are watching to see if we drop our guard; the visible enhancement of 2d Regiment's combat readiness during Deep Water will help assure our enemies that they should not test our Corps.

"'This training event will improve our warfighting proficiency and prepare us for tomorrow's battles. 'Tarawa' (2d Marines call sign) Marines will fight and win if called,' he concluded."[71]

---

71. "2D Marine Regiment Executes Exercise Deep Water," (November 5, 2020), https://www.2ndmardiv.marines.mil/News/Press-Releases/Article/2406048/2d-marine-regiment-executes-exercise-deep-water/.

During my visit to 2nd MAW in the first week of December 2020, I had a chance to discuss the exercise and its focus and importance with Major Rew, the exercise's air mission commander.

I learned from Major Rew that this exercise combined forces from pickup zones in North Carolina and Virginia.

MV-22B Ospreys with Marine Medium Tiltrotor Squadron 266 and Marines with 3rd Battalion, 6th Marine Regiment conduct Exercise Deep Water 2020 at Marine Corps base Camp Lejeune, North Carolina, July 29, 2020. Photo by Maj Binford Strickland, 2nd Marine Aircraft Wing.

The exercise consisted of a force insertion into a contested environment, meaning they used air assets to clear areas for the Assault Force, which included both USMC (AH-1Z, UH-1Y, F/A-18A/C/D, and AV-8B) and USAF aircraft (F-15E and JSTARS). Once air superiority was established, the assault force was inserted by USMC MV-22Bs and CH-53Es. The exercise also included support aircraft such as the KC-130J and RQ-21.

The planning and execution focused on bringing a disaggregated force into an objective area that required integrated C^2 with Ground, Aviation and Logistics Combat Elements. This C^2 functionality was delivered in part by an Osprey operating as an airborne command post with a capability delivered by a "roll-on/roll-off" C^2 suite, The use of MAGTF Tablets (MAGTAB) provided a key means of digital interoperability that allowed for real-time information sharing to ground elements and aviators. The MAGTAB provided the visual representation of the integrated effects and outcomes to the command element. ISR was provided by USMC assets and by a USAF JSTARS aircraft. They used their Network-on-the-Move Airborne (NOTM-A) system to provide interoperability for the commander and assault force.

As Major Rew put it, "I think having the NOTM-A kit on the Osprey is a big win because it provides so much situational awareness. With the Osprey as a C^2 aircraft, there is added flexibility to land the aircraft close to whatever operational area the commander requires. There are many capable C^2 platforms across the DoD but not all of them also have the ability to immediately land adjacent to the battlefield like the Osprey does."

Capt Peter M. Lamoe, a V-22 Pilot with Marine Medium Tiltrotor Squadron 262 (Reinforced), 31st Marine Expeditionary Unit, flies behind an MV-22B Osprey with Marine Medium Tiltrotor Squadron 262 (Reinforced), during a Networking On-the-Move Airborne (NOTM-A) training exercise from amphibious assault ship USS America (LHA 6). September 22, 2020.Photo by LCpl Brienna Tuck, 31st Marine Expeditionary Unit.

One aspect of mission rehearsals the Marines are developing is to leverage joint assets in support of an assault mission and to be able to provide information to that mission force as well. To be clear, the Marines did not march to the objective area; they flew to their objectives in various USMC lift assets accompanied by USMC rotary wing and fixed wing combat aircraft. They were moving a significant number of Marines from two different locations, hundreds of miles apart, to nine different landing zones.

As Major Rew explained it, "We were working with a lot of different types of aircraft, and one of the challenges is trying to successfully integrate them to meet mission requirements. As the air mission commander, I was co-located with an infantry colonel who was the overall mission commander. We were in an Osprey for a significant period of time leading the operation from a C^2 perspective. In the exercise we sometimes had to solve problems during execution that required rapidly sending information to an asset so that they could complete a crucial battlefield task. We work with commander's intent from the outset of an operation, and this is especially critical during distributed operations."

The coming of the F-35 to both Air Assault and Distributed Operations is crucial as well. According to Major Rew, "The F-35 has incredible sensors and they have the capability to be able to see what's happening on the battlefield, assess things real time, and then send that information to the individual who needs to make a decision. Incorporating them into future exercises of this magnitude will be value-added to the entire Marine Corps."

In effect, the Marines are working on an ecosystem for integrated and distributed force insertion. As they build out that ecosystem, new ISR, C^2 and strike capabilities that enter the force can be plugged into the ecosystem that will allow for a continued evolution of that system. In that sense, the future is now.

Working the Light Attack Helicopter Piece

December 30, 2020

During my December 2020 visit, Marine Light Attack Helicopter Squadron 269 (HMLA-269) was commanded by LtCol Short and is a squadron consisting of the AH-1Z Viper attack helicopter and the UH-1Y Venom utility helicopter. They are known as the Gunrunners, and next door within the same hangar are the Warriors of Marine Light Attack Helicopter Squadron 167 (HMLA-167), commanded by LtCol Hemming.

They are part of Marine Aircraft Group 29 within the 2nd Marine Aircraft Wing. The Gunrunners operate what they refer to as "attack utility teams." What that means is that they operate the Viper (AH-1Z) and the Venom (UH-1Y) as an insertion and support package. They share 80% commonality of parts, operate from a small logistical footprint and are extremely maintainable in the field, which make them a significant expeditionary warfare asset.

Recently, both squadrons retired their last AH-1W Super Cobra attack helicopter in favor of the AH-1Z Viper. LtCol Hemming noted in the interview, "The hydraulics, the engines, and some of the systems on the aircraft and the air frame, are significantly more durable and reliable than the old AH-1 Whiskey in terms of the amount of hours you can put on before you have to conduct maintenance on it. These significant upgrades result in your ability to operate the aircraft for an extended periods of time compared to the legacy Cobra and Huey."

The Viper brings significant firepower to an expeditionary unit with the Venom providing lift and support to that unit as well. The helicopters have evolved from their legacy ancestors to be more capable as well.

An AH-1Z Viper with Marine Light Attack Helicopter Squadron 269 flies over Marine Corps Base Camp Lejeune, North Carolina, July 31, 2020. HMLA-269 practiced close air support and aerial surveillance to maintain mission readiness. U.S. Marine Corps photo by Cpl Cody Rowe, 2nd Marine Aircraft Wing.

As LtCol Short put it, "We are the most expeditionary and resilient attack helicopter platform there is in terms of the scale and the ability to survive in the field or operate forward. Our hydraulics, our control systems, our powertrain systems are the most expeditionary maintainable as an attack utility team in operation today."

LtCol Short added, "We are the, as somebody described it, 'the punchy little friend in the overhead that's there when no one else is.'" LtCol Short argued that their attack utility team was very "risk worthy" in terms of the "logistical, the manpower, the cost investment for the capability gain, you would give a ground force, or you would give a supported force by putting them forward, putting them into a position to offer support."

The Viper is adding Link-16 and full-motion video so that it can be even more supportable for or supported by an integratable insertion force. It is also very capable because of its relatively small footprint able to land in a variety of ground or ship settings and get refueled. If one focuses on the ability to operate virtually in any expeditionary setting, at sea or on land, the Viper is extremely capable of refuelability for an insertion force. They can do this onboard virtually any fleet asset at sea or at a FARP.

From a concept of operations perspective, notably with regard to an ability to operate from multiple bases, the attack utility package certainly can keep pace with the "pacing threats" facing the Marines. The Commandant has asked the Marines to rethink how to do expeditionary operations, and to promote tactical innovations to do so. HMLA-269 has been focused on this effort. Notably, they have been exercising with the Ground Combat Element (GCE) at Camp Lejeune to work small packages of force able to be inserted into the combat space and able to operate in austere locations for a few days to get the desired combat effect and then move with the GCE to new locations rapidly.

HMLA-269 has been working closely with 3rd Battalion, 6th Marines to shape innovative ways to deploy expeditionary force packages. "We are working ways to work distributed force operations with the battalion." They have a security mission currently with regard to II MEF in reinforcing

Norway. The question being worked is: how, in a multi-basing environment, can one provide the kind of firepower that the maneuver force would need?

The Gunrunners took a section of aircraft to work with a ground combat unit and to live together in the field for a period of time and sort out how best to operate as an integrated force package. They operated in the field without a prepared operating base and worked through the challenges of doing so. They worked with an unmanned aircraft ISR feed as part of the approach.

Obviously, this is a work in progress, but the strategic direction is clear. And there are various ways to enhance the capability of the force to be masked as well. Movement of small force packages, operating for a limited period of time, moving and using various masking technologies can allow the attack utility team which is operational now to be a key player in shaping a way ahead for Marine Corps expeditionary operations.

In short, the attack/utility team of 2nd MAW are taking the force they have, and their significant operational experience, and adapting to the new way ahead with the next phase of change for expeditionary warfare.

The Osprey Piece

January 4, 2021

During my visit to 2nd Marine Aircraft Wing, and to New River Marine Corps Air Station, I had a chance to visit Marine Aircraft Group 26. Over the years, I have had a chance to come often to MAG-26 and to discuss the MV-22B Osprey, its introduction, its evolution and its progress. Each time I have come, I have had a chance to meet with the MAG and its commanding officer, who have been without exception, experienced, very competent leaders. This visit proved no exception.

Col John Spaid has been with the Osprey since 2005. Indeed, he was part of the first Osprey deployment to Iraq in 2007, under LtCol Rock (now MajGen Rock) and then with the first MEU deployment in 2009. And we went back in history to discuss his initial experiences with the introduction and initial maturation of the Osprey.

A V-22 Osprey lands at Baghdad International Airport Saturday, Oct. 27, 2007. Photo by Staff Sgt Curt Cashour, Defense Imagery Management Operations Center.

Indeed, my first exposure to the Osprey was in a 2007 visit to MAG-26. In that discussion, we focused on how what was referred to me early on, as the Osprey Nation, was stood up and shaped a core group of combat warriors who brought such an innovative plane into combat and reshaped really how the Marines have operated since then.

In a discussion earlier this year with LtGen (Retired) George Trautman, the Deputy Commandant of Aviation when the Osprey was introduced into combat, he underscored that the approach was to introduce the Osprey into Iraq through an 18-month period with three groups of Marines, each operating in Iraq for a six-month period. The first was headed by now MajGen Rock, the second was commanded by now LtGen Heckl and the third by Col (Retired) "Mongo" Seymour.

Col Spaid was part of that first squadron and indeed, with his copilot, was the first to enter Iraq flying from the Middle East. His CH-46 squadron transitioned to Ospreys and he flew with that squadron to Iraq. He had flown with the HMM-263 in Iraq and was aware of its limitations and vulnerabilities and saw the Osprey as providing capabilities for a different operational approach in Iraq. "We could now operate at altitude with speed and range and able to circumnavigate the battlespace and then insert in a favorable point into that battlespace. We also had a more survivable aircraft with the new materials used for the air frame as well."

The airplane was so different from legacy aircraft that he jokingly compared his transition to the Osprey as equivalent of him being inconceivably selected for the space program, with new technologies, new capabilities and very different operational possibilities. The tiltrotor capabilities were certainly, and still are, revolutionary, but the maneuverability side of the aircraft was also a challenging part of the Osprey revolution. "The fly by wire capability and unique flight control system of the aircraft was new for the legacy rotary-wing community. And learning to fly it and get used to what it could do was exciting and a challenge to transition from the old ways of doing things. When I started working precision landings, it took a couple of days to adjust. It was not a normal aircraft and doing precision landings was different as well. Indeed, when I was first learning how to fly the aircraft in the simulator and even first flights in the aircraft, I believed that it was going to be an area weapon. There's no way I'd be able to land precisely where I wanted to, but soon learned to do so with ease. Then there was the tactical adjustment. Being able to operate high and fast while minimizing our time in the climb and dive then coming in unexpected, that was a tactical advantage that no one else had or seen."

As the Marines were learning to use the aircraft in combat, my own observation was that inside the Beltway, the aircraft started to get support from top leaders because it could take them around all of Iraq for inspections in a day, rather than having to operate over longer time within the limitations of how far a helicopter could fly.

Col Spaid noted that indeed he had that experience of flying senior military around Iraq and doing so as I described it. For example, "On Christmas Day in 2007, we flew General Petraeus around to three or four different FOBs in a single day, and he loved the plane."

Col Spaid described the operational difference from a CH-46 in these terms: "A year and half earlier, I would fly a CH-46 from al-Assad out to al-Qa'im once a week. For rotary wing assets, you are going out West and the weather could be bad, and it was just a long-legged journey. With the Osprey, we did it daily."

The Osprey started small in terms of deployment numbers for sure, but there was an esprit de corps to the team that would lead them to call themselves the Osprey Nation. It started by bringing back lessons learned from operations to then shape the TTPs for the follow-on squadrons. As Col Spaid put it: "In Iraq we spent a lot of time in the dust doing reduced visibility landings. We worked some initial tactics and procedures and brought those back to the squadrons. And that started an earnest process of refining tactics. We were a small community, but we came from a variety of aviation settings and platforms. And that mix of different experiences informed our approach on how best to operate the Osprey. We had a very good mix of healthy work ethics which drove innovative thinking. It was a melting pot of Marine Corps aviation. We all brought our best professional military aviator qualities into this effort, which means we had a unique opportunity to filter out bad habits that may have been lingering in our previous communities. We were working objective area mechanics and tactics for the aircraft and learning to fly the aircraft in those settings."

But as the community grew, standardization needed to be shaped. "In the period from 2010-2012, we focused heavily on standardization as West Coast squadrons were standing up."

Then in 2009, he deployed with the first MEU for the Osprey. Col Paul "Pup" Ryan was their squadron commander. They operated in the CENTCOM area with Fifth Fleet. They were in Bahrain, Kuwait and Iraq during the first MEU tour for the Osprey. This was the first time the aircraft operated from the sea base to project power from the sea.

Col Spaid served as the Aviation Maintenance Officer for that deployment. Among the 29 aircraft assigned to the composite squadron, 12 Ospreys were deployed with 8 on the LHD and 4 on the LPD. This was a learning challenge for the Navy as they had to adjust to Osprey operations and learn how it could operate from the ship, just as the Marines were learning how to maintain the new aircraft afloat. Eventually, the Navy officers onboard learned, in Spaid's words, that "we could fix it faster, we could launch it faster, we could fold it faster than originally expected. In the end, the confidence of the Navy officers and crew grew."

This experience clearly impacted CENTCOM leadership for it set in motion what would become known as Special Purpose MAGTFs, and in EUCOM and AFRICOM is now called the North Africa Response Force, or the NARF. Combatant Commanders learned, in Spaid's words, "that we could offload in Kuwait but operate all throughout Iraq. That was an eye opener for them."

In effect, with the Osprey the Marines were finally demonstrating what a long-range shipboard assault support asset could do while the entire concept of an ARG-MEU was transforming. Then in 2010, the squadron took the Osprey to Afghanistan, where LtCol "Buddy" Bianca was the commander, and I interviewed him prior to Afghanistan and after the first operations of the Osprey in Afghanistan as well.

This initial experience clearly has made Col Spaid a plank holder in Osprey nation. As Spaid put it: "Being a plank owner and setting up a squadron is one thing but taking that aircraft with the first squadron and doing the first MEU, doing the first combat deployment in Iraq, you're not just the plank owner, you're driving the ship that you built the plank on. It is liking being a plank owner for a revolutionary military advantage."

But he noted that at the time you really did not focus on that. "We were just doing our jobs. You focus on mission accomplishment; you don't really understand the historical significance of the event at the time. There were some really significant contributions there from the whole team, but I don't think you really appreciate it until later."

When I first visited the flight line at New River in 2007, there were four aircraft on the tarmac. When looking at the tarmac, now there are a large number of Ospreys at rest, at least for a brief period of time between flights and operations. Thirteen years has brought significant change both to the Marine Corps and to the airplane and now will do so for the Navy as they introduce their variant of the Osprey. As Col Spaid put it: "All our Marines are smarter. You still have hard working maintainers fixing the planes, but they are better armed with experience. Baseline pilot intellect is now through the roof. We've normalized what we thought was creative thinking and training. And now we're asking them to be even more creative and train for the next strategic challenge."

I asked him, what was a primary focus during his time as CO of MAG-26 with regard to the aircraft itself? For Col Spaid, the answer to that question is sustainment, sustainment, sustainment. "A good number of the software upgrades we are making are with regard to reliability and benefit the maintainer and the maintenance process. We are working hand in hand with the program office and with industry to find the best way to keep this aircraft reliable."

We then discussed the decision by the Navy to buy the Osprey for its resupply role. Col Spaid highlighted several advantages. First, there was enhanced prioritization to sustainment of the aircraft throughout the entire Naval Aviation Enterprise. Second was the benefit of training, as the Navy pilots are trained at New River, and as the West Coast squadrons are stood up, there will be refresher training opportunities for Marines on the West Coast as well. Third, with the Osprey deployed to both the carrier and amphibious fleets, there will be greater opportunity for parts availability across the fleet. Fourth, there will be shared opportunities for upgrading the aircraft as well.

One area where I think this is clearly the case will be with regard to passive sensing on the aircraft, and having the new MISR officers involved will bring benefits to both Marine Corps and Naval operators. The initial training for USAF Osprey pilots and maintainers is at New River as well, but because of the specialized mission and equipment on the USAF variant, there is less impact from commonality than will occur with regard to the Marines and the U.S. Navy working together, notably with the new emphasis on ways to shape enhanced Navy–Marine Corps integration as well.

But one area of partner training has occurred as the Japanese have acquired the Osprey and their pilots and maintainers trained at New River. For Col Spaid, the Japanese maturation at New River has been very significant and prepares the future for new FMS partners. "As new FMS opportunities arise, we'll be able to leverage off the great success we have had with our Japanese allies. We'll change some things up a little bit, but it was a really good experience," he said.

In short, Col Spaid was on the ground floor with the birth of the Osprey nation. And he is driving the change as the next phases of Osprey operations unfold.

The Heavy Lift Piece

December 23, 2020

During my visit to 2nd MAW during the first week of December 2020, I had a chance to visit MAG-29, with regard to both the CH-53 and H-1 units. Then I had a chance to discuss the way ahead for the assault force with the Commanding Officer of MAG-29, Col Robert Finneran.

It would hardly surprise you to learn that the CO was a very experienced combat aviator who had worked on assault operations for a significant period of time, including tours in Iraq and Afghanistan and at MAWTS-1. He also served at United States Special Operations Command (SOCOM) where he broadened his experience as well. His own operational experience is associated with the AH-1W and AH-1Z, but as the CO of MAG-29, he serves as the Naval Aviation Enterprise's fleet lead for the CH-53. This role includes the transition to the CH-53K. Later in my visit I would have a chance to "fly" the CH-53K in the simulator at New River.

We discussed three major issues: the CH-53K, the H-1 transition with digital interoperability and the key role which Marine Corps aircraft play in mobile or expeditionary basing, or as he put it: "They are key elements ensuring that a distributed force is integrable, rather than being dispersed and isolated."

We started by discussing the CH-53K and I asked him a direct question: Why is it so hard to explain how different the K is from the E? It is indeed so different that I recently wrote an article suggesting if they had named the aircraft the CH-55, people might get the point of how different it is.[72] Col Finneran: "It starts with the silhouette of the two aircraft. They are very similar, but that is about it. The Kilo [CH-53K] is a generational leap in technology. It is a completely different airplane as far as capabilities and technology. But because it is for now a Marine Corps-only aircraft, there is no widespread recognition in the joint force of how different the aircraft is and what its impact will be."

The digital capabilities of the aircraft certainly will enhance the situational awareness of the combat team, and its speed and range provide a significant advantage for force insertion. "Anything we can do to enhance the situational awareness for the pilots, and take the workload off of them, allows them to focus on their mission. And mastering the aircraft in terms of flying will be fairly easy for the converting CH-53E pilots, but for the CH-53K generation, they will need learn how to manage all of the information that can be worked in that aircraft to enhance situational awareness and maximize its utility for the mission."

He also argued that the CH-53K will affect risk calculus for force insertion as well. "With the aerial refueling capability of the CH-53, we can extend range and move a force and needed sustainment quickly and across great distances. This provides both the Marine Corps and the Joint Force Commander flexibility and complicates the problem for any adversary."

We also discussed the coming of digital interoperability to the H-1 family and how significant he saw that, notably as the Marines focused on integration with the U.S. Navy. "We're in the early stages of talking to the Seahawk Weapons Schools, both the MH-60S and MH-60R, to figure out how we can find complementary ways to employ our airframes. We bring a lot to the table for maritime operations, notably in terms of the weapons we

---

72. Robbin Laird, "What if it was called the CH-55," *Second Line of Defense* (December 8, 2020), https://sldinfo.com/2020/12/what-if-it-was-called-the-ch-55-transformation-in-the-vertical-heavy-lift-fleet/.

carry on the Viper, and we need to figure how best to integrate that capability with the maritime force.

"Once we're networked and we can become part of the maritime kill chain, there's a lot that this airframe can bring to bear in the role of both sea control and sea denial. I just don't think we've explored it enough, and we're in the early stages of taking a look at that. Because it is significant, what we bring from a weapons standpoint to the maritime domain, I think it's really on us to explore how we can expand our operational reach in that domain."

But as the Marine Corps focuses its attention on naval integration, a key part of that effort is upon working mobile, multiple and expeditionary basing, and how to do that with the current force as the force transforms. Obviously, a key challenge is having effective logistical connectors. As Col Finneran put it: "Logistical connectors are key to expeditionary basing. For example, the CH-53E and then the CH-53K can provide crucial support as they can bring fuel to an expeditionary base directly, rather than having to work through a series of basing locations. Fuel is certainly critical to distributed operations and our heavy lift helicopter is a key enabler, and frankly, I only see it increasing in importance to such operations. I don't see how the force goes and does any of the new operational concepts without that capability."

With regard to risk mitigation or being "risk worthy" as it pertains to distributed operations, Col Finneran argued that the force under his command is clearly suited to that mission challenge or requirement. With the attack utility team which the Viper and Venom create and with the heavy lift capability of the CH-53 family, the time to maneuver to get the desired combat effect is less compared to slower paced basing enablement methods. And it is sustainable as well with regard to bringing what is need to the mission, rather than depending upon ship-based support in an expeditionary basing maritime environment. He added, the CH-53K versus the CH-53E provides "a lot more options" for this kind of scenario based on performance improvements in terms of range and payload.

MAG-29, along with MAWTS-1, are working on new TTPs to maximize their capability to deliver the evolving basing capability and the kind of combat effect desired for sea control and sea denial. My visits to MAWTS-1 and NAWDC this year certainly underscore this shift as well. Col Finneran concluded: "If we really want to be risk worthy, and we really want to challenge the risk calculus for our adversary, we've got to outmaneuver them in both time and space, and that is what my command is focused on delivering to the fight."

The Coming of the CH-53K

January 5, 2021

During my visit to 2nd Marine Air Wing during the first week of December 2020, I had a chance to visit New River Marine Corps Air Station and meet with LtCol Frank, VMX-1, to get an update on the coming of the CH-53K. LtCol Frank showed me the simulator as well, giving me a chance to experience the flying qualities and, notably, the ability to hover using the automated systems to operate in difficult visual and operating conditions.

He joined the USMC in 2002 and has flown a wide variety of rotorcraft during his career and served as a pilot for former U.S. President Barack Obama. He came to VMX-1 in 2018. He has stayed in large part to follow through the CH-53K to fruition, that is into operations. As he put it: "It is crucial to have a CH-53 fleet that works effectively as it is a unique capability in the USMC crucial for our way ahead operationally. It is the only aircraft we have that can move an expeditionary brigade off of our amphibious ships."

"We have about a hundred Marines here at the test detachment. We've been training our maintainers and our air crew on the 53K for two years now. The maintainers have been working on it since 2018, when we started the logistics demonstration, which is essentially the validation of maintenance procedures on the 53K. I have 10 pilots in the det including myself and I'm responsible for ensuring that everyone goes through the proper training syllabus. All 10 of our pilots in addition to our crew chiefs and our maintainers will be the first unit to be allowed to operate a 'safe aircraft for flight,' which is a term we use for the maintainers.

"Our job is to conduct initial operational test and evaluation training for six months, beginning this month and ending in May or June of 2021, where we will establish five aircraft commanders, myself being one of them, five co-pilots, that'll be our 10 pilots. We'll qualify 10 crew chiefs, and our maintainers will continue to advance in their maintenance quals. In June of 2021 is when we enter into IOC evaluations.

"We're going to evaluate the reliability and maintainability of the aircraft. We're going to collect all our maintenance data, determine how long it takes to fix, how long it's down before it's fixed and how many flight hours it accomplishes per maintenance man hour to evaluate it.

"We will evaluate Its shipboard compatibility in June and July 2021. We are to evaluate its desert mountainous capabilities in Twentynine Palms, beginning of August and September 2021. And we also have a sorties generation rate demonstration where we will execute a surge capability of sorties from a ship in November 2021; we'll do that for a period of about 72 hours straight, where we will fly every aircraft every day and see what they deliver."

We discussed the importance of the fly-by-wire system in the aircraft, which he considers "very mature." He did note that the USMC subjects its aircraft to some of the harshest environments in the DoD: "salt spray, open ocean, desert heat and freezing cold." Robustness is a crucial aspect of determining reliability. "We do not operate runway to runway. We do not store them inside; we use them in challenging conditions," he added.

LtCol Frank referred to his team as "the learning curve for the CH-53K," similar to what happened with the Osprey or the F-35B. He underscored that the aircraft is well along the path to initial operating capability (IOC). "We've had a lot of time with the aircraft. Our Marines have been working on it for two years now. During logistics demonstration, we took the publications, which were in their infancy, and we went through every work package. The bulk of the Marine Corps' CH-53K personnel, equipment, aircraft, and support will be located at VMX-1 when the Marine Corps declares the CH-53K program is IOC."

LtCol Frank described the innovation cycle as follows: "When problems come up with the aircraft, we bring up to the program office, the program office sends it out to engineering and industry. They implement changes. They implement engineering fixes, and they incorporate them."

The author with LtCol Frank at New River, July 13, 2021.

While at New River, we visited the first of the CH-53Ks delivered to VMX-1, which I had seen earlier in the log demo program but now was on the tarmac. At the time of our meeting, LtCol Frank indicated that VMX-1 was to receive six aircraft overall. "We are to receive our next aircraft on January, February, June and September of 2021, and the last one on January of 2022. By January 22, when the sixth aircraft is delivered, we should be done with IOT and E and we should carve out a detachment size group of maintainers, pilots, and aircraft from VMX-1 to form the initial cadre of HMH-461."

How does he compare the Es to the Ks? "I've started in the Ch-53D in 2004, they're my first love. I'll always love them. They were much harder to fly. And the ease of flying this, the flight control system is probably the biggest game changer for the 53 community. We're not used to anything like this. It's very intuitive. It can be as hands off as you know, a brand-new Tesla, you can close your eyes, set the autopilot and fly across country. Obviously, you wouldn't do that in a tactical environment, but it does reduce your workload, reduces your stress.

"And in precision hover areas, whether it's night under low light conditions, under NVGs, in the confines of a tight landing zone, we have the ability to hit position hold in the 53 K and have the aircraft maintain pretty much within one foot of its intended hover point, one foot forward, lateral and AFT, and then one foot of vertical elevation change. It will maintain that hover until the end of the time if required. that's very, very stress relieving for us when landing in degraded visual environments. Our goal at VMX-1 is to create tactics that employ that system effectively.

"Some communities struggle with how they use the automation, do they let the automation do everything? Do they let the pilots do everything? How to work the balance? We're working on a hybrid where the pilots can most effectively leverage automation.

"If you know you're coming into a brownout situation or degraded visual environment, you engage the automation at a point right before the dust envelops you. And then in the 53-K, you can continue flying with the automation engaged. You continue flying with the automation engaged, and you can override it, but as soon as you stop moving the controls, it will take your inputs, estimate what you wanted and keep the aircraft in its position.

"It's a very intuitive flight control system, and it blends very well with the pilot and the computers. It allows you to override the computer. And then the second that you stop overriding it, the computer takes back over without any further pilot input. That's probably the biggest game changer for our community."

The Impact of the CH-53K

January 25, 2021

In recent visits to both II MEF and 2nd MAW, it is clear that the coming of the CH-53K to the North Carolina–based Marines is crucial. As the Marines work enhanced naval integration and expanded force mobility in dealing with the evolving strategic environment, the capabilities which the CH-53K brings to the force are not nice to have but a critical capability. And the new digital aircraft provides a solid foundation for evolution not only of the platform but for changes in concepts of operations as well.

Both the CG of II MEF and the CG of 2nd MAW indicated in interviews I did with them in 2021, that the coming of the CH-53K is especially important for their force generation capabilities to deal with the evolving threats in the Euro-Med region.

During my July 2021 visit to 2nd MAW, I had a chance to visit the VMX-1 CH-53K detachment at New River Marine Corps Air Station and to continue my discussions with LtCol Frank, Officer in Charge of the CH-53K Operational Test Detachment at New River. During the July 2021 visit, LtCol Frank provided an update on progress through the testing process, and we took the opportunity to also discuss the wider impacts which the CH-53K has on training and operations as the USMC works its evolving approach to crisis management as part of the high-end fight.

Since my visit in December 2020, LtCol Frank indicated that they had received new aircraft and had begun and then ramped up the flying hours. With their flight certification, they have now flown around 235 flight hours on the aircraft. They have certified five aircraft commanders, five copilots, ten crew chiefs and more than a required number of maintainers with the appropriate level of qualifications for the next phase of training. That next phase will occur in August 2021 at 29 Palms.

They have completed their initial operational training but are waiting for certification to begin initial operational test and evaluation. In the meantime, they have engaged in a number of "rehearsal test and evaluation" sessions with Marines at 2nd MAW and Camp Lejeune to prepare for the August training efforts at 29 Palms.

The digital aircraft has many advantages and one can be seen on the training dimension. As with the F-35, pilots can train to core proficiencies more rapidly, which leaves room for expanding training options for the evolving mission sets which the Marines are clearly focusing on for full-spectrum crisis management.

With regard to conversion training, they have discovered at VMX-1 that hours and flight events could be reduced for the pilots. As LtCol Frank put it: "the initial conversion syllabus from the CH-53E to the CH-53K was tailored based on our best guess of what events and flight hours would be required for the conversion aircrew. Following our initial foray into our own flight and simulator training and through our evaluations of the current syllabus we realized we could reduce those numbers by around 25%.

"Currently, we are focusing heavily on the co-pilot series-conversion syllabus which began as 17 total flight events for 26 flight hours. After our pilots completed this period of instruction, surveys taken at the end indicated that we could pare those numbers down by 7 events and 10 less flight hours. My hope is that this 25% savings will result in a typical Marine Heavy Helicopter Squadron saving 6 months over the duration of their transition. So now, if we can capitalize on the flight hours savings and pair that with an enhanced focus on the higher-level syllabus, we could expand training for those missions to meet high end events that the Marine Corps has decided is important in the evolving context."

We then discussed what he saw as the clear advantages of the K over the Echo for the USMC. As he put it: "There is nothing sexy about assault support. Horsepower's our weapons system, and reliability is the key to providing the horsepower for the heavy lift needed for assault support."

Reliability is crucial, and the K is focused on enhancing reliability over the legacy aircraft. As he put it: "If the grunts want a lift, and they need six to eight helicopters; it would take a whole MAG effort of 53 ECHO to put the package in the air for a battalion. With more reliability, we would not need a whole MAG to do this.

"We're hoping that's where the K is going to help, with its digital systems, engine, rotor, and drivetrain system reliability. The Full Authority Digital Electronic Control (FADEC) provides enhanced control, health monitoring, maximum power and efficiency as often as possible. They also provide what we call automatic power assurance checks and integrated power assurance checks. So we know exactly how engines are performing all the time. And it's providing real-time data.

"Automatic means the FADEC is just pulling numbers all the time. It's a behind the scenes process. It's just going all the time and it gets downloaded onto our maintenance data card, which then the maintainers will plug into their ground module, their ground computer, and they can see the engine health.

"Also, we can initiate power assurance checks as pilot, and the pilot can then bring up the summary of those and I can see, okay, power is doing good. Based on the spec engine performance, I'm actually plus 38 from the spec engine. So I've got more power than even the spec engine should have. The engine power available and limitations will be reflected on the primary flight display so we can be aware of that in the plane.

"Such accuracy and certainty is critical when you do a high altitude and a high ambient air temperature lift. That's when the K would be power limited. Knowing exactly how much power the engines are putting out, if I'm called to extract a platoon of Marines from a mountain top that's very high and it's very hot, and I have a lot of fuel on board, so I might be power critical, I can do a power assurance check and know that I'll be able to do it. Unlike the Echo, the K will give you a visual readout of your power status in real time while you are executing the lift."

LtCol Frank then addressed the reliability piece which the Integrated Vehicle Health Management System (IVHMS) delivers. "Our main gearbox pressure sensor will say it's starting to fail or it's getting a false reading. It's still performing, but it's getting a false reading. And what our maintenance

Marines will do is they'll interpret that maintenance data when we give them the data card and they'll say, 'Okay, your main gearbox pressure sensor reported itself. Your intermediate gearbox reported itself for vibrations. That means there's a bearing failing in it.' As opposed to the ECHO where we would fly, and we would see chip light, caution light, oil pressure failures in the gearbox. That means the gearbox literally seizes or fails itself. That's when we know it's failed. In the K we'll get proceeding indications of that. Ideally, it leads to parts being removed before they fail. That should lead to increased maintenance readiness. Things fail a lot in the legacy aircraft. As a flight crew, you build an anecdotal seat of the pants data base. I have had dozens of hydraulic system failures, multiple engine failures, oil system failure, electrical components failing, attitude gyros failing at night and in IMC. All those things create the seat of the pants sense that you need a lot of hours to accumulate, those failures help you get the experience you need."

One benefit of these machine-aided pilot systems in the K clearly is that the less experienced pilots can approach capability levels of more experienced pilots. This will enable the man-machine system to deliver more safety for flights, and enhanced combat capability for the Marines as well. Assuming you're an experienced pilot, you have combat experience from which you could make judgments. But if one is a less experienced pilot, now they have actually some machine aids that can help them.

Given that Marines are onboard one is talking about a lot of lives. And when the USMC Commandant and the Sergeant Major of the Marine Corps visited VMX-1 at New River in March, this was a key point which LtCol Frank underscored. "Pilot vertigo can be a Marine killer and has been in past accidents. With the ability to push a button and let the aircraft fly itself, this should not happen in the future."

The advantages of a digital aircraft are very clear. But this also means that cyber threats need to be dealt with on an ongoing basis, and clearly, the CH-53K program is not only aware of this but also working it. Regular upgrading of software on the aircraft is part of the solution, as well as cyber defensive capabilities. Both are being pursued with regard to the aircraft and its support systems.

A Marine Corps CH-53K King Stallion lowers a Navy MH-60S Knighthawk helicopter to the ground after recovering it from the nearby mountain ranges after it conducted a hard landing near, Bishop, California, Sept. 5, 2021. The two-day operation was the first official fleet mission for the CH-53K King Stallion, as it is currently undergoing an operational assessment while the Marine Corps modernizes and prepares to respond globally to emerging crises or contingencies. U.S. Marine Corps photo by LCpl Colton Brownlee.

What does LtCol Frank conclude with regard to the aircraft coming to the Marine Corps? "With the 53-K I would fly it 1,000 times over with my hair on fire before I would set foot in an ECHO again. Don't get me wrong, I love the old iron, still wear a 53D patch. I cherish my time in that plane. It's my first love. It's like an old Jeep, simple and reliable but unrefined, the ECHO is similar. However, most of the time I would prefer to drive the Denali, that is the KILO. Its operational capabilities are much enhanced over those legacy aircraft simply by the awareness and aides it can provide to the flight crew, our crew chiefs and maintainers feel the same."

Being a generational shift, the new digital aircraft is in LtCol Frank's words "a blank slate."

"You have an aircraft that can carry significant supplies or Marines inside and can carry 36,000 pounds externally. They can carry a lot of stuff. It has automated flight control systems that allows you to land in the degraded visual environments that you would not dare land an ECHO or a DELTA in. It can fly long distance without the air crew being fatigued. If you're aerial refueling and flying 1,000 miles in the E, the air crew would be wet noodles getting out after the flight. In the K you can relax a little, take a breath, allow the aircraft to help you fly and thus reduce aircrew fatigue significantly.

"I think when the necessity for conflict rears its head the K will be able to respond, and using human ingenuity, the operators will be able to find a way to support any mission that the Marine Corps needs it to do. The K is so versatile that I don't see people being pigeonholed into not being able to do something with a K. I think they'll be able to answer the call 99.9% of the time.

"It'll be able to pick up its combat payload. It'll be able to transport it, fly it any distance and land it anywhere. And you're not going to be afraid to do it. In the ECHO, if it was low light at night, the visibility was bad, you didn't have a moving map, and you were headed to a dusty and tight zone the pucker factor would be through the roof. The altitude hold was suspect, it didn't have lateral navigation and flight director capability, your attitude gyros would fail often. So you get this hair on the back of your neck stands up that,

I don't want to be flying in this environment. The aircraft's not going to help me, and I can't help myself because I don't have my sensory cues.

"But in the K, you know the aircraft's going to help you. We've sat in brown out dust, just sitting there hovering and talking to each other with position hold on. And we've been debriefing the landing, and the aircraft's just holding a hover perfectly. So that's what I like about the K is that I think it will be able to answer the call for the mission most anytime the Marine Corps needs it, whether we know what the mission is going to be, or not."

Visiting MAG-26

August 3, 2021

I first visited Marine Aircraft Group 26 (MAG-26) in 2007 when they were beginning the MV-22B Osprey transition. Now, the Osprey is the backbone of the Marine Corps combat assault support community. And with both heavy-lift and light-attack helicopter squadrons, the 2d MAW is the cornerstone of all rotorcraft support for North Carolina-based Marines.

During my recent visit, I had a chance to discuss the way ahead for combat assault support with three members of MAG-26. Maj Mazzola is MAG-26 Operations Officer. Maj Kevin O'Malley is assigned to Marine Medium Tiltrotor Squadron 263 (VMM-263), an operational MV-22 squadron, and Maj Tom Gruber is a member of VMM-365. We focused on the challenges of transition from the Middle East land wars as well as the work on shaping a new way ahead for the assault force. Up front, the shift was described by one participant as "a total paradigm change." 2nd MAW Marines will perhaps lessen expeditionary operations in Mesopotamia and increase engagements in the North Atlantic area operations. In fact, the Marine Corps has already made gains towards this goal.

Two MV-22 Osprey aircraft with Marine Medium Tiltrotor Squadron, Marine Air Group 26, approach Landing Zone Bluebird during a confined landing area exercise aboard Camp Lejeune, N.C., Aug. 4, 2015. Marines with VMM-365 rehearsed different drop off and extraction scenarios at Landing Zone Bluebird and Landing Zone Bat aboard Camp Lejeune to maintain skills and standards within the squadron. U.S. Marine Corps photo by Cpl Alexander Mitchell.

Since 2018, focus on specific challenges such as cold weather training and exercises have increased at a pace not witnessed since the Cold War. Case in point: one interviewee noted that in March 2022, they would once again train with the Norwegians in the Cold Response exercise—one of the largest Norwegian and coalition exercises since the Cold War.

As the Marine Corps conduct force design, they must figure out how to supply that force. For example, when operating in the Mediterranean, the Ospreys can fly to several support facilities. This will not be the case when operating in an environment like the North Atlantic. This means working the logistical support challenge with the Navy to provide for afloat support and to work on pre-positioning of supplies and work the arc from North America to the Baltics.

How will the supply chain to support North Atlantic operations be shaped going forward? Clearly, the renewed focus on Naval integration is part of the answer. This will be a function of how the Navy reworks its own logistical support; this will be a function of how ashore support is built out in the region (the arc from North Carolina to the Baltics) and how the amphibious fleet is reshaped.

Clearly, the coming of maritime autonomous systems can be part of evolving support solution sets. As one participant put it: "Perhaps the supply shortfall can be mitigated by logistical movers. Having unmanned aircraft or unmanned surface vessels will undoubtedly be able to contribute going forward." There is clearly a shortage of amphibious shipping both in terms of combat ships and connectors for the North Atlantic mission against a peer competitor. We did not discuss the broader challenge which can be referred as shaping a new family of systems to deliver the amphibious warfare capability to the extended littoral engagement in the North Atlantic, but this is a key challenge which must be met going forward.

Another aspect being worked is how to integrate the ARG-MEU in wider fleet operations. The Marines and the Navy are working exercises in the North Atlantic to find ways to do so, and the recent BALTOPS 50 did provide some insight with regard to this. And the evolving relationship between 2nd Expeditionary Strike Group and II MEB will clearly focus on this challenge.

An aspect of the way ahead for the ARG-MEU is its participation in fleet defense and shaping ways in which the amphibious force can better defend itself afloat. The F-35 has already demonstrated in the Pacific that it can contribute significantly to this role and with the F-35 coming to 2nd MAW's operational force, it can play a similar role in the Atlantic. But given the nature of the arc from North Carolina to the Baltics, allied F-35s will play a key role in all of this, as has already been demonstrated in BALTOPS 50 with the role of Norwegian F-35s.

The participants indicate that indeed they are engaged in discussions with the Navy about how to better integrate capabilities for the extended littoral operational fight. As one participant highlighted: "As the Navy focuses on integration of their fleet operations, they want to be able to use all of the assets available to them. And that is why the MEU is now part of the discussion."

One key question which is a shaping function moving ahead was posed by one participant this way: "How does the Air Combat Element (ACE) participate effectively in defense of the amphibious force?"

Deputy Commandant for Aviation LtGen Mark Wise is noted as saying that "the Marine Corps as an expeditionary force must be agile, mobile, and survivable. That means looking to, and building upon, current warfighting philosophy and our way of doing business. This vision is built around distributed maritime operations, littoral operations in a contested environment, and expeditionary advanced based operations: DMO, Littoral Operations in a Contested Environment (LOCE), and EABO. The Marine Corps will not abandon, but rather will refine and improve upon, these concepts for operational design for a littoral fight."

A final aspect of the potential evolution of assault support which we discussed briefly is the potential contribution of roll-on roll-off systems onboard the Osprey. This was demonstrated at last year's Deep Water exercise where MV-22 onboard capabilities allowed it to play a key role in providing C^2 to a distributed force. The Marines further contended that several pertinent future capabilities are being shaped for the Osprey. All in all, this is a good news story, something that back in 2007 I did not even think was possible.

The MV-22 Osprey is not only leading the way in combat assault support but is also a centerpiece as the Marine Corps and 2d MAW train for operations in any clime or place.

The Tactical Fighter Piece
MAG-14 Preparing the Transition

August 11, 2021

During my July 2021 visit to 2nd Marine Air Wing, I had a chance to meet with the leadership of MAG-14. I met with Col Williams, the MAG-14 Commanding Officer; LtCol Harrell, the MAG-14 Executive Officer; and Maj Cunningham, the MAG-14 Operations Officer. Based at Cherry Point, MAG-14 operates AV-8B Harriers, KC-130Js and the RQ-21A Blackjack. It is in transition from the Harriers to F-35s, and their KC-130Js are key enablers for the entire MAGTF.

2nd MAW includes Marine Fighter Attack Training Squadron 501 (VMFAT-501), the Warlords, which is an F-35 training squadron at MCAS Beaufort.

But the coming of operational F-35s to MAG-14 and 2nd MAW will be another driver of transformation of 2nd MAW capabilities. Operationally, 2nd MAW deploys all over the globe to include working with allied F-35s in the North Atlantic and European theaters in the recent BALTOPS 50 exercise.

But transition is always challenging, and one can see significant construction in preparation for the standup of the F-35 at the base. As Col Williams put it: "We are in transition as we wind down the Harriers and get ready for the arrival of the F-35s in the 2023 timeframe. We are scheduled to receive the first six aircraft in late FY23, while VMU-2 will transition from the RQ-21 to Reapers in the FY25 timeframe. We will continue to support the East Coast MEUs with Harriers and will be sustaining the Harrier force through fiscal year 2028. When the F-35s take over the East Coast MEU's duty that will represent a significant transformation."

The first hangar is being built, as well as the simulator building for the F-35s coming to the base. As Col Williams noted: "We will eventually have two more hangars. A new headquarters will be built for MAG-14 as well." The challenge is to make the transition and yet maintain the readiness of the current force. Managing the two dynamics is the challenge which the

MAG-14 leadership is facing. The Harriers deploy with the MEUs as the MEUs transition towards more North Atlantic defense missions as opposed to Eastern Mediterranean missions.

The pilot and maintainer force will transition as the F-35s come onboard at Cherry Point as well. And this aspect is a key one in managing the transition as well. The service has used incentive programs, such as Selective Retention Bonus, to encourage reenlistment and continued service of highly qualified Marines—particularly aviation maintainers.

We then discussed the KC-130J. My own observation over the years is that the KC-130J is crucial to Marine Corps operations by providing logistic support, air-to-air refueling and close air support to fleet operating forces. As a multi-sensor image reconnaissance and close air support platform, the KC-130J aircraft may be equipped with the Harvest Hercules Airborne Weapons Kit (HAWK) configuration as well. The Marine Corps has integrated the Harvest HAWK system that provides the Battlefield Commander with a limited, persistent surveillance capability with the onboard Production Target Sight Sensor (TSS). The TSS can also provide the ability to employ precision weapons using laser guidance.

A U.S. Marine Corps KC-130J Super Hercules is staged on the flight-line at Marine Corps Air Station Miramar, California, Feb. 27th, 2019. Marine Aerial Refueler Transport Squadron (VMGR) 252 is expanding its mission capabilities by providing close air support and surveillance for ground forces. VMGR-252 is a subordinate unit of Marine Aircraft Group 14, 2nd Marine Aircraft Wing. U.S. Marine Corps photo by Cpl Paige C. Stade.

A core focus for MAG-14 is ensuring the readiness of the aircraft and crews for the KC-130Js. Given the aging inventory of aircraft, this is a key challenge going forward.

There has been a new focus on the long-range firing function which the USMC could participate in as they address evolving concepts of operations for extended littoral operations, such as the Marine Littoral Regiment (MLR). The MLR is a purpose-built unit designed to enable the Marine Corps' new service strategy and employs three uniquely designed subordinate elements: A Littoral Combat Team (LCT), a Littoral Anti-Air Battalion and a Littoral Logistics Battalion.

The LCT is designed to provide the basis for employing multiple platoon-reinforced-sized expeditionary advance base sites that can host and enable a variety of missions such as long-range anti-ship fires, forward arming and refueling of aircraft, intelligence, surveillance and reconnaissance of key maritime terrain and air-defense and early warning.

It has seemed to me that the Harvest HAWK experience could be leveraged here in terms of either working with longer range missiles or adapting a Harvest HAWK capability for the Ospreys to provide rapid insertion fires into the fight. There is also the clear possibility that airlifters can be modified by using missiles in the box to be able to carry weapons that can be launched from the back of the aircraft. Clearly, kill-web approaches can allow for that, and setting up advanced expeditionary bases of C^2 or sensor operating Marines supporting air-delivered fires is more expeditious than trying to move first to EABOs themselves.

MAG-14 is in transition, but it can be viewed as maintaining the competitive edge within a larger transition of the USMC itself.

Nordic Training

August 6, 2021

During my visit to 2nd Marine Aircraft Wing in July 2021, I had a chance to talk with MAG-31, notably the VMFA-115 operations officer, about their squadron's time in Finland training with the Finnish Air Force the preceding month. MAG-31 Operations Officer LtCol Waller and VMFA-115 Operations Officer Maj Simmermon discussed the training effort with me.

Originally, VMFA-115 was to participate in a multi-national exercise, Arctic Challenge 2021. But because of COVID-19 restrictions, their engagement became a bilateral exercise with the Finnish Air Force. This provided an important window on how one might modify training going forward.

What VMFA-115 learned was how the Finns fight. How they operate their air force in a truly distributed manner. How they use their roads for landing sites, distribute logistical support and work under the shadow of Russian long-range fires. Clearly, Marines learning to fight as the Finns fight is a good thing, and part of the cross-learning process, which is necessary for U.S. forces to be familiar with various concepts like distributed maritime operations, littoral operations in a contested environment and expeditionary advanced-base operations. All concepts that provide an understanding of how to operate in the High North back to the Baltic Sea.

This is how Maj Simmermon described the experience: "A year ago, we were preparing for Arctic Challenge 21. If we had participated in an Arctic Challenge exercise, it would have been a big mission planning exercise and very scripted. We would have most likely used our own tactics and tried to incorporate into what the other countries were doing for their own tactics.

"But it became a bilateral exercise called ILVES (Finnish for "Lynx"). We were able to train with them in their tactics. A great tactic VMFA-115 was able to observe was the Finns diverting and spreading out to reduce the effects from a potential strike on their location. They showed us how they're able to set up expeditionary arresting gear, where they put their support and how they taxi the aircraft. We then had one of their instructor pilots get in their simulator with us, where we practiced road landings which was a relatively benign mission, really just taking off and landing on small, short expeditionary runways. The whole system relies largely on the logistics support and the infrastructure for their road runways, which are already in place."

He added: "Doing the bilateral training that we did during ILVES, exposed us to smaller level tactics, techniques, and procedures, which I had never seen before. Those conversations and briefs would not have been available in a big exercise like 'Artic Challenge,' but it was as you mentioned, a whole logistics and infrastructure aspect of aviation, as well as a unique divert strategy, and changing the way your force is employed by consolidating in the air and understanding their TTPs.

"It reminds you that even as a globally deployable force, it's important to see that there are a lot of different ways and different geographical locations, specifically Finland and their neighbors that change the way an aviation unit fights or how a conflict in general is executed. Seeing how other nations fight was very valuable. I would emphasize that going to any country that has a different defense strategy or offensive strategy for that matter is very eye opening, if they're willing to share with you some of their considerations and how they employ their forces."

U.S. Marines with Marine Fighter Attack Squadron (VMFA) 115 fly alongside Finnish Air Force Fighter Squadron 31 over Rissala Air Base, near Kuopio, Finland, June 18, 2021. Photo by LCpl Caleb Stelter, 2nd Marine Aircraft Wing.

I would note that when visiting Finland in 2018, I discussed with a senior Finnish defense officer, who was former head of the Finnish Air Force, the unique way the Finns use their air combat capabilities in the defense of Finland.

As LtGen Kim Jäämeri, the former head of the Finnish Air Force put it: "It is becoming clear to our partners that you cannot run air operations in a legacy manner under the threat of missile barrages of long-range weapons. The legacy approach to operating from air bases just won't work in these conditions. For many of our partners, this is a revelation; for us it has been a fact of life for a long time, and we have operated with this threat in the forefront of operations for a long time."[73]

I also discussed with Norwegian Air Force officers their ramped-up cooperation with the Finns and Swedes in airpower integration. This is being done in part with their cross-border training. As I noted in a 2018 interview: "From 2015 on, the three air forces have shaped a regular training approach, which is very flexible and driven at the wing and squadron level."

Major Ertsgaard added: "We meet each November, and set the schedule for the next year, but in execution it is very, very flexible. It is about a bottom-up approach and initiative to generate the training regime. The impact on Sweden and Finland has been significant in terms of learning NATO standards and having an enhanced capability to cooperate with the air forces of NATO nations. And the air space being used is very significant as well. Europe as an operational military airspace training area is not loaded with good training ranges. The range being used for CBT is very large and is not a cluttered airspace, which allows for great training opportunities for the three nations, and those who fly to Arctic Challenge or other training events. And the range flies over land so there is an opportunity for multi-domain operational training as well."[74]

Since 2018, the Marines have ramped up their efforts to train in the Nordic region and to operate in cold weather. With the Nordics ramping up

73.   Robbin Laird, "Distributed Operations, Exercises and Building Out Finnish Defense Capabilities," *Second Line of Defense* (March 2, 2018), https://sldinfo.com/2018/03/distributed-operations-exercises-and-building-out-finnish-defense-capabilities-the-perspective-of-lt-general-kim-jaameri/.

74.   Robbin Laird, "The Nordics Rework Defense: The Role of Cross Border Air Combat Training," *Second Line of Defense* (July 3, 2018), https://sldinfo.com/2018/07/the-nordics-rework-defense-the-role-of-cross-border-air-combat-training/.

their defense capabilities and working greater integration with each other and with their North Atlantic partners, there are enhanced opportunities for Marines to work in the region as well.

I discussed the importance of Nordic defense and its impact on U.S. forces learning with VADM Lewis, in my interview with him on July 16, 2021, the day after the ceremony launching the Allied Joint Forces Command Norfolk for full operational capability, in the period in which 2nd Fleet was re-established and the Nordic nations clearly ramped up their defense efforts and cooperation with each other and with the United States and NATO. This "learn from others" approach is a key part of how VADM Lewis has led his command. As he commented: "That has been my mantra from day one here: learning from our regional operations. As we work how best to operate in the region, we are learning from our regional partners some of the best ways to do so."[75]

And for the Carolina-based Marines, this means expanded opportunities to learn from our Nordic partners as they work enhanced integration with the U.S. Navy.

Visiting the Warlords

April 29, 2019

During my most recent visit to 2nd Marine Air Wing, I had a chance to visit MCAS Beaufort and meet with LtCol Adam Levine, the CO of VMFAT-501, otherwise known as the Warlords.

As the base was busy for the airshow being held the weekend of the 26th of April 2019, the CO graciously provided some time for an update on the USMC training efforts and shaping the pipeline for the training aspect of the fast jet transition in the Marine Corps.

---

75.   Robbin Laird, "VADM Lewis: Shaping a Way Ahead for C2F and Allied Joint Forces Command, Norfolk," *Second Line of Defense* (July 23, 2021), https://sldinfo.com/2021/07/vadm-lewis-shaping-a-way-ahead-for-c2f-and-allied-joint-forces-command-norfolk/.

I first dealt with the Marines getting ready for F-35 as Eglin stood up the first training efforts. My guide to those efforts was Col "Turbo" Tomasetti. Then when the Warlords were first set up at Eglin, the CO was a Marine, whom I knew from his F-22 flying days, LtCol Berke. The Marines have had a very significant impact on the global standup of the F-35, both because they were the first to IOC the aircraft and because the kind of integration which the Marines embody is very similar to what the smaller air forces of partners and allies seek from their F-35s.

My visit to LtCol Berke took place during a visit of Secretary Wynne to Eglin in 2013. And LtCol Berke has embodied the impact of the Marines on the partners for he appeared at the Williams Seminar in 2014 in Canberra, Australia, which highlighted fifth-generation aircraft in the context of Australian defense transformation and then in the 2015 Williams Foundation Seminar in Denmark, where the same opportunity to speak and to shape the understanding of the fifth-generation revolution for allies was highlighted.

Then in 2015, Murielle Delaporte and I visited Beaufort shortly after the warlords had transitioned to Beaufort from Eglin. I later met members of the Warlords onboard the USS Wasp during sea trials.

But I have not been back to Beaufort for four years, and the Marines have been busy ramping up their training efforts during that period. LtCol Levine provided a comprehensive update on those efforts. It was obvious from the flight line that more planes, pilots and maintainers were populating the base since I was last there. The command has obviously scaled up since the last time I was there, with more than 100 pilots trained, and with the standing up of the second training squadron at Beaufort over the next few months, that scaling up would be accelerated as well. The challenge is a significant one, as the USMC will transition from their legacy force to an all F-35 one within the next two decades, and the task of the training squadrons will be to train the "newbies" and the experienced pilots from legacy aircraft to fly and operate the F-35.

The training cycle is eight months, during which the pilots learn to fly the new jet and then take the jet through its paces with regard to variety of missions for which the Marines use their fast jets.

When I was last there, no "newbies" were present, only experienced pilots. Now the "newbies" are the majority of the pilot trainees. I asked the CO, who is an experienced Hornet pilot, how the two cohorts' experience was different. It must be remembered that at the heart of fifth-generation aviation is a man-machine revolution, where the pilot is getting comfortable with the performance of his aircraft generating data providing situational awareness and the pilot interacting with his screens while operating the aircraft.

He made the point that the "newbies" had never experienced the much more pilot-intensive processing of data which legacy pilots have had to do. In other words, they already assumed the new baseline of man-machine interaction and wanted that interaction to speed up. The pilots of legacy aircraft had much more appreciation of the fact that the F-35 was working from a very different baseline than their legacy jets did. The training of the two cohorts was handled a bit differently, as the more experienced combat pilots could do more training in the simulators, with the "newbies" doing more time in the cockpit.

F-35B from the Warlords flying at the 2019 MCAS Beaufort Air Show, April 17, 2019. Photo by author. Credit: *Second Line of Defense*.

I wanted to discuss with the CO the challenge of training with regard to a software upgradeable aircraft. I have discussed this challenge with regard to other software upgradeable aircraft in Williamtown Airbase with the Royal Australian Air Force and the P-8 with Jax Navy. Put simply, the advantage of the software upgradeable aircraft is that the historical type/model/series understanding of an aircraft now transitions the type by the software-enabled combat systems onboard and which variant is onboard the particular aircraft or squadron of aircraft.

This is the concurrency issue, which is built into a software upgrade process, although the defense press has incorrectly only identified this challenge with that of the F-35. What this means is that the training command will certainly operate the early software versions of the aircraft as the Marines are pushing the 3F version to the operational squadrons. But what it also means is that pilots in the training process need to become familiar with both variants of the aircraft and understand the interaction of the two.

This is not a bad thing because in the operational world they will need to work with aircraft operating globally which are at various software levels, both with regard to services and partners.

LtCol Levine has been flying the F-35 for more than seven years and has witnessed first-hand the software road map taking shape from block 1A through 3F. He underscored that the evolution onboard the Hornets flown by the Marines compared to flying the early variants of the F-35 did not demonstrate the generational differences which now are evident with the 3F. "There is simply no comparison between a 3F F-35 and a legacy aircraft. They are in different worlds," he said.

The Marines at Beaufort have and are working closely with allies. The Brits stood up their training at Beaufort and have jets, pilots and maintainers working with the squadron until this summer. Now the training squadron is being stood up at RAF Marham, and the RAF and Royal Navy will train there.

But with the departure of the Brits, the Italians are coming next and will train for the next couple of years before their carrier comes to the U.S.

for final certifications in a couple of years. And with the Japanese and Singaporeans likely to become F-35B users, one might assume that they will learn of the charm of this lovely Southern city as well. If you are in the F-35 program, you can decide to change the mix of variants, and I would not be surprised to see partners starting to add Bs to the mix, given its inherent basing advantage in a world where mobile basing is clearly becoming a strategic requirement.

The Training Piece

September 12, 2021

During a July 2021 visit to 2d MAW, I talked with LtCol J. Eric Grunke and LtCol Jessica Hawkins. Grunke just relinquished responsibility to Hawkins for the Marine Aviation Training Systems (MATS) ecosystem within 2d MAW, encompassing all aviation simulators and the necessary infrastructure. There is a MATS site at each of the major 2d MAW air stations: MCAS Cherry Point, MCAS New River and MCAS Beaufort.

In order to remain America's Force in Readiness, the Marine Corps must continue to adapt as the world changes. Major General Michael Cederholm, Commanding General (CG) 2d MAW, emphatically believes that training must evolve exponentially to strengthen the Marines enduring advantages and allow them to prevail in strategic competition with China or any other nation.

Keeping with this vision, the CG directed the integration of multiple, disparate platform simulators along with CAC2S to better prepare his force and support II Marine Expeditionary Force missions. China has fundamentally transformed the operating environment and the Marine Corps must modernize the force and its capabilities in order to continue to deter adversaries.

A key element of the combat learning process is integrating live, virtual, constructive training; a technique that combines simulation with real-world flights and ground maneuver. This technique is a force multiplier when shaping tactics and concepts for new and emerging technology like the F-35. War-gaming is a time-tested element of the planning process for informing a commander of the strengths and weaknesses in an operational plan. However, advances in modeling, simulation and workforce integration provide an alternative to the traditional war game.

Commanders that leverage the advancing capabilities in virtual and constructive environments are provided with a dynamic operational environment that truly exercises real-time risk and force employment decision-making at all levels. More importantly, it will allow commanders to engage a "thinking" enemy and the associated friction often lacking in a static set of assumptions used by traditional war gamers, ideally, thereby providing a more accurate assessment of an operational plan's efficacy.

Maj J. Eric Grunke, pictured here at Cherry Point, was named 2011 Marine Corps Aviator of the Year by the Marine Corps Aviation Association. Grunke, an AV-8B Harrier pilot, played an instrumental role in a mission to recover a downed Air Force pilot in Libya. April 24, 2012. Photo by Cpl Brian Adam Jones, II Marine Expeditionary Force.

LtCol Grunke's experience in Operation Odyssey Dawn (OD) provides an example of the operational plan not playing out to script. LtCol Grunke was flying Strike Coordination and Reconnaissance (SCAR) sorties in support of OD when he had to quickly change mindset and serve as the on-scene commander for an innovative downed pilot recovery effort using a combined flight of Ospreys and Harriers. The team launched from an amphibious ship to rescue a downed USAF pilot in record time. His actions were a potential war-changing event war-game modeling can easily overlook.

Much of my discussion with LtCol Grunke and LtCol Hawkins focused on how to enhance integrated training and increase pilot proficiency against enemy aircraft and weapons systems.

To address the pacing threat, the Marine Corps is evolving and innovating as part of the larger naval expeditionary force. One theme we discussed is the 2d MAW effort to improve realistic wing-level training. One critical step is having real pilots operating in their platform-specific simulators (e.g., a qualified Cobra or Harrier pilot flying in the simulators) and integrating with the Marine Aircraft Control Group (MACG) to conduct coordinated missions in support of the exercise scenario.

This concept was recently tested in 2d MAW's Cope Javelin exercise. Achieving a higher level of simulator integration was described by LtCol Grunke as a crawl, walk, then run process.

"The crawl phase was to get a Cobra pilot in their sim and a Harrier pilot in their sim and make sure they share the same visual representation to both fly and see the same terrain. They can then work together in that common operating picture. The walk phase is to take that pairing and work with a Joint Terminal Aircraft Controller in their sim to execute a single sortie in the simulator. In that phase we still did not have the MACG (the C^2 arm of the wing) fully virtual. They were purely constructive and travel to the various sites to participate. They were sitting in our simulator center just talking on the radio, doing their jobs, but not on their own equipment, and not in their own space. The run phase which was seen in COPE JAVELIN was the C^2 element at the DASC controlling the close air support assets coming in and out of objective areas on their own gear, while Harrier pilots in their sims and Cobra pilots in their sims participate in the engagement. The goal here is to shape readiness at the wing level – Marines must be ready for anything, anywhere, especially when the nation is the least ready."

LtCol Grunke highlighted the focus of the effort as follows: "This is a working mission rehearsal. What I want to happen is a force-on-force exercise. We have a red team acting as the Russian commander; they do as they please with their forces. I want to ensure no telegraphing to the blue side of their intentions. The Harriers and the other air assets get their targets assigned and then the red force take force-on-force action appropriate to the enemy mission. This is how we truly achieve a force-on-force event; where we basically get to see whether our tactics work or not, given our assumptions, as the scenario unfolds. They're met with limited success in really achieving a true force-on-force, which is something we'll want to work on for the next time."

A second theme discussed was the challenge of networking individual platform simulators to deliver a more integrated operating space for the training effort. When I visited Jax Navy, the challenge there was linking MH-60 Romeo with MQ-4C Triton and P-8 simulators, which is crucial, as these three platforms operate as an integrated system to deliver a coordinated set of effects. A similar challenge faces the trainers at 2d MAW.

As LtCol Hawkins put it: "We are working to streamline the data flow across not only the different flight simulators, but the other simulation systems as well, in order to run a more effective exercise. All of these systems have been developed somewhat independently and speak their own language. To work around that problem all the networking information has to run through a Distributed Information System (DIS) bridge which essentially interprets the various coding languages used by each simulation device, processes and converts it into usable language for each to understand. With the scale of COPE JAVELIN, the number of virtual and constructive friendly and enemy entities, the DIS bridge can become rapidly overwhelmed."

A third theme discussed was training in the environment where operational plans are intended to be executed. As LtCol Hawkins underscored: "We need to obtain a more comprehensive visual data base in order to conduct true mission rehearsal exercises. All of the different platforms, represented by their own program offices have purchased visual imagery databases based on their own assessed priorities. This has resulted in a disparity between the platforms; they don't all have the same images. For example, a MV-22 might be able to go to Northeastern Europe in the simulator but the Harrier may not. The Cobra might be able to go to the Horn of Africa, but another platform might not. These are problems Aviation Training Systems are working through."

A fourth theme discussed was how the training way ahead will allow warriors to drive innovation beyond traditional war-gaming outputs. As LtCol Grunke put it: "Instead of war gaming, let's train for a real war. Let's get into the areas where we expect to fight, with the actual terrain in a simulator, with the G/ATOR where we think it's going to be, where we think the force is going to launch from, and see how we do.[76] There's no reason why we can't do something like that, so long as all the imagery is unified in all the trainers, and we can see the effects of operations from the various simulator locations."

---

76. Ashley Calingo, "Inside Acquisition: How the G/ATOR Modernizes the Corps for the Future Fight" (July 14, 2021), https://www.marines.mil/News/News-Display/Article/2694135/inside-acquisition-how-the-gator-modernizes-the-corps-for-the-future-fight/.

A U.S. Marine Corps AN/TPS-80 Ground/Air Task Oriented Radar, a part of Air Defense Company Alpha, Marine Air Control Squadron (MACS) 4, sits in a field at Andersen Air Force Base, Guam, July 25, 2021. Marines with MACS-4 use the G/ATOR to provide real time airspace surveillance, command and control while coordinating air and missile defense actions in support of U.S. Marine Corps, Navy, and Air Force aircraft during exercise Pacific Iron 2021. Photo by LCpl Tyler Harmon, 1st Marine Aircraft Wing.

A fifth theme we discussed was the allied aspect of training for an integrated combat effect.

I highlighted the discussion I had with the BALTOPS 50 team, where Norwegian F-35s played the F-35 role in the exercise. As LtCol Grunke underscored: "The Norwegian F-35As carry a much different ordnance load from the F-35B flown by the USMC. They also have different rules of engagement (ROE) considerations. So to work the virtual aspect we need to have a constructive role player from Norway to come over and indicate how they approach the operation."

We closed with a question I posed to the new director of the MATS: What key capabilities would you most like to add in the near term to accelerate the way ahead for training? LtCol Hawkins underscored: "I think there are two things. First, would be building and operating from a common global visual database. Second, simulators that are easily connected to one another and can talk and transfer data back and forth with ease."

Shaping a Way Ahead for the Assault Support Community

August 10, 2021

During my visit to 2nd Marine Air Wing in July 2021, I had a chance to discuss the way ahead for the assault support community with the commanding officer of MAG-29, Col Joyce, and the operations officer for MAG-29, Maj Bowing. In terms of aircraft, MAG-29 has CH-53E in the heavy-lift squadrons, and AH-1Z Vipers and UH-1Y Venoms in their light-attack helicopter squadrons. The Marine Corps is scheduled to deliver the CH-53K to MAG-29, as well as add Link 16 and full-motion video capabilities to the H-1 assets. These upgrades will provide significant options for the aircraft to support the way ahead as part of the evolving capabilities for the assault force.

For Col Joyce, the return of naval integration is really the return to his roots in his initial operational time in the USMC. He has also served on the Navy staff in the N98 Air Warfare Division as the Marine Corps officer working with Naval aviation, where discussions of how to leverage and integrate the Marines' role as Naval aviators into the future maritime fight were a daily event. Non-Marines often forget that Marine Corps aviators are indeed naval aviators and as such provide a key access point in the effort to find new ways to integrate the two forces.

As Col Joyce put it: "We are really talking about reintegrating our Naval Force. Getting back to our roots as a Corps to provide Fleet Marine Forces for service with the Fleet. Our history over the past six decades may be filled with periods of sustained operations ashore, but our legacy as a Corps is that of naval campaigning, amphibious operations, and the conduct of such land operations as may be essential to the prosecution of a naval campaign. Today's reintegration focus is oriented on a vision of maritime warfighting designed to posture the Naval Force for the next six decades."

Col Joyce entered the Marine Corps towards the end of the Cold War and is one of the officers I have interviewed in the Navy or the USMC over the past three years who bring real operational experience in this strategic competition environment. Major Bowing has been part of the Huey community from the beginning of his time in the USMC and has served for three years in MAWTS-1 working assault support training and concepts of operations.

One issue we discussed was the integration of Link-16 and full-motion video upgrades for the H-1s and their potential impact. Col Joyce put it this way: "I believe the integration of Link-16 along with many other digital interoperability (DI) efforts should help us look at ourselves differently moving forward. I would argue the attack and utility community over the last 20 years largely viewed our pursuit of DI efforts such as Link-16 from a consumer's perspective. Meaning, we wanted the ability to ingest mostly targeting data via Link-16 to create a tactical effect on the battlefield from our own platform.

"I would also suggest this idea is consistent with the way we've been tactically employed over the past two decades. But the future of naval campaigning and maritime warfighting, especially within the close-in, confined, and contested key maritime terrain of the littorals, requires the HMLA community to view ourselves much more as participants and enablers of larger kill chains and kill webs. This means attack and utility capabilities out forward – acting as an extension of the Marine Littoral Regiment (MLR) – to screen, scout, and sense within both the landward and seaward areas of the littorals.

"As participants in a larger kill web, we must be able to gather, disseminate, receive, exploit, and/or act on the information depending on the tactical task assigned. Our core missions within Assault Support Aviation will remain vital in future littoral battles – conducting assault support operations, providing forward arming and refueling points, conducting aviation reconnaissance and surveillance, and conducting aviation delivered fires remain core competencies of the future force.

"What is different from our recent past is the explicit focus on supporting Surface Warfare and Sea Denial operations. What do we bring to that fight? Where are the warfighting gaps? Can we fill those gaps? Should we fill those gaps? How do we contribute to anti-surface warfare (ASuW) missions?

"These are some of the questions we're looking at right now within MAG-29. We are the only Service viewing this future environment through the lens of a Stand-In (versus Stand-Off) force.

"How do we contribute to Surface Warfare and Sea Denial operations as part of the Stand-In force? How do we continue to provide close-in support to the MLR maneuvering throughout the landward area of the littorals in a high-threat non-permissive environment, while enabling the larger kill web oriented on Sea Denial operations within the seaward area of the shallow blue waters? Are we postured through ongoing DI initiatives to gather, disseminate, receive, and exploit information across subsurface, surface, air, and information domains?

"I would argue this is a paradigm shift in mindset from our operations over the past 20 years in the desert. Lethality across Assault Support Aviation, including our heavy lift platform, remains a critical as ever in the future fight. But our ability to screen, scout, and sense within the littorals and then contribute to the larger kill web may be even more important in the years to come."

Looking ahead, the leadership of 2d MAW is clearly focused on working towards the tactical missions that are likely to be dominant in the 2030 timeframe. As Col Joyce hammered home: "There is absolutely a critical role for Assault Support Aviation looking forward. When you look at the shear expanse of geography, force dispersion and distribution, and challenges with our maritime logistics fleet in just one example, I can't envision a situation where somebody tells me we have too much heavy lift capability.

"What we must do as a community to help the larger Force Design effort is to focus our analysis on capabilities, rather than specific platforms. We must experiment ruthlessly with those capabilities through the lens of future tactical tasks and missions. And then focus our platform modernization efforts and develop aviation tactics, techniques, and procedures to deliver those needed capabilities to the Fleet Marine Force."

His earlier discussion with regard to how assault support can contribute to sea control and sea denial is an example of what he means by looking at capabilities through different tactical or mission lenses. Rather than define the mission sets by the primary operations of the past twenty years in the Middle East, the aperture is being opened to correlate capabilities with evolving mission sets.

For example, the Marines are adding the CH-53K to the force, and Col Joyce underscored that the new platform brings new capabilities to the force. But rather than simply describing how the platform is replacing the CH-53E, the focus needs to be upon how to leverage new capabilities to deal with evolving mission sets. The Marine Corps has been investing in capabilities to respond globally to crisis and contingency and build the capabilities to compete and blunt a potential adversary's aggression.

As Col Joyce put it: "Logistics is our pacing function. It doesn't matter if it's the High North or the Indo-Pacific. Assured logistics, assured movement, and assured sustainment of the force requires the capabilities that the heavy lift team brings to the fight. And the CH-53E and future CH-53K is the only heavy lift rotary-wing capability within the Department of Defense. The CH-53K is simply an exponential leap in heavy lift capability in terms of range, payload, and digital interoperability. No one can predict with precision what the future holds. Advances in long-range precision strike, unmanned systems, loitering munitions, low earth orbit system sensing, and AI/ML will change how we currently perform our warfighting missions. But Close Air Support, Strike, Aerial Delivery, Assault Transport, Air Evacuation, and Tactical Recovery of Aircraft and Personnel to name a few absolutely have a future role in the Nation's Crisis Response force."

Major Bowing built on the discussion and added a core point, namely, the weaponizing of communication. The sharing of information and data as part of the shaping of enhanced capabilities for an integrated distributed force is a key part of the way ahead for shaping the role for the assault support community.

We did not discuss the following point specifically, but if one combines a number of thoughts which have been shared by Marines at both II MEF and 2nd MAW with me, the blending of assault support with C^2/ISR warfare could well emerge from the process of working integration with the Navy. In an August 2021 exercise, we will see the establishment of an advanced expeditionary sensor base built around the new Ground/Air Task-Oriented Radar or G/ATOR.

The assault support community—notably by heavy lift—can deliver that radar to such a base.

The C^2 community is very capable of not only supporting G/ATOR at that base but also flying in the Osprey, which is an assault support asset, and with a roll-on roll-of capability, providing the C^2 linkages from that sensor base to the key combat nodes in the kill web, as was done in the 2020 Deep Water exercise discussed earlier.

One could establish on another advanced expeditionary base information warfare Marines or MIG-combat members who could contribute to spoofing, jamming or various disinformation efforts in support of the deployed force, and again that would be a payload delivered by the assault support force.

In other words, the assault support community can deliver a wider array of payloads than simply direct kinetic force. Indeed, if one focuses on maritime kill webs, the Marines really do not need to carry weapons to the point of attack; they can deploy capabilities which can find targets, communicate those targets to other fire solution combat capabilities and contribute to the electronic warfare aspects of the fight.

With the flexibility inherent in roll-on roll-of capabilities on the Osprey, a variety of mission support elements could be put on the unique tiltrotor-enabled range and speed asset. And with an ability to put interior fuel cells into the Osprey, endurance is enabled as well. In other words, capabilities seen through the lens of expanded mission sets can drive the transformation process.

CHAPTER SIX:

THE VIEW FROM THE PACIFIC

When I visited MARFORPAC in 2014, it was the beginning of what the Obama Administration called the "Pivot to the Pacific." But that really did not happen, as the Russians seized Crimea and the wars in the Middle East ramped up. Those demand sets still weigh heavily on the U.S. military and its ability to generate forces for Pacific operations.

But the basic template for the Marines in the Pacific was already being shaped, namely, a distributed laydown, from which the Marines could operate with greater strategic depth than their operating locations in Hawaii and on the West Coast of the United States would allow.

In a 2014 article, I highlighted the basic template which was being put in place as follows:

> The U.S. Marine Corps is in the throes of a significant shift in the Pacific in the disposition of its forces. Because two thirds of Marines are deployed to the Pacific, such a shift is a key event in re-defining the Marine Corps stance in the decade ahead.... The demand to support distributed forces is rising and will require attention to be paid to the connectors, lifters and various support elements.
>
> Part of that demand can be met as allies modernize their own support elements, such as Australia and Singapore adding new Airbus tankers which could be leveraged to support Marine Corps Ospreys as well as other aircraft.

Indeed, a key element of the distributed laydown of our forces in the Pacific is the fact that it is occurring as core allies in the region are reshaping and modernizing their forces as well as partners coming to the table who wish to work with and host USMC forces operating on a rotational basis with their forces. The military and political demands for the kind of forces that the Marines are developing also are what allies and partners want for their operations. In turn, this drives up the importance of exercises in the Pacific with joint and coalition forces to shape new capabilities for the distributed force.

The distributed laydown, the evolution of the capabilities for distributed forces, the modernization of allied forces and the growing interest in a diversity of partners to work with the USMC are all part of shaping what might be called a deterrence-in-depth strategy to deal with the threats and challenges facing the United States and its allies in shaping a 21st-century approach to Pacific defense....

It is clear that as the distributed approach is shaped in the Pacific, the demand on support, connectors and lift is going to increase. There will be a need for Military Sealift Command ships and amphibious ships and to draw heavily on new ships like the T-AKE and USNS Montford Point (MLP-1). The demand on airlift is significant, and it's clear from developments in the Pacific and new approaches like Special Purpose MAGTFs that KC-130Js need to be plussed up.

Senior military commanders from Australia, Japan and the United States pause for a quick orientation before boarding a U.S. Marine Corps MV-22 Osprey that will transport them to the USS Peleliu (LHA-5) amphibious assault ship for a discussion on Maritime Power Projection. Shown in the photo are (from left to right): LtGen Terry G. Robling, Commander, U.S. Marine Corps Forces, Pacific; Gen. Kiyofumi Iwata, Chief of Staff, Japanese Ground Self-Defense Force; Adm. Harry B. Harris, Jr., Commander, U.S. Pacific Fleet; Adm. Katsutoshi Kawano, Chief of Staff, Japanese Maritime Self-Defense Force; Gen. Vincent K. Brooks, Commander, U.S. Army Pacific; and Major General Peter Warwick "Gus" Gilmore, Deputy Chief of Army, Royal Australian Army. July 14, 2014. Photo by Gunnery Sgt Christine Polvorosa, U.S. Marine Corps Forces, Pacific.

LtGen Robling, the MARFORPAC commander, underscored the nature of the challenge: "The demand signal goes up every year while the cost of using the lift goes up every year as well. This has me very concerned. The truth of the matter is the Asia Pacific region is 52 percent of the globe's surface, and there are over 25,000 islands in the region. The distances and times necessary to respond to a crisis are significant. The size of the AOR [area of responsibility] is illustrated in part by the challenge of finding the missing Malaysian airliner.

"If you don't have the inherent capability like the KC-130J aircraft to get your equipment and people into places rapidly, you can quickly become irrelevant. General Hawk Carlisle uses a term in his engagement strategy which is 'places not bases.'

"America doesn't want forward bases. This means you have to have the lift to get to places quickly, be able to operate in an expeditionary environment when you get there, and then leave when we are done. Strengthening our current partnerships and making new ones will go a long way in helping us be successful at this strategy," the general added. "We have to be invited in before we can help. If you don't have prepositioned equipment already in these countries, then you have to move it in somehow.

"And, right now, we're moving in either via naval shipping, black-bottom shipping, or when we really need it there quickly, via KC-130J aircraft or available C-17 aircraft. Right now, we are the only force in the Pacific that can get to a crisis quickly, and the only force that operates as an integrated air, sea and ground organization. Allies see the Marines clearly on the right path, and that path is a powerful one. But funding for the capabilities needed and the proper training will not happen by itself."[77]

---

77.   Robbin Laird, "Meeting the Challenges of the Demand Side of the Distributed Laydown in the Pacific," *Second Line of Defense* (July 28, 2014), https://sldinfo.com/2014/07/meeting-the-challenges-of-the-demand-side-of-the-distributed-laydown-in-the-pacific/.

The Pacific laydown strategy of the USMC as envisaged by MARFORPAC in 2014. Unclassified slide from *Second Line of Defense* article in 2014.

In my return to MARFORPAC in August 2021, the core template put in place in 2014 remains valid and a sound basis for moving ahead. The major changes since then are clearly how both the Chinese and Russians are reaching out further into the Pacific, and the North Korean nuclear challenge has deepened.

During my MARFORPAC visit in August 2021, I had a chance to be briefed by Joe Sampson, Director of Strategic Engagement, which provided an opportunity to talk about what has changed and what has not. And there are a number of takeaways from that discussion which provided an overview on how to view the Marines and their evolution in Pacific defense.

The first major takeaway from our discussion is that the push further out into the Pacific by the Chinese and the Chinese military build-out and engagements in the Pacific require the Marines to operate forward of their basing in the United States and in Hawaii. One way to do so is to work on more effective operational capabilities to project force from three trajectories for operations in the Pacific. The first is from Okinawa, which is in the first island chain and where the F-35s of the Marines provide a key element for projecting power. The second is from the rebuild of Guam with the Marines having a base from which to rotate forces for operations. The third is working with the Australian Defence Force from the Northern territories.

When I first visited MARFORPAC, the F-35 was not yet there, and the Marine Rotational Force-Darwin (MRF-D) was just in its infancy. Both of these additions highlight how the Marines are working their approaches to operating in the Pacific. The F-35 allows the Marines to work closely with allies in the region who also have F-35s, and, notably, prepare to operate with the South Koreans and Japanese who will operate F-35Bs as well off of their amphibious ships and integrate closely with the USAF.

The Australian working relationship is a key one, and having spent many years working with the Australians, the key impact will come as the Australians rework their military strategy in the region, and the Marines sort through how to most effectively work with the Australians as they do so.

But the core takeaway is simply the importance of being able to project force from multiple trajectories.

The second major takeaway is the central role of training. Training is a weapon system. But shaping a USMC trained properly for Pacific operations is challenging, as there is no one place to do so. Marines operate off of Hawaii and multiple islands but are limited in what they can do in specific training situations. Bringing the whole capability together is crucial and difficult. For the U.S. Navy and the USAF, bringing the full spectrum of capabilities into the current training environment is virtually impossible, and I mean literally impossible in either a live or virtual setting. For the Marines to work through how to integrate more effectively with the Navy or USAF is a major challenge going forward.

Sampson underscored the importance of training from another perspective as well. It is crucial to train with partners and allies, not simply from the standpoint of bringing what the U.S. can do to an allied or partner training event. Rather, it is crucial to understand the approach of those partners and allies not only to military training but also to their tactical and, inferentially, their strategic purposes for national defense in the region.

A third takeaway is how really crucial aviation is for the USMC to operate in what is lovingly called the "tyranny of distance." The Marines as the only tiltrotor/fifth generation force in the world need clearly to leverage those capabilities going forward.

A fourth takeaway is the enhanced importance on naval integration, but the shortage of amphibious or expeditionary sea-basing ships is certainly a barrier to getting full value from what is possible for the fleet as an integrated fighting force. When I was at MARFORPAC in 2014, there was a growing emphasis on the importance of "amphibiosity." This emphasis remains significant as the Marines are focused on how to influence Naval operations from their sea bases to their expeditionary bases.

Now partner and allied nations are clearly ramping up their amphibious capabilities which provides a significant operational set of opportunities for the Marines going forward. And working naval integration is not limited to the U.S. Navy, of course. Marines operating off of HMS Queen Elizabeth in the Pacific or landing on Japanese amphibious ships is also part of the broad-scale integration with naval forces in the Pacific.

An MV-22B Osprey from Marine Medium Tiltrotor Squadron 161 prepares to land aboard the JS Shimokita during Dawn Blitz June 14, 2013. Photo by Sgt Isaac Lamberth, Marine Corps Air Station Miramar.

A fifth takeaway is the enhanced emphasis on force distribution including expeditionary basing which MARFORPAC and the USMC is working on in following General Berger's Force Design 2030 approach. Sampson provided a very helpful slide in his briefing which highlighted the modernization priorities which reflected the Commandant's 2030 force design-led effort. That slide highlighted the following with regard to the Marine Corps modernization priorities:

- A Lighter, More Mobile and Versatile Infantry. Shoot, move, communicate, and survive within range of enemy weapon systems while seizing and defending key maritime terrain in order to conduct sea denial missions in addition to our other traditional missions.

- Expansion of Long-Range Fires: Capability to lethally strike a moving maritime target with precision at range.

- Investments in Unmanned Systems: Increase the number of unmanned aerial systems to enhance our ability to sense and strike targets at range.

- Maritime Mobility and Resilience: Seek new capabilities to increase mobility and resilience (i.e., light amphibious warship, etc.)

- Mobile Air Defense and Counter-Precision Guided Missile Systems: Directed energy systems, loitering munitions, signature management, electronic warfare, expeditionary airfield capabilities, and structure to support manned/unmanned aircraft in austere environments.

U.S. Marines with Kilo Company, 3rd Battalion, 8th Marine Regiment, patrol at Combined Arms Training Center, Camp Fuji, Japan, Jan. 21, 2021. Marines patrolled in disaggregated units towards a common objective for Joint Exercise Littoral Strike, the culminating event for Fuji Viper 21.2, that strengthened interoperability and challenged infantry formations to facilitate joint force multi-domain maneuver in support of naval operations. 3/8 is forward-deployed in the Indo-Pacific under 4th Marine Regiment, 3rd Marine Division. Credit Photo: 3rd Marine Division.

In short, the Marines are a key part of the effort to shape the kind of integrated distributed force crucial for full-spectrum crisis management in the region.

The Perspective of LtGen Rudder, the MARFORPAC Commander

My last visit to Hawaii and meetings with the MARFORPAC commander and his staff was in 2014. In August 2021, I visited again and spent several days in the islands, during which I visited both MARFORPAC and PACAF. Since my last visit, what the Marines refer to as the "pacing threat" has gained enhanced momentum. The People's Republic of China, both in policies and capabilities, have ramped up the threat and challenge envelope for the United States and its allies. The Russians are a Pacific power as well, and the direct threat posed by North Korea is an evolving one as well.

At the onset of my visit to the Marine Corps in Honolulu, I had a chance to talk with LtGen Steven Rudder, commander, U.S. Marine Corps Forces, Pacific. I have known "Stick" ever since he served as deputy to the then deputy commandant of Aviation, LtGen George Trautman.

We started the conversation by focusing on how he sees the challenge facing the Marines in the Pacific.

This is how LtGen Rudder put it: "Our first challenge is about having the right force postured with the right capabilities. Our starting point is today's posture, which for the most part is centered in Northeast Asia. Because of the vast distances in the Pacific, our additive challenge is being able to maneuver capabilities into places where you may not have a dedicated sustainment structure. Regardless, you have to be able rapidly to get there, set up, and operate using organic lift and logistics."

LtGen Rudder underscored that part of the USMC current posture means that on a daily basis, the Marine Corps must operate inside an adversary's threat ring. He said, "I think the key advantage for us is the daily posture of Marines in Japan and within ongoing partner operations in Southeast Asia.

We are persistently in the first island chain ready to maneuver to seize or defend key maritime terrain. Continued integration with the joint force in Japan and in the Republic of Korea is critical within the context of any contingency. The question then becomes: What capabilities does the Marine and the Joint Force need to maneuver into the right tactical position to get the desired effects?"

In 2013, when we published our book on rebuilding American military power in the Pacific, we highlighted the strategic triangle of U.S. force generation and the strategic quadrangle for force employment.[78]

Strategic Geogrpahy

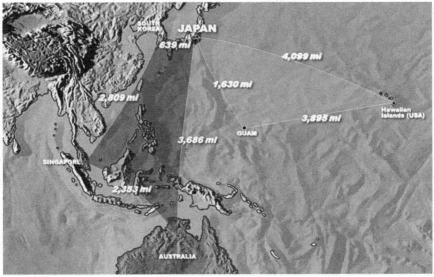

Conceptualizing the strategic triangle of force generation in the Pacific by U.S. forces and the strategic quadrangle of the operation of those forces in the Pacific. Graphic credited to *Second Line of Defense*, 2013.

---

78.   Robbin Laird, Edward Timperlake and Richard Weitz, *Rebuilding American Military Power in the Pacific: A 21st Century Strategy* (Praeger, 2013).

Since we shaped this graphic, and since I last visited MARFORPAC in 2014, the Marines have reworked the force projection trajectories and are in the process of making these trajectories realities to shape a more effective engagement force in the region. Notably, since 2014, the initial Marine Rotational Force in Australia (MRF-D) has deepened its cooperation with the Australian Defense Force. And Australia has itself enhanced its joint force capabilities, including the introduction of the F-35 and an amphibious surface fleet and air/ground capability. The focus on operations in the direct defense of Australia and wider Indo-Pacific region creates significant and evolving opportunities for U.S.–Australia interoperability.

Also, the Marines are building up their presence in Guam at Camp Blaz. This is the first new Marine Corps base since 1952. This is how LtGen Rudder highlighted several opportunities for force projection: "We are focused on shaping an effective posture that combines forward bases with rotational partnerships with key Allies. I have already highlighted how important our posture is in Japan. Employing infantry and MV-22s from Okinawa and F-35s from Iwakuni (in southwest Honshu). we readily integrate with Japan's Amphibious Rapid Deployment Brigade.

"MRF-D plays a role as well. Six months out of the year, we rotate 2,000 Marines into Australia with ground forces, MV-22s, fires, and logistics capability. Now that the Australians are operating the F-35 and routinely exercising amphibious operations, we can work jointly on expanding high-end bi-lateral and multi-lateral operations. As a combined force, we have already increased the complexity of operations as recently demonstrated during Talisman Saber 21.

"And as we build up and deploy greater numbers of forces to Camp Blaz, Guam, we will use this location as an additional posture location for 5,000 Marines and Sailors. All of these posture developments allow us to have various operational touch points from which one could aggregate force capabilities. With a combination of air and sea lift, we are designing a force with the ability to rapidly move into positions of advantage."

We then discussed the evolution of fires which the Marines can bring to the Pacific fight.

With the end of the INF (Intermediate-Range Nuclear Forces) Treaty, the United States can now build longer range conventional capabilities. The Marines are looking to participate in this effort and employ them from expeditionary forward bases well inside the adversary's weapons engagement area. The objective is to contribute to SLOC defense or be additive to offensive naval fires.

LtGen Steven R. Rudder, commanding general of Marine Forces Pacific (center), speaks to the Marines of Marine fighter Attacks Squadron (VMFA) 323 at Marine Corps Base Hawaii, June 21, 2021. Photo by Sgt Dominic Romero, 3rd Marine Air Wing.

According to LtGen Rudder: "If we look forward in the not-too-distant future, we'll have the ability to have land-based long-range fires, aviation fires, and persistent high endurance ISR (Intelligence, Surveillance and Reconnaissance) with the MQ-9. We'll be able to move those capabilities with KC-130s, MV-22s, or amphibious lift allowing us to project long-range fires forward anywhere in Asia, much like we do with the HIMARS (High-Mobility Artillery Rocket System) today.

"HIMARS fits in the back of a KC-130 allowing rapid mobilization and insertion. We will exercise the same operational tactic with anti-ship capability. We want to project sea denial capabilities to cut off a strait of our choosing or maneuver into positions to create our own maritime chokepoint. As we saw with hunting mobile missiles in the past, having long-range fires on maneuvering platforms makes them really hard to hit. As we distribute our long-range fires on mobile platforms, we now become a hard platform to find.

"Our desire is to create our own anti-access and area denial capability. For the last several years, we were thinking about the adversary's missiles, and how they could be used to deny us access to forward locations. Now we want to be the sea denial force that is pointed in the other direction. Land based fires are perfectly suited to support naval maneuver.

"We want rapidly to move by air or sea, deliver sea denial capabilities onto land, maneuver to position of advantage, deliver fires, maneuver for another shot, or egress by air or sea. We are training current forces on concepts for sea denial missions supported by maneuver of long-range fires. This is a key element of the naval integration."

With the growing capability of joint sensor networks, the potential for more effective joint targeting is a reality. As the joint force focuses on dynamic targeting, services are closely coordinating fires networks and authorities. The advantage of land-based expeditionary fires is that it provides persistence cover within an established air and surface targeting solution.

This is how LtGen Rudder characterized how he saw the way ahead: "We are completely integrated with naval maneuver and working hand and hand with the joint force. I MEF and III MEF have been operating seamlessly as three-star naval task forces astride Seventh and Third Fleets. During crises, I become the deputy JFMCC (Joint Force Maritime Component Commander) to the Pacific Fleet Commander. The MARFORPAC staff integrates with the PacFleet staff. Even during day-to-day operations, we have Marines at

PacFleet planning and integrating across multiple domains. Should we ramp up towards crisis or conflict, we will reinforce our JFMCC contribution to ensure we remain fully prepared for all-domain naval force execution.

"This means that our anti-ship missiles will integrate into naval maneuver. We also aggressively pursue PACAF integration for bomber, fighter, and 5th Generation support. Daily, our F-35s are integrated into the PACAF AOC (Air Operations Center). We are focused on better integration to insure we have a common operating picture for an integrated firing solution."

The USMC F-35s play a key role in all of this. Although there is a clear focus on enhanced integration with the U.S. Navy, the integration with the USAF is crucial for both the U.S. Navy and the USMC. LtGen Rudder highlighted the role which USMC F-35s play in Pacific defense and force integration. "We count on pulling fifth-gen capability forward in time of crisis. We are committed to having forward deployed F-35s conducting integrated training on a regular basis with our PACAF counterparts. We will also conduct integrated training with our Korean, Japanese, Singaporean and Australian partners. We are also training with aircraft carriers when they operate in the region, such as the USS Carl Vinson, the first U.S. Navy F-35C variant carrier aircraft, is currently.

"And the F-35B has caught the operational attention of the rest of the world. The United Kingdom's HMS Queen Elizabeth is the largest fifth-generation fighter deployment ever conducted on an aircraft carrier. We are proud to be a part of that UK deployment, with a Marine F-35B squadron, VMFA-211, embarked and operating with our British partners. They are currently doing combined operations in the Western Pacific.

"We are excited to see the Italians operating F-35s off the ITS Cavour, and we hope by the fall of this year that we'll be landing an F-35B on the Japan Ship Izumo, as the Japanese look ahead to the purchase of F-35Bs. The South Koreans are considering going down a similar path, with Singapore also adding F-35s to their inventory.

"Aside from shipboard operations, the F-35B can do distributed operations like no other combat aircraft. We can go into a variety of airfields which may not be accessible by other fighter aircraft, reload and refuel, and take back off again, making both the aircraft and the airfields more survivable."

The Marines are the only combat force that tactically combine fifth generation with tiltrotor capabilities. This combined capability is crucial for operations in an area characterized by the tyranny of distance. The MV-22 Ospreys can also carry a wide variety of payloads that can encompass the C^2 and ISR revolutions underway. And if you are focused on flexible basing, the combination of the two aircraft provides possibilities which no other force in the world currently possesses.

But shortfalls in the numbers of aircraft forward create challenges to unleash the full potential of the amphibious fleet to enable the Marines as a crisis management force and to enhance the Marine Corps' contribution to the joint force. The nature of distributed operations in the Pacific demands long-range aircraft like the MV-22 to sustain the force.

This is how LtGen Rudder put it: "We can reconfigure our amphibious ships to take on many different assault functions. I think when people talk about amphibious assault, they have singular visions of near-beach operations. Instead, we need to think of our amphibious capability from the standpoint of our ability to maneuver from range. Rather than focusing on the 3,000 or 5,000-meter closure from ship to shore, I think about the 600, 700, 1,000-mile closure, with amphibs able to distribute and put people in place or to conduct resupply once you're there.

"Amphibious lift, with its ability to bring its own connectors for logistics support, is increasingly significant for the operational force. In addition, we have to make sure that we're able to close the force when lethal and non-lethal shaping has done its course.

"At some point, you're going to need to seize and defend land. We have two ways to tactically accomplish this mission, either by air or by surface assault. There's no other way to get forces ashore unless you secure a port that has the space to offload and a road network to move ashore. Open port options are highly unlikely during crisis, thus amphibious lift is increasingly becoming more valuable for maneuvering forces in the maritime domain."

The Marines are launching a new capability in the next couple of years, the Marine Littoral Regiment (MLR). According to the MARFORPAC commander: "We are working towards initial operating capability (IOC) of the MLR in 2023. We want to demonstrate the maneuverability of the MLR as well as the capabilities it can bring to naval operations. Near term, we will work to exercise new capabilities in the region, such as loading the NEMESIS (Navy/Marine Corps Expeditionary Ship Interdiction System) system on the KC-130s or Landing Craft Air Cushion (LCAC) for integrated operations with F-35s, MQ-9s, and other maritime targeting capabilities."

In short, the USMC is in transition in the Pacific and working towards greater interoperability with the joint force, notably, the U.S. Navy and the USAF.

The Perspective of LtGen Heckl, I MEF Commander

July 9, 2021

During my lifetime, the USMC has been the initial crisis management for the nation. It continues to do so, but after a long interlude of becoming land centric due to the demands of the nation's leaders. With the return of direct defense in Europe and with the changing strategic situation in the Pacific, the USMC is in transformation to recalibrate how to play its crisis management role with the presence of peer competitors.

The Marines, as we underscored in our book on Pacific defense published in 2013, already have several key elements necessary to play a more agile and flexible role in the Pacific. The Osprey, coupled with the F-35, provides significant tools in providing an entry insertion point which is a significant one. The Marines are building on this advantage and looking to find new ways to shape their force forward in the Pacific and to do so with enhanced joint and allied cooperation.

I had a chance to discuss the way forward with the CG of I MEF, LtGen Karsten Heckl. I last talked with him when he was the CG of 2nd Marine Air Wing. Before that, I talked with him in Norway when he was COS STRIKEFORNATO, and before that when he was the deputy to the deputy commandant of Aviation.

From Left to Right, Major Morten "Dolby" Hanche, the first Norwegian F-35 pilot, Major General Tonje Skinnarland and Brigadier General Heckl, COS STRIKFORNATO at the Norwegian Airpower Conference February 2017 in Trondheim, Norway. Photo by author. Credit: *Second Line of Defense*.

We started by discussing how he saw the challenge. He underscored that a key part of understanding the nature of the threat environment is to understand the nature of the Chinese regime. Although this can be labelled great power competition, in the Pacific the great power is run by leaders of the Chinese Communist Party. They are communists, they are authoritarians and they wish to play by their rules and to impose those rules on the global community.

It is not simply a military challenge but a political-military and cultural one as well. Certainly, a key part of working the Marine Corps role in the Pacific is political-military as well as a narrowly warfighting role. We often hear about hybrid war and the gray zone; with a Marine Corps well respected in the Pacific and working relationships with partners and allies in the region, the Marine Corps can play a more effective role as a crisis management force.

LtGen Heckl underscored that a major challenge facing I MEF was enhancing its ability to operate forward or west of the international dateline.

"I have a 7,000 nautical mile physics problem, but we're doing a lot of things already that have us operating west of the international dateline."

He noted that the strategic shift provided in the defense guidance to focus on the great power competition is a key driver for change, but the transformation necessary to do so needs to be accelerated. This includes the question of augmenting Indo-Pac exercises as well.

Clearly, the Marines, like the rest of the joint force, are working through how best to deter the Chinese and to engage in operations over an extended area or an extended battlespace. This is clearly a work in progress. He noted that I MEF has a great working relationship and is enhancing integration with the Third Fleet, but both are located on the West Coast of the United States. How best to operate forward?

This entails the question of how to do effective blue water expeditionary operations. How best to work the Pacific geography with allies and partners to get the maximum political-military and combat effect? It is also a question of taking advantage of new ways to operate. How might the Marines assist more effectively the Navy in sea denial and sea control in the Pacific?

A key limitation for the Marines in the Pacific for sure is the size and state of the amphibious fleet. It is clear that operating at sea and from the sea with Marine Corps air assets provides very agile and powerful force insertion assets to deliver crisis management effects. But the decline in the numbers of amphibious ships is a critical problem, and how best to rebuild the fleet is a work in progress.

When I was last in Hawaii, the MARFORPAC team was focused on ways to expand the amphibious force in the Pacific with allies, or to enhance what they referred to as "amphibiosity." That was five years ago, and now allies are indeed expanding their amphibious forces, in South Korea, Japan and Australia. And allies are adding F-35Bs and Ospreys to their force. How can the USMC best leverage this upsurge in capabilities? It makes little sense to further devolve the U.S. amphibious fleet, as allies themselves see greater utility in this force for crisis management and warfighting.

As LtGen Heckl put it: "My biggest concern right now is amphibious shipping and connectors." And in this sense, the expeditionary force leverages what the Navy and Marines have now, but creative thinking about how to build out an amphibious fleet is clearly needed. As LtGen Heckl put it strongly : "The challenge seen from I MEF is that for us to be effective we need to be credible. To be credible, we need to be forward with credible forces. We are focused on positioning the MEF to be in a position to be an effective deterrent force."

Three Key Weapons Systems for the Marines in the Pacific

September 14, 2021

As the Marines focus on enhancing their capabilities for Pacific defense both with the joint and coalition forces, three key weapon systems enabling the effort are the F-35, the Osprey and C^2 capabilities at the tactical edge. Each of these systems brings different capabilities to the fight, but together they provide a core ability to operate from flexible bases, to be able to aggregate desired combat effects and to morph into flexible task forces at the point of interest.

I had a chance while visiting MARFORPAC during my August 2021 visit to discuss the way ahead with Marines involved with F-35s, Ospreys and C^2 evolution in a single roundtable. The participants in the discussion from MARFORPAC were Col Manlee Herrington, AC/S Aviation; LtCol Shane Bursae, Fixed Wing Air Officer; Maj Paul DiMaggio, Rotary Wing Air Officer; and Maj James Arnold, Aviation C^2 Officer.

As one participant put it: "We need to have the ability to close forces at the decisive point. We are operating as an expeditionary force which means we have to deploy agile and close rapidly. We need to combine speed with expeditionary flexibility and reach. That is why the F-35/Osprey combination is so critical for the Marines."

The F-35 Piece

The coming of the F-35 to the Pacific is a major difference from my earlier visit to MARFORPAC in 2014. The Marines operate two squadrons of F-35s from Iwakuni, with a third rotational squadron to be added in the future. The Marines operate the most forward-deployed F-35s in the region and operate from the first island chain. Now the USAF has deployed the F-35 into the region, and the Marines are working closely with them in shaping what the USAF calls "agile combat employment," something for which the F-35B is ideally suited.

A U.S. Marine Corps F-35B Lightning ll aircraft with Marine Fighter Attack Squadron (VMFA) 121 soars over Marine Corps Air Station Iwakuni, Japan, April 8, 2021. VMFA-121 is the first forward deployed Marine F-35B squadron. Photo by Cpl Jackson Ricker. 1st Marine Aircraft Wing.

The U.S. Navy is deploying F-35Cs into the Pacific with the introduction of the USS Carl Vinson carrier group. Marines are also involved, as they are F-35C operators as well. Marine Fighter Attack Squadron (VMFA) 314 operates those aircraft.

With allies buying F-35s and working towards ship-based F-35B operations, the envelope of engagement of the Marines in shaping shared coalition operational concepts and capabilities has expanded as well. They are working with allied F-35As as well as F-35Bs, which means that working the first island chain through to South Korea is clearly a work in progress.

Working closely with Japan and Australia, as those allies deploy and develop their F-35 fleets, provides significant opportunities to shape collaborative con-ops as well. Singapore is becoming an F-35 Security Cooperative Participant, which extends the operational envelope as well for Marines working with allies in shaping collaborative defense capabilities and approaches.

The Marines as well are working new concepts like the Lightning Carrier, whereby operating of a ship like LHA-6 (the USS America), allows a larger number of F-35 to support USMC operations from the sea or from the sea to the shore. And intersecting the capabilities coming off the USS America with allies and the joint force afloat or based ashore provides an opportunity to expand significantly the impact of USMC F-35Bs can have in a combat situation in the Pacific. The reach of the sensor systems of an integratable F-35 fleet is a core enabler for the joint and coalition force in the Pacific.

But to get the full value out of a USMC F-35 force, it is crucial to fund the enablers. The weapons development calendar is behind schedule, and there is a clear need to ramp up the weapons planned for development for the F-35 enterprise. As the U.S. shifts from the land wars, it is important to ramp up high-end capabilities in the missile domain for sure.

A second key enabler is tanking. The KC-130J fleet is a key asset for USMC operations, and they are in short supply. If you want to focus on their role to supply bases spread throughout the Pacific, then you are not highlighting their tanking role. If you are highlighting the tanking role, then you are reducing the ability to supply bases. There is no way around this other than ramping up the buys of KC-130Js.

The Osprey Piece

When I was last at MARFORPAC in 2014, the Osprey was making its presence known. It was the key bedrock for shaping what was then possible with regard to the strategic approach for the distributed laydown. In fact, I would argue that the Osprey was the bedrock for the initial transition of the Marines to a distributed laydown ecosystem which underlies the current approach to shape a more integrated distributed force.

At the outset of the meeting, we discussed the significant nature of the transition from the CH-46 to the Osprey and the impact of that transition on the rest of the Marine Corps force. The shift away from a rotorcraft mindset has been a challenging one for the Marine Corps, and indeed one which the U.S. Army or allied armies have yet to do. It is not just about speed and range; it is about rethinking how one operates in the extended battlespace.

Two U.S. Marines with Marine Medium Tiltrotor Squadron 363 (Reinforced), Marine Rotational Force – Darwin, observe an MV-22B Osprey preparing to land at the East Arm Wharf, Darwin, NT, Australia, Sept. 20, 2021. MRF-D's Aviation Combat Element prepared their aircraft to depart Australia after a successful 2021 rotation. Photo by Sgt Micha Pierce. MRF-D.

And that thought process is still a work in progress. When the Ospreys first came to the Pacific, an immediate impact was filling the gap caused by a shortage of KC-130Js. The Ospreys could move supplies and Marines around in ways that the KC-130J would traditionally do, with the role of the KC-130J in air refueling then highlighted.

Now as the Marines look to operate from multiple launch points, and to do so with working from a network of sea and expeditionary bases, the role of the Osprey is without doubt enhanced.

At the same time, the ways an Osprey can support or work with such a force have expanded significantly. What the participants underscored was the importance of working new capabilities for the Osprey and the F-35 to work together, to shape various payloads, which the tandem could deliver to a distributed integrated force.

For example, the East Coast Marines have recently worked a distributed G/ATOR system deployed on an expeditionary base in support of the fleet. How might this be worked in the Pacific? Can the G/ATOR be reconfigured to be delivered by a platform other than the KC-130J? Could it be done by Ospreys and CH-53Ks, for example, and provide for even greater basing flexibility? How to configure Ospreys to deliver unmanned surface vessels (USVs) into the battlespace with ISR systems for information or deception? In other words, how best to leverage what the revolutionary duo of F-35 and Osprey can deliver to the force?

The C² Piece

C² is a weapon system for shaping and synchronizing the delivery of fires and maneuver for an integrated distributed force. One participant drew an analogy between the USMC transition from CH-46 to the Osprey in terms of what was going on with C². He argued that with the focus on the land wars, we are just beginning to see the implementation of a generational leap forward with the latest sensors and information systems.

But with a shift to working in contested environments, and one prioritizing expeditionary operations, new capabilities and new concepts of operations were necessary. Technology is at hand to shape a way ahead, but ensuring that a distributed force can work in an integrated manner is an ongoing challenge.

As the Marines reshape themselves for operating as an inside force, how best to ensure that the C^2 for the inside force integrates with the air combat element for the Marines, or the naval strike force or PACAF's agile employment force? As one participant put it: "This is uncharted territory." And with regard to the deployment of the new Marine Littoral Regiment, how to ensure that it has the appropriate reachback capability to ensure mission success?

In short, as one works the USMC transition, the Marines already have in their hands a number of key tools for the transition. It is just important to realize and remember that going forward.

Seam Warfare, Exercises and Deterrence

September 15, 2021

Effective crisis management requires escalation control ranging from HADR operations through gray zone conflict to higher levels of lethal combat. A core challenge to be met is what one might call the ability to conduct effective seam warfare, namely, through working with partners and allies to reduce the seams left open in either in Pacific or European defense which the authoritarian powers can exploit.

I discussed this approach during my visits, and in one session with MARFORPAC future operations planners, we discussed how exercises are a key part of shaping the force precisely to deal with this challenge. That session was a discussion with Dr. Dave Hudspeth and Mr. Juan Zapata, G-35 Future Operations Planners. Shaping ongoing exercises allows a meshing of the capabilities and commitments of U.S. with those of partners and allies.

In my own view, the USMC in the Pacific is a linchpin between the USAF and the U.S. Navy, and a player which can deliver integrated combat force to a seam in times of crisis. What emerged from the discussion was a renewed focus on innovative exercises which built off the operations of competitors in the region and which drove innovative approaches with regard to shaping more effective joint and coalition operations.

INDOPACOM and the Marines are not focusing on what one participant called "wash and rinse" repetitive exercises, but instead focusing on expanding both the number of like-minded international participants in each exercise and the exercise objectives themselves to create more realistic and innovative deterrence approaches that measurably change how peer competitors are operating. The goal is to generate concepts of operations which present challenges to those adversaries in terms of seams which they would have difficultly closing in a crisis or more extended conflict. The goal is to be able to place the right combat capability at the right place at the right time to deliver the desired combat or crisis management effect. As one participant put it: "We need to look beyond traditional military measures of performance in exercises – such as number of sorties flown – to understanding how we are actually impacting the operational environment."

This means that working exercises is about determining how to shape the right capability to work outcomes desired in terms of crisis or extended conflict. Training and exercises are becoming core weapons. The challenge is to determine how best to do so from the standpoint of both the joint force and coalition partners and allies. And those determinations are not always going to be the same. The aperture has been opened with regard to shaping a way ahead for innovations in Pacific defense, and the introduction of new capabilities in the near to mid-term will be evaluated in terms of how these capabilities impacts in the real world in ways that allow the force to operate more effectively in influencing adversary behavior.

Allies, Partners and Marines in the Indo-Pacific

September 19, 2021

I had a chance to discuss the partnering challenges with the MARFORPAC team responsible for working those challenges. I met with Mr. Rich Hill, G-5 International Affairs Branch Head; Maj Zach Ota, G-5 NE Asia Desk Officer; Maj Dylan Buck, NE Asia Desk Officer; Mr. Justin

Goldman, TSC Plans Specialist; and Mr. Scot Hasskew, TSC Plans Specialist. This is an impressive team and we had a wide-ranging discussion of allied and partnering issues in the region.

Because of my engagement with the Australians as a research fellow with the Williams Foundation, and because the Marine Corps Rotational Force-Darwin had just been set up when I was last visiting MARFORPAC in 2014, we discussed the Australian relationship at length.

But we also discussed the tapestry of change in the Indo-Pacific as the Chinese reached out with both their economic and military power deep into the Indo-Pacific as well.

The team articulated a key point underlying the Marine Corps approach in the Indo-Pacific. They are focused on working with allies and partners from the standpoint of crafting approaches to operations and not just taking a U.S.-built template and incorporating allies into that template.

As one participant put it: "We use our training exercises to experiment with what particular allies or partners wish to do, and to work through how we can build that into an effective coalition warfighting capability."

With the concern about what is referred to as "gray zone operations" by adversaries, deterrence delivered through interactive training throughout the region is a key focus of USMC activity in the region. Training is a weapon system, and no more so than in shaping the ecosystem for combat operations in the Indo-Pacific through training with partners and allies. A key point which emerged from the conversation was how training as a weapon system actually shaped joint coalition warfighting capability.

The argument went like this: The Marines are training with partners and allies throughout the Indo-Pacific and through these efforts are shaping distributed, survivable, and agile network of training areas with partners and allies. This, in essence, creates combined joint task forces of varying sizes and varying locations that are scalable and agile. And by exercising through the various training events, one is creating a deterrent effect.

By working throughout the entire geographical areas of the Indo-Pacific, the Marines are able to operate from multiple vectors, which is a core strategic focus of the Marines in the Indo-Pacific today. A key element of innovation in the Indo-Pacific is working through a way ahead for coalition amphibious operations, from ships to the shore, from the shore to the sea, and shaping distributed and flexible combat clusters throughout the region.

We discussed how ARG-MEUs coming from CENTCOM through the Indo-Pacific both on the way and on the return have been part of the training regimes. But clearly, a renewed emphasis on building amphibious task force capabilities in the Indo-Pacific is required going forward, in terms of not simply the U.S. Navy and the USMC but also broadening the efforts to shape coalition wide amphibious task force capabilities.

We spent much of the time discussing the Australian relationship with the USMC. In my view, there is a significant evolution of Australian strategy underway, and how that evolution crosscuts with how the Marines work their own relationship in the Pacific can provide a powerful stimulus for shaping effective deterrent forces in the region. In part it is about the evolution of MRF-D in the future. How do the Aussies and MRF-D expand how they work together and with what focus? If the Australians focus significant attention on shaping distributed but integrated forces from Western Australia to their first island chain (the Solomon Islands), that area of operation which encompasses significant interaction with the partners in the region provides a very innovative and significant area in which the Marines can themselves work their cross-cutting innovations.

An airman from the Royal Australian Air Force helps guide a U.S. Marine with High Mobility Artillery Rocket Systems platoon, Marine Rotational Force – Darwin, as he backs up a HIMARS onto a RAAF C-17 Globemaster III aircraft at RAAF Base Darwin, NT, Australia, Aug. 12, 2021. Photo by Master Sgt Sarah Nadeau. MRF-D.

For example, bringing the newly formed Marine Littoral Regiment into an area of operations from Western Australia to the Solomon Islands and building out relationships with the Australian Army as that force rethinks its role in the region would drive significant cross-cutting operational changes important for both the Marines, more widely in the Pacific, and the Australians in reshaping their own defense capabilities.

I introduced another idea which we discussed, but I am not holding the team responsible for my own conclusions. There clearly needs to be an area to hold regular coalition amphibious task force training. This is no longer limited to operating as a greyhound bus delivery of capability ashore; the amphibious task forces of today are radically different and more capable in working the full spectrum of operations. It might make sense for the Aussies to sponsor an annual amphibious task force training exercise. It would be bilateral at its core but of course, India, Japan, South Korea and others who have capability to be tested in the 21st-century concepts of operations for an amphibious task force could engage in this ongoing combat learning and innovation effort.

The Marines face a challenge with regard to allies and partners and training which should be recognized as well. The Marines have built an integrated force capability which can deliver Marine Corps combat capability where needed. If the Marines go down a path of redesigning their force only to fit uniquely into a U.S. Naval joint force integration package via a hyper-specialization focus, they become less useful to the kind of force integration which allies, and partners, are engaging in to deal with the current and evolving Indo-Pacific defense threats.

But it is clear: the USMC in the Indo-Pacific will be most effective when it can integrate effectively with partners and allies throughout the entire gamut of operations from gray zone to higher levels of conflict.

Operations in the Information Environment

September 22, 2021

During my August 2021 visit to MARFORPAC, I had a chance to talk with the specialists in information operations within the command. In particular, I met with Mr. Justin Bogue, Information Maneuver Branch Deputy; Maj Melissa Giannetto, MARFORPAC PsyOp Officer; and Maj Nick Mannweiler, COMMSTRAT Operations.

Clearly, one major change since my last visit to MARFORPAC in 2014–2015 has been a renewed focus on information operations. With the Russian seizure of Crimea, which involved significant use of information warfare and the ramp-up of information operations including cyber in the Pacific—China, North Korea and Russia—a focus on crisis management operations needs to incorporate information operations as a core capability. It needs to be, in the words of one participant in the discussion, "not a bolt-on capability but a core integrated capability."

A key change which the Marines have made to build out modern IO capabilities has been the formation of MEF Information Groups (MIG) in each Marine Expeditionary Force. And those MIGS are operating as centers of excellence to shape the practical side of information operations and also as magnets for change throughout the Marine Corps as a whole. It is about forging a coherent capability to build in information operations elements within operations. As one participant put it: "It has taken time but over the past few years, we have been able to get wider recognition of the importance of information operations for the Marines and there is now much greater practical focus on how to do this more effectively going forward."

U.S. Marine Corps Meteorology and Oceanography (METOC) Analyst Forecasters with 3rd Intelligence Battalion, III MEF Information Group (MIG) participate in a Field Exercise (FEX) at Kin Blue, Okinawa, Japan, Nov. 3, 2021. The Marines conducted the exercise to test their capabilities in providing communication services in field environments. III MIG functions as the vanguard of III MEF, operating in the Indo-Pacific region's information environment, and supports Marine Air-Ground Task Force operations with communications, intelligence, and supporting arms liaison capabilities. Photo by LCpl Manuel Alvarado. III MEF Information Group.

And one aspect of that challenge going forward is working through what the relationship between what has been traditionally called public affairs is with operational information war. Or put another way, what is the relationship between COMSTRAT and Information Operations?

Another participant underscored that information operations were a key part of how the U.S. and allied militaries operated in the Cold War.

Some of these skill sets need to be recreated but to do so in the digital age and one where cyber war is a key reality as well. In the briefing given by the information operations team, one slide highlighted "how the Marines fight in the information environment." And the focus was upon how the MIG was positioning itself as a core element within the MAGTF to shape a way ahead for integrated information operations. The slide highlighted that the MIG "coordinates, integrates, and employs capabilities for information environment operations to ensure the MAGTF Commander's ability to facilitate friendly forces maneuver and deny the enemy freedom of action in the information environment." They concluded that "presence in an area is not complete if you are not present virtually."

Because the Marines are a full-spectrum crisis management force, IO needs to be addressed across the spectrum of operations from Humanitarian and Disaster Relief Operations (HADR) to higher end forcible entry operations. And to do so MIGS need to work seven functions of OIE or Operations in the Information Environment were identified: Assure enterprise command and control and critical systems; provide information environment battlespace awareness; attack and exploit networks, systems and notifications; inform domestic and international audiences; influence foreign target audiences; deceive adversary target audiences; and control information capabilities, resources and activities.

With a focus on more joint force integration of the Marines with the Navy, in particular, it was increasingly important that coordination among service-based IO needs to be coordinated, and common approaches and language shaped to execute more effective joint operations. And IO against peer competitors was at a very different scale than what has been learned and practiced in the Middle East land wars. Events at the local level in INDOPACOM can become strategic in character rapidly: how best to handle the management of IO at local levels and ensure that they work hand in glove with effective strategic-level decisions?

The exercise piece is of growing importance as well. Training and exercises are becoming of increasing importance in shaping joint and coalition force capabilities. But they are messaging events as well. How to bring these two strands within exercises more effectively together, namely, effective combat training and effective political impacts through messaging?

We discussed the crucial importance of collating information and lessons as well learned in crises, exercises or other information operational events. And here the team highlighted that from the beginning the MIGS are working closely with one another, and there are clear efforts to shape a coordinated community which can indeed share experiences and knowledge gained from those experiences.

In short, part of the strategic shift which the Marines are undergoing from the land wars to full-spectrum crisis management is learning how to master information operations. And to do so in a way that is integrated within kinetic operations as well.

The Logistics Challenges

September 24, 2021

The distributed laydown which started in 2014 has now been re-calibrated to focus on Marines operating further forward in the Pacific and doing so with closer joint force integration while retaining the capabilities to contribute significantly to full-spectrum crisis management with allies and partners. To do this with the force structure and budgetary limits facing the Marines will be challenging.

Underlying the strategic shift is the effort to find ways to shape sustainment capabilities. Obviously, the sustainment system used for the past twenty years in the land wars has little or no relevance to providing for sustainment for a both distributed force in a maritime environment, as well as one that may need to aggregate from multiple locations.

As one Marine put it during my visit to MARFORPAC: "We need to have the ability to close forces at the decisive point. We are operating as an expeditionary force, which means we have to agilely deploy and rapidly close. We need to combine speed with expeditionary flexibility and reach."

How do you shape a logistics system which can support such an approach? I had a chance to discuss the logistics challenges and the evolving approach to meeting those challenges during my visit with Maj Katie Petronio, G-4 Engineer Planner, and Mr. Jorge Diaz, G-4 Logistics Plans and Exercises. And as one participant put the challenge: "It is all about space. How do position ourselves to sustain the force where it needs to operate?"

Broadly speaking, the Marines have a number of ways to support their force projection force.

The first is to pre-position supplies throughout the region, and working with allies and partners in exercises provides such an opportunity. Similar to how the Marines store supplies in Norway, there are opportunities in the region to build out pre-positioning options.

The second is to work integration among the sea bases and to leverage not only what the amphibious fleet can deliver ashore but also leverage the broader fleet. The coming of the CMV-22B to the fleet adds a common capability shared with the Marine Corps, which allows cross-decking support and projection to mobile or expeditionary bases ashore.

The author with Capt Dewon "Chainsaw" Chaney, then the Commander of COMVRMWING (or Fleet Logistics Multi-Mission Wing) at North Island in front of the first CMV-22B at the Naval Air Station. June 2020. Credit Photo: U.S. Navy

The Marines are seeing an enhancement of their lift capability with the coming of the new CH-53K, along with the enhanced capabilities of the H-1 family (newly enabled with Link 16 and full-motion video capabilities). Such organic lift can play an important role in working sea to mobile or expeditionary basing cross-linkages as well.

The third is to rely on longer range lift provided by the KC-130J to move Marine Corps forces around the Pacific chessboard. The KC-130J fleet does face major demands for tanking missions which compete with lift missions and that constitute a constraint on moving the force on the chessboard.

A fourth way to deal with the logistics challenges is to work joint force support more effectively. This primarily will be done with the Navy but there is no reason this cannot be highlighted with the USAF as well. And over the past few years, the Marines have worked with the Military

Sealift Command to build new ships which allow the Marines to deploy and be supplied by new ships that are not classic amphibious ships. A good example of this is the purpose-built expeditionary mobile base ships, like the Lewis B. Puller.

A fifth way, and one underscored in the current Commandant's Force Design 2030 effort, is to reshape the force to reduce the logistical footprint required by Marines operating from expeditionary bases. This certainly can be done as part of an overall approach to the demand side with regard to sustainment with the insertion of a C^2 or ISR cell supportive of a broader joint force effort.

A key point was underscored by one participant on the importance of what was raised earlier in the conversation about sustaining a joint task force. "The focus here is not only the Navy supporting us but how do we support the Navy. The Navy needs to work with us to identify gaps which they have which we can solve. By coming together more effectively, we can co-learn as well reshape how we work together to support combat operations."

By opening the aperture of the Navy working with the Marine Corps differently, that is, baselining integration, there was an opportunity to expand ways to support one another in joint combat situations. But combining these various options into an overall logistics enterprise to support the strategic shift, the Marines are undergoing will be very challenging indeed. Logistics enablement is clearly a weapon system in terms of ensuring that the Marines "can have the ability to close forces at the decisive point."

The way ahead is to shape logistics network which is adaptive and can sustain a forward-engaged distributed force. And a major part of the challenge is to adapt service logistics systems to be able to provide for support for integrated force operations or to operate on a functional level. How will a modular task force which includes Marines, Sailors or Airmen, in an integrated operation, be sustained?

Shaping a Way Ahead for Force Design 2030 in the Pacific

Another change since my last visit to MARFORPAC in 2014–2015 was how the distributed laydown begun in that period was being reworked in terms of expanding basing flexibility and force distribution associated with the current Commandant's Force Design 2030 effort.

I have had a chance both with the East Coast Marines and with the Commander of I MEF and with the LtGen Rudder and his team in Honolulu to discuss the changes being worked as part of the Force Design 2030 effort.

A very helpful briefing and discussion on the overall effort during my visit was provided appropriately by the head of G-9 Capabilities and Requirements branch within the command, Col Steve Fiscus.

I have had a chance certainly with the East Coast Marines to discuss and observe changes associated with Force Design 2030, and in my time with MARFORPAC have been given the ability to do so with regard to Marines in INDOPACOM. Col Fiscus provided really one of the best explanations of how the Force Design 2030 effort was helping shape the Marines after their very significant engagement for twenty years in the Middle Eastern land wars.

The Marines have been working a shift for some time, but the ability to make a dramatic shift has been constrained by the Middle East land wars and the priority demands from CENTCOM. For the Marines to succeed more effectively in making the shift, it is crucial for them to be able to focus on reworking their forces in line with joint and coalition forces in both Europe and the Pacific.

A key element of the Force Design effort is to work with the Joint Force in reshaping how that force can work more effectively together against peer adversaries. And as Col Fiscus put it: "Within the joint force, someone has to be able to work within the WEZ and to be able to identify mobile and fleeting targets for the joint force to engage." He put it this way: "The Marines are working towards becoming a light force focused on forward positioning and persistence inside the weapons engagement zone of the adversary to be able to conduct reconnaissance, counter-reconnaissance and to be able to hold key capabilities of the adversary at risk."

He noted that the Marines really do not currently have the kinds of sensors that they need for such a mission focus. And a good deal of the experimentation and force redesign going forward is to identify, acquire and reshape a land-based force (agile in terms of expeditionary basing) which possesses sensors for reconnaissance and counter-reconnaissance and to have the kind of low-signature C^2 which would allow them to use those sensors as part of a wider kill web.

Col Fiscus made an extremely important point about enhancing the role of sensor and C^2-engaged Marines: "We need to get much better in understanding the Red Side and how they operate." And as I saw when visiting East Coast–based Marines, there is a growing realization of the importance of ramping up Red Side understanding more akin to how the Marines operated in the Cold War.

These are what the Marines refer to as stand-in forces. According to Headquarters Marine Corps, stand-in forces are defined as follows: "Stand-in Forces are designed to generate technically disruptive, tactical stand-in engagements that confront aggressor naval forces with an array of low-signature and affordable platforms and payloads. They must remain resilient under demanding conditions.

"When other elements of the Joint force are outside the weapons engagement zone, preparing for deliberate actions, our forward elements will remain operationally unpredictable, combining lethal and non-lethal capabilities with continued maneuver to facilitate denial activities and otherwise disrupt or deter adversary operations. They don't have to get to the fight, they're already there.

A U.S. Marine Corps light tactical all-terrain vehicle is offloaded from an MV-22B Osprey with Medium Marine Tiltrotor Squadron 262 (Reinforced), 31st Marine Expeditionary Unit (MEU), during exercise Noble Tempest on Camp Hansen, Okinawa, Japan, March 8, 2021. Noble Tempest is a force-on-force exercise designed to enhance the MEU's ability to operate and maintain communication between smaller, more dispersed elements. Photo by Cpl Alexandria Nowell, 31st Marine Expeditionary Unit.

"Stand-in Forces will be supported from expeditionary advanced bases and will complement the low signature of the bases with an equally low signature force structure comprised largely of unmanned platforms that operate ashore, afloat, submerged, and aloft in close concert to overwhelm enemy platforms."[79]

This is an important part of the redesign effort. But at the same time, the Marines operate on the basis of Marine Expeditionary Units as a standing force. The MEUs operating off of the amphibious fleet play a key role in crisis response and contribute significantly to the joint force's full-spectrum crisis management capabilities.

---

79. "Stand-in Forces," Headquarters Marine Corps (August 2, 2021), https://www. marines.mil/News/News-Display/Article/2708140/stand-in-forces/.

We concluded by my posing the question of where one would look to see the focal point of changes unfolding for INDOPACOM Marines. He responded that changes will most readily be apparent in the experimentation being undertaken at III MEF, as well as the innovations being generated by the MEUs.

CHAPTER SEVEN:

THE MARSOC CASE

The Marine Forces Special Operations Command provides an interesting case study for the USMC transformation path. It was stood up in 2006 and was clearly part of the response to the land wars and to enable the Marines to work more effectively within the key role which Special Operations Forces were playing in how the land war was being fought.[80]

With the land wars over (although counter-terrorism operations sadly not) should MARSOC be abolished? Some have argued this. But as the Marine Corps is reworking how to operate force distribution and integration, why isn't the small unit operational capabilities of the Raider teams not a key element of the next phase of transformation?

The idea behind the Inside Force is to find ways that smaller clusters of Marines can deploy within a Weapons Engagement Zone, and connect with an Outside Force, either to empower that Outside Force or to deliver decisive effect in a special area of operations.

Also, a key element of the peer fight is to understand how to deal with a core challenge posed by our peer competitors, namely, being able to counter their focus on operating at a level of lethality below outright war but using military and other means to coerce outcomes in their favor.

---

80. Sgt Jesula Jeanlouis, "Marine Forces Special Operations Command Celebrates 15th Anniversary," (February 22, 2021), https://www.dvidshub.net/news/389559/marine-forces-special-operations-command-celebrates-15th-anniversary.

It would seem that MARSOC forces could contribute significantly to working at this level of warfare, and with a key focus on ways to connect more effectively with indigenous or partner groups with the Outside Force, whether Marines, or the joint or coalition forces, the work which MARSOC has done with joint and coalition forces in the past would seem as well to be a key asset to leverage going forward.[81]

MARSOC while preparing for a peer fight could also provide a significant real world force element for innovation at the small group level, which can be leveraged and introduced into the wider Marine Corps force. They also could assist in rethinking how to use the assets the Marines already have to enhance combat capability now rather than waiting for whatever innovations arrive and are credible the decade out.

Given the importance of small group operations distributed but integratable with a larger force, the Marine Raiders should be a key part of this next phase of transformation. In effect, the Marines have the opportunity to take full advantage of MARSOC and to leverage their potential contributions to shape change going forward.

MARSOF 2030

In March 2018, the USMC released its long-term plan for the MARSOC command.[82] It was published March 2018, and more generally, 2018 was a year in which the Marines started focusing deliberately on the shift to conflict with peer competitors. For example, the Marine Information Groups were established in 2018 and 2nd MAW flew to Trident Juncture in Norway which as a major refocus by the Norwegians on the Russian threat and challenge.

---

81.   An interesting look at some of these dynamics is an article by Paul Baily, "Enabling Strategic Success; How MARSOC can help overcome 'simple minded' militarism," *Small Wars Journal* (January 11, 2021), https:// smallwarsjournal.com/jrnl/art/enabling-strategic-success-how-marsoc-can-help-overcome-simple-minded-militarism.

82.   https://www.marsoc.marines.mil/Portals/31/Documents/MARSOF%202030. pdf?ver=2018-03-29-143631-557.

After describing how they saw the future operating environment, the assessment highlighted the kinds of capabilities which MARSOC would need to possess to succeed in that environment. The document interpreted these capabilities as four core pathways for shaping a way ahead.

The first is focusing on MARSOC as a connector whereby they would be able to bring greater and more diverse capabilities on the problems facing the force and the nation. This is how the document described this pathway:

"The lines between war and peace will be ever more stretched and blurred as opponents seek to exploit U.S. vulnerabilities and reorder the world to their advantage. SOF will continue to be the premier choice for policy makers seeking to mitigate political risk and avoid direct confrontation while providing a scalable, effective response across a range of problem sets.

"To compete in the future operating environment, Raider formations will need to leverage the increasing reach of national and theater level capabilities, particularly those within the information space. MARSOC's facility in building cohesive, task organized teams provides us with the opportunity to develop into the ideal integrator and synchronizer of U.S. global capabilities with USSOF and partner nation actions. This concept aims to extend the idea of integration beyond traditional battlefield functions like ISR, Fires, Information Operations, and Electronic Warfare. MARSOC seeks to leverage its command-and-control architecture to provide a foundation from which U.S. and coalition actors and capabilities can be brought to bear on problems whose solutions require the synergy of military and non-military instruments.

"As competitors and adversaries refine approaches within what we today call 'Hybrid Warfare', the challenges will routinely defy strictly military responses, while requiring the expertise of players from across the government. Nonetheless, the nation will continue to gravitate to the Department of Defense. Within the military, SOF will be viewed as the tool to organize/coalesce whole of government approaches to difficult, complex problems. MARSOC's strength in task organizing and integrating across functional capabilities will provide a natural foundation on which to integrate and enhance theater, national, and interagency capabilities at every echelon. Our emphasis on relationships and mission command naturally positions our forces to be the connector, synchronizer, enabler, and integrator, particularly in cases where interagency or foreign partners possess limited command & control capability. Facility in matching and coordinating military and non-military instruments against multi-faceted, complex problems will provide MARSOC with a truly unique capability to produce valuable operational and strategic level effects in areas that currently stymie DoD.

"Integrating tactical, theater, and national capabilities with a relatively small 'boots on the ground' presence, as well as providing a venue for coordinating interagency actions, holds the potential to provide the nation with a unique set of capabilities. This concept comes with significant challenges. It will require an ambitious effort to change current authorities and permissions. It will also require a long-term effort to build the interagency relationships, understanding, and trust that must necessarily underpin such a concept. Lastly, it will require investments in select regions to cultivate the required partner relationships above the tactical level.

"Although this concept has inherent challenges, it builds on MARSOC's existing strength in command and control. Raider formations can become preferred partners; the 'glue' that binds wide ranging capabilities and disparate entities to achieve meaningful effects."

The second pathway is an ability to intertwine information, intelligence and cyber in shaping combined arms for the connected arena. This is how the document described the way ahead:

"Our units must be able to thoughtfully combine intelligence, information, and cyber operations to affect opponent decision making, influence diverse audiences, and counter false narratives. Furthermore, we must be able to synchronize operations, activities, and actions in the information environment with those across operational domains and, when necessary, fuse cognitive and lethal effects. Given current trends, effects in the information environment will become increasingly decisive across the conflict continuum."

A U.S. Marine Corps CH-53E Super Stallion is staged during a Marine Corps Forces Special Operations Command night raid exercise at Tactical Air Combat Training System Airfield, near Yuma, April 21, 2016. This exercise was conducted during Weapons and Tactics Instructor (WTI) course 2-16. Photo by LCpl Zachary Ford, MAWTS-1.

An additional way to characterize the way ahead from the information warfare perspective was highlighted as follows: "Building awareness and acting across the information environment requires deliberate effort that will challenge current roles, missions, and authorities. Where our Raiders identify operational requirements that we lack the ability to fulfill, we must have the means to connect to responsive capabilities from the Joint force or interagency. Raider formations will increasingly operate in the information environment and integrate those operations across physical domains.

"This demands our units view information and cyber tools as foundational, not just complementary, and develop facility in combining them as naturally as we combine direct and indirect fires today. To achieve this, we must change the manning, training, and equipping of our force. The creation of an enhanced combat development capability is one of the more important aspects of achieving MARSOC's goals for the future. Capabilities held at higher levels today may be accessed (with effort) in the near term, routinely incorporated into operations in the midterm, and perhaps become habitually associated or organic over the long term."

Such a perspective requires new training approaches and reshaping skill sets for the evolving conflict environment. This is how the document highlighted this pathway: "Sharp regional competition by adversaries with the ability to mitigate or deny traditional U.S. military strengths will increasingly drive missions demanding a high degree of skill and nuance to discern the sources of the problem and develop meaningful solutions. These problems will strain current conceptions of conflict and joint phasing, thus requiring SOF capabilities that can effectively address them while minimizing open hostilities.

"The Raiders we send into such environments must be able to understand them and then adapt their approaches across an expanded range of solutions. While tough, close-in, violent actions will remain a feature of future warfare, MARSOF must increasingly integrate tactical capabilities and partnered operations with evolving national, theater, and interagency capabilities across all operational domains, to include those of information and cyber.

"Creating operational and strategic effects in the future operating environment will require a SOF operator with an equal amount of brain to match brawn; foresight in addition to fortitude. Raiders must be able to seamlessly integrate a wide range of complex tasks; influencing allies and partners; developing an understanding of emerging problems; informing decision makers; applying national, theater, and interagency capabilities to problems; and fighting as adeptly in the information space as the physical. This set of competencies defines the 'Cognitive Operator' and is necessary to achieve 'MARSOF as a Connector' and 'Combined Arms for the Connected Arena'.

"Built upon a solid foundation of continued tactical excellence, the 2030 Raider must be as comfortable working as a part of interagency or multinational effort as serving inside of a MARSOF formation. This concept will place increased emphasis on the qualities of intellect, judgment, creativity, and teamwork while maintaining attributes like determination and endurance that have been critical to our success to date. The cognitive operator must have the curiosity and intellect to see the whole picture and infer underlying problems, the skill to convey those layers to leaders, the creativity to recommend effective multi-domain action, and the drive to see those actions through to completion."

And the fourth pathway is precisely for the MARSOC operators to understand how to operate in the wider environment and link up with right partners, at the right time and the right place. This is how MARSOF 2030 put it: "MARSOC possesses the advantage of being a relatively small force with its own component headquarters. Our cohesive, focused force confers an organizational agility that allows the Command to rapidly reorient the organization to confront new challenges as they emerge.

"In other words, the unity of purpose and organizational dexterity over which MARSOC presides provides SOCOM with an agile, adaptable force to meet unexpected or rapidly changing requirements. Seen from the bottom up, forward deployed Raider echelons are able to reach directly back into a responsive component command headquarters to assist in innovating solutions for operational problems. In this context, MARSOC's small size becomes a significant strength; one that can provide both organizational and operational agility to the USSOCOM Commander."

The document added: "Success will require SOF that is adaptable to changing environments and versatile across a diverse range of challenges. An institutionally agile MARSOC provides USSOCOM with a component that can rapidly orient, focus, or retool capabilities to meet emerging requirements or work a discrete transregional problem set with full spectrum SOF from onset through resolution. This tactical adaptability and operational agility will enable MARSOC to contribute more meaningfully within USSOCOM and be a bid for strategic success against rapidly emerging and changing threats."

Shaping a Way Ahead for MARSOC

On April 28, 2021, Major General James F. Glynn, the CG of MARSOC, provided his assessment of the way ahead for MARSOC in his testimony before the Subcommittee on Emerging Threats and Capabilities of the Senate Armed Services Committee.[83] In his testimony, he underscored the need for shaping a transition from the land wars to the new strategic environment, characterized by the reality of dealing with peer competitors. Excerpts from that testimony follow:

> We continue to uphold our Marine Raider legacy and forge the path of providing the nation and Geographic Combatant Commanders a Marine Special Operations Force capable of strategic impact while dynamically adjusting to meet the demands of the future operating environment. As the smallest SOF Component, we continually seek opportunities leverage our agility to maximize the effectiveness of our force and bring outsized benefit to the SOF enterprise and our parent Service. Over the past two decades, we have rightfully been focused on the global counterterrorism fight. We concentrated our efforts on the skills required to be successful in the military fight against violent extremist organizations (VEO), becoming highly effective in this arena.
>
> As we move forward however, we are in the midst of reassessing the skills and organizational capabilities required to maintain our military advantages in every domain. Our Commandant has set forth reimagining the Marine Corps to answer this challenge through ongoing Force Design efforts. These changes have broad effects that compel MARSOC to follow suit rapidly to ensure we bring the capabilities and organizational construct required to conduct strategic shaping and reconnaissance in support of the Joint Warfighting Concept, the Special Operations Command Vision, and Service concepts like Expeditionary

83.   https://www.armed-services.senate.gov/imo/media/doc/20210428_MAR-SOC%20Posture%20Statement_SASC-ETC-FINAL.pdf.

Advanced Base Operations (EABO) and Littoral Operations in a Contested Environment (LOCE).

With our Marine ethos and "Gung-Ho" attitude, MARSOC is well suited as an experimentation force, test bed and innovation engine for distributed operations in contested environments. As we continue to implement the tenets of Marine Special Operations Forces 2030 vision, it will be of utmost importance to leverage our size as an advantage to be the nimble, flexible, and pliable force that can understand, wargame, and experiment with developing operating concepts, leading edge technologies, and the latest equipment to develop competitive advantage and enable the joint force. As with the Marine Corps writ large, MARSOC is undergoing a capability review to ensure we integrate and enhance the capabilities to operate in the information environment, increase our understanding of developing situations, create asymmetric advantages, and further evolve the role of SOF in competition and conflict. The ability to compete in multiple domains simultaneously and synchronize those effects is an essential element as we refine objectives from the traditional kinetic realm.

In our role as a connector between United States Special Operations Command and the Marine Corps, MARSOC remains positioned to capitalize on the forward deployed placement and access to help prepare the operating environment for potential future operations in competition and conflict. As a complementary force in the contact layer, Marine Special Operations Forces are poised to do the advanced work to assess strategic locations, operational imperatives and tactical capabilities, while also working as part of the Stand-In Force to trade time and space for Joint Force physical and virtual maneuver. All aspects of multi-domain operations (Electromagnetic Spectrum Operations (EMSO), Cyberspace Operations, Space Operations, Influence Operations, Deception Operations, and Information Operations) will require to be enabled by SOF, and MARSOC is posturing for such and remains prepared to support the Nation's expeditionary force in readiness. These capabilities, more effectively integrated into our operations, facilitate actions SOF can take to support the resilience of our partners, support resistance movements against adversaries, influence populations to align with our ideals, and conduct precision direct operations as required....

Over the past year, MARSOC personnel deployed in support of 7 named operations across 14 countries. Reinforced Marine Special Operations Companies (MSOC), made up of Marines and Sailors from the Marine Raider Regiment (MRR) and the Marine Raider Support Group (MRSG), were persistently forward deployed in order to conduct full spectrum operations in the Indo Pacific, Central, and Africa Command areas of operation, with elements also episodically deployed in support of the European and Southern Commands.

In addition, MARSOC has maintained a forward deployed O-5 level headquarters, Special Operations Task Force (SOTF), in support of combat actions in Iraq and Syria for the last 5 years and has also deployed a MARSOC–led Combined Joint Special Operations Task Force – Iraq (CJSOTF-I), an O-6 level headquarters, to Iraq multiple times during the same period.

Inherent in all MARSOC deployable formations is the ability to collect and fuse information that illuminates adversary actions and networks and then conduct activities to shape and influence the environments, contribute to partner resilience, and conduct combat operations.

MARSOC efforts in the Indo-Pacific are of note, where Raiders are deployed in several key areas throughout the region gaining access and placement to build relationships and partner resilience. Notably, MARSOC elements in the Philippines are paired with significant support from III MEF forces to provide robust assistance to partner nation forces as they work to root out the final remnants of ISIS capabilities while providing reassurance of the United States commitment to the region in an active competitive location....

Though MARSOC is not a platform centric organization, we realize the use of specialized technologies and equipment can significantly enhance our operations across the spectrum. SOCOM guidance outlines areas that the SOF enterprise will focus its modernization efforts. These areas include Increased Lethality, Improved Interoperability, Next Generation Mobility Platforms, Network and Data Management, Next Generation ISR/Targeting, Biotechnologies and Human Interface, Hyper-Enabled Operators, Autonomy, Edge Computing, and Alternative Precision Navigation and Timing (PNT).

In coordination and partnership with other SOF elements, the Service, and a broad array of government and industry partners, MARSOC Combat Development continues to pursue the integration of intelligent unmanned, automated, and robotic technologies across the force. At the forefront of these development efforts is the pursuit of a technological fusion of our unmanned systems technologies with our advancing Cognitive Raider, Broadband Tactical Edge Communications, and Organic Precision Strike efforts.

Our planned unmanned systems (air, ground, and maritime) will operate with greater autonomy and serve as an increasingly important force multiplier, extending the operational reach, capability, and capacity of Marine Raiders by teaming them with intelligent and interactive robotic partners. Coupled with other capabilities, this human-machine teaming effort will increase survivability and increase the tempo of operations in the physical and virtual realms. These capabilities are effective operating against both Violent Extremist Organization (VEO) networks, as well as near peer competitors.

Given that our most prized asset is our people, it should be no surprise that our innovation efforts are centered on the skills, training, and equipment we provide the future Cognitive Raider to be a blend of elite commando, intelligence collector, and information operations expert with a deep understanding of the environment. The future Marine Raider needs to possess the knowledge of how to blend, synchronize, and apply a wide variety of capabilities to accomplish the given mission. To achieve that, MARSOC will continue to be an evolving force that enhances the way we approach the operating environment and how we leverage and facilitate Joint, Governmental, and Partner capabilities.

Over the next five years, you will see an organization that operates with the same intensity as we currently do, but with potentially smaller, more specialized and capable elements focused on discreet indirect actions that counter peer adversaries.

These teams are intended to shape adversary/competitor behavior through enabling partners, assuring sovereignty, and eroding confidence in their own systems through a variety of low visibility methods. This may call for organizational and capability enhancements that allow us to stay ahead in this mission area.

Specifically, we anticipate increased demand for organic capabilities in the areas of Cyber, EMSO, Space, and Information Operations. Skills in these areas are increasingly important at every echelon of action, especially as we operate in the increasingly complex and sensitive future operating environments.

A Discussion with Major General James F. Glynn

November 18, 2021

I had a chance to discuss in November 2021 the challenges and opportunities for shaping the way ahead for MARSOC within the overall transformation of the USMC and its role in the Joint Force with Major General James F. Glynn, the CG of MARSOC. Major General Glynn assumed command of Marine Forces Special Operations Command (MARSOC) in June 2020. His previous assignment was the Commanding General of Marine Corps Recruit Depot Parris Island and Eastern Recruiting Region. A native of Albany, New York, his service as a Marine began in 1989 after graduating from the U.S. Naval Academy with a Bachelor of Science Degree in Mechanical Engineering.

His initial assignment was with 3rd Battalion, 3rd Marine Regiment, in Hawaii where he served as a rifle platoon commander throughout Operations Desert Shield/Desert Storm and later as the Mortar Platoon Commander. He has served in a variety of command and staff billets at: Marine Barracks 8th & I, Washington, DC; 1st Battalion, 4th Marine Regiment, Camp Pendleton, California; Marine Corps Recruiting Station, San Antonio, Texas; I Marine Expeditionary Force, 2nd Battalion, 4th Marine Regiment, Camp Pendleton, California, and Marine Corps Forces Special Operations Command's (MARSOC) Special Operations School, Camp Lejeune, NC.

More recently, MajGen Glynn served as the Deputy Commanding General of Special Operations Joint Task Force, Operation Inherent Resolve (Forward).

Previously, he served at Headquarters Marine Corps (HQMC)—first as the Military Assistant to the Assistant Commandant of the Marine Corps, and then as the Director of the Office of U.S. Marine Corps Communication.

Marine Forces Special Operations Command hosted a change of command ceremony, June 26, 2020, as the Marine Raiders bid farewell to MajGen Daniel D. Yoo and welcomed MajGen James F. Glynn. Glynn returns to MARSOC to serve as its eighth commander, having previously served as the commanding officer of the Marine Raider Training Center. Photo by LCpl Christian Ayers, Marine Forces, Special Operations Command.

We started by discussing the nature of the change being focused upon at MARSOC. As MajGen Glynn put it: "From the outset of the standing up of MARSOC, we focused on a concept often referred to as I-3: Interoperability, Integration, and Interdependence. And I believe, based on competitors and what their study of our Joint Force capabilities are, the time is now to focus very purposefully on interdependence as a core element going forward."

"How are we going to be ready for the future? A stand in force approach means that we need to be very deliberate about the development of our capabilities going forward, with a thought towards the interdependencies of what special operations forces are expected to do in support of, and as part of, such a force."

"By virtue of Title 10, services tend toward the responsibility to engage in crisis response as a core function, and certainly the Marine Corps is crucial to such a mission. The Navy performs some actions in competition, such as freedom of navigation, and all the services focus on reassuring partners and allies. But SOF in general, and MARSOC in particular, focuses on activities that begin before crisis. We are part of the overall engagement in pre-crisis actions and do so by operating and developing relationships with partners and allies to enable them to do their own crisis prevention and response and enable them to tamp down violent extremist organizations that can turn into insurgencies. What we do on behalf of the naval services is provide access and placement to friends, partners and allies in shaping relevant capability in that pre-crisis to crisis phase."

We then discussed the advantages which flow from smaller group operations to drive innovation in the larger force. I argued that one of the advantages of having small groups like MARSOC is you can be more cutting edge because you're smaller, and you have less large force consensus building to try something new. And in my view, the Marines have capabilities from the aviation side, right now, Ospreys, F-35s, Vipers/Yankees, and CH-53Ks which can be tapped in new ways to shape innovation going forward while other innovations are shaped in the decade ahead, which in my view will be shaped by actual modular task forces in operations and combat.

MajGen Glynn provided his perspective on this aspect of driving change as follows: "Our size is our strength. We have the agility to make a decision, take one step and pivot 90 degrees to enable that decision. We've demonstrated that in a number of areas. That's obviously considerably more cumbersome to larger formations."

"What that enables SOCOM, and the Marine Corps is an outsized return on investment for a relatively miniscule investment in time, money and equipment. We can leverage the SOCOM acquisitions mindset of buy, try, decide; in other words, get one, try it. If it's not good, then don't use it. If it just needs to be modified, make some modifications, and try it again. And if it's worthy of investment, then on behalf of the service we can turn it into a program of record and a larger scale investment."

"We are focused on strategic shaping and reconnaissance with a specific emphasis in the electromagnetic spectrum and information environment. Our ability to bring multi domain awareness and effects to the pre-crisis and crisis phases to, for example, the MARFORPAC commander in his role with the Joint Force Maritime Component Commander, is a key focus for us."

"Returning to my point with regard to interdependencies, I look at MARSOC operations as part of a Venn diagram, or the image of the Olympic rings. If the capabilities of the service and the SOF component are thought of as rings, how purposeful can we be about where, how, and why they overlap? What are those capabilities that intersect and represent purposeful interdependencies? The Marine Corps prides itself on mission analysis and task organizing for the mission. We have that opportunity on a larger scale right now, and MARSOC, as the Service SOF component, is optimized to be the vanguard of experimenting with interdependencies required for stand-in forces."

The focus on MARSOC as an Inside Force or Stand in Force, as the Marines call it, does highlight the interdependent nature of their operations. What do they bring to an area of operation? What do they link to enhance their own impact, and to enhance the other elements of the force which operates in or comes to an area of interest? Working innovations in interdependencies to shape effective pre-crisis and crisis responses is a core driver of change for the evolving MARSOC force.

This is how MajGen Glynn put it: "Our name, Marine Raiders, highlights an innovative tradition dating back to 1942. Our company commanders in this organization are Majors and each unit has the capability to engage in multi-domain operations. Throughout these initial 15 years, MARSOC units have significant experience in expeditionary operations, sets and reps as expeditionary advanced operators and that experience is crucial in shaping the way ahead as we work with new approaches and new technologies. At the same time, we have joint and coalition experience, and working with partners and allies is a key part of our operational DNA.

"For the naval forces, our approach to basing and logistics is a key driver of change as well. We are agnostic to where we operate from, but it is influenced by aspects of support like logistics. As long as we get what we need to operate, we are not concerned with how it arrives. If it is by CH-53s, or an unmanned USV, the logistics capability contributes to enabling where we are. We operate from ships, ashore, can be air dropped, however, we will stay where necessary for the time needed, and a noteworthy aspect of it is about logistical enablement for what can be done in the area of interest."

"From this perspective, we are clearly interested in adopting new technologies. We can operationally test, evaluate, and take equipment and techniques to a remote location where we're training or deployed and learn from it. With that experience, we've said, "Hey, we're going to need to fix that thing, but the other thing works. From there, we've been able to influence the pace of investment and adoption. I think this approach can become very impactful to the way ahead for the coming Marine Littoral Regiments."

"Our ability to leverage what we already have, but to do so in new ways, is crucial to innovation with today's force, as we develop tomorrow's force. Our ability to operate with the Viper, with the 53K, with the F-35 now, we definitely have an opportunity and are working towards realizing enhanced combat effects from such interdependencies."

We then concluded by discussing the changing nature of warfare, and how MARSOC can enable the force to enhance its ability to prevail within that changing warfare calculus. In my view, the 21st century authoritarian powers who are peer competitors operate in the warfare spectrum from the use of lethal force designed to achieve tactical or strategic objectives below the threshold of triggering a wider conventional conflict up to the level of nuclear force informed conventional operations.

MARSOC from this perspective is a clear player in frankly both ends of the spectrum, but certainly is a meat and potatoes player in deploying to counter the lethal force supporting the political objectives of what people like to call "hybrid warfare" or operating in the "gray zone." And with its focus on shaping the kind of relevant interdependencies with other force elements, which can play from either partner or coalition or joint forces, can learn how to be an effective tip of the spear, but even more importantly help shape what indeed the most relevant spear would be in such situations. From this perspective MARSOC is not a force focused on irregular warfare, but on regular warfare 21st century peer competitor style.

MajGen Glynn noted that from such a perspective one could consider MARSOC as focused on optimizing for the 21st century version of regular warfare. "We're leveraging capabilities in order to bring cross domain awareness of peer adversary actions and activities that are going on right now."

He argued that bringing their combat experience to the evolving warfare context is a key advantage for the MARSOC force. "The reality of our deployments around the world is that our force is getting very relevant warfighting sets and reps. They know what it's like to be in a denied environment, at least for a period of time, they know what it's like to be in a contested environment for extended periods of time. That they're adapting and adopting both the technology, the techniques, and the manner in which they do business on an evolving basis to operate in such environments.

"We take lessons from our deployed forces now and apply them into the process that we have to certify, validate and verify every formation that we send in support of Special Operations Command. We run a validation process flexible enough to adapt to emergent requirements to make sure we stay relevant and remain current, because that's our assessment of how quickly things are changing, particularly below the threshold of declared armed conflict."

CONCLUSION:

CHALLENGES FACING THE WAY AHEAD FOR THE USMC

As the Marines work their capabilities and concepts of operations for full-spectrum crisis management engaging peer competitors, they face several key challenges, many of which are outside of their control.

The first major challenge is the question of what the overall U.S. warfighting strategy will be going forward and where the Marines will fit into that strategy. Associated with that is the question of the size of the overall joint force, the joint force building priorities and where the Marines fit into that overall effort.

The second major challenge is what the nature of the core military challenges will actually be going forward. Crises will shape our domain knowledge of such desired capabilities, but uncertainties abound with regard to how our various adversaries will develop their own strategies and capabilities going forward. China is referred to as the pacing threat, but that tells us little about how they will act and how their force would really perform in direct combat. The Russians remain a direct threat to the United States and to our European Alliance. And although we have had a blitzkrieg withdrawal from Afghanistan, that tells us little about how the United States will engage in the broader region which has exported global terrorism as a global commodity.

The third major challenge is sorting through the overall configuration of the USMC itself. As noted earlier, the Marines have built an integrated force capability which can deliver Marine Corps combat capability where needed. If the Marines go down a path of redesigning their force only to fit uniquely into a U.S. Naval joint force integration package via a hyper-specialization focus, they become less useful to the kind of force integration which allies and partners are engaging in to deal with the current and evolving Indo-Pacific defense threats. But it is clear: the USMC in the Indo-Pacific will be most effective when it can integrate effectively with partners and allies throughout the entire gamut of operations from gray zone to higher levels of conflict.

And that raises a core question of how to balance the role of the Marines as an inside force for the joint force with their own role of being a unique outside force which can project power from the sea to the littorals and operate throughout the extended littoral combat space.

In this chapter, I will discuss each of these challenges prior to closing with an interview with LtGen (Retired) Robling, who was Deputy Commandant of Aviation and the MARFORPAC commander, in his last assignments before he retired from the USMC. He provides an overall perspective on the challenges which I highlight in this chapter.

The Way Ahead for the U.S. Military Strategy and the Joint Force

Although the Trump Administration underscored the need to focus on the return of great power competition, what will be the stance of the Biden Administration, the Congress and successor administrations?

A key element of shifting focus to China and Russia with the growing nuclear threat from North Korea is very clear: nuclear arms competition is a pacing threat which makes any thought of an all-conventional military competition ramping up to the high end very difficult to believe to be credible. The U.S. military and the U.S. political elite need to refocus on the realities of what Paul Bracken has called the Second Nuclear Age and how nuclear weapons affect the escalation management challenge which peer competition entails.

As Paul Bracken put it in a 2018 piece: "The key point for today is that there are many levels of intensity above counterinsurgency and counter terrorism, yet well short of total war. In terms of escalation intensity, this is about one-third up the escalation ladder. Here, there are issues of war termination, disengagement, maneuvering for advantage, signaling, — and yes, further escalation — in a war that is quite limited compared to World War II, but far above the intensity of combat in Iraq and Afghanistan....

"A particular area of focus should be exemplary attacks. Examples include select attack of U.S. ships, Chinese or Russian bases, and command and control. These are above crisis management as it is usually conceived in the West. But they are well below total war. Each side had better think through the dynamics of scenarios in this space. Deep strike for exemplary attacks, precise targeting, option packages for limited war, and command and control in a degraded environment need to be thought through beforehand.

"The Russians have done this, with their escalate to deescalate strategy. I recently played a war game where Russian exemplary attacks were a turning point, and they were used quite effectively to terminate a conflict on favorable terms. In East Asia, exemplary attacks are also important as the ability to track U.S. ships increases. Great power rivalry has returned. A wider range of possibilities has opened up. But binary thinking — that strategy is either low intensity or all-out war – has not."[84]

At the opposite end of higher-level conventional conflict shaped by the nuclear effect is the other challenge posed by our peer competitors, that is their focus on operating at a level of lethality below outright war but using military and other means to coerce outcomes in their favor. How will the U.S. military and civilian leaders manage this challenge?

Working both challenges, higher end escalation management and lower lethality levels to contest authoritarian regimes, and their efforts to prevail in "gray zone operations," are both critical.

How to shape a strategy to do so? And how to size an appropriate joint force to do so as well?

---

84.   Paul Bracken, "One-Third Up the Escalation Ladder," *Second Line of Defense* (April 25, 2018), https://sldinfo.com/2018/04/one-third-up-the-escalation-ladder/.

The Marines are a leverage force within the joint force. The USAF will look to the Marines to provide airpower to supplement their own operations and to work effectively together with allies. The U.S. Navy is shaping a more integrative approach with the USMC, but the question of what is most valued by a U.S. Navy in fundamental transformation is an open question. The U.S. Army is seeking to redefine its missions and roles in the peer fight and will add some of the capabilities which the Marines have operated, such as higher speed assault forces. And the Army is in charge of a number of key items which the Marines have indicated they intend to deploy, notably longer-range ground strike weapons.

The challenge is that with the uncertainties of the overall strategy for the nation, coupled with the sister services themselves all in transformation, how will the Marines fit in most effectively? And some of the tools they would like to have will have to come from the sister services because of the Marines own budgetary limitations.

Adversaries and Allies: How Will They Shape the Dynamically Evolving Strategic Environment?

In an interview I did with three admirals in Norfolk, Virginia, in February 2020, we discussed the challenge of understanding both how our adversaries are shaping a way ahead and how that interacts with our own efforts for the evolution of our own capabilities and concepts of operations. The host for the meeting was Rear Admiral Peter Garvin, and he invited two other admirals as well to the discussion. The first was Rear Admiral John F. Meier, then head of the Navy Warfare Development Command, and the second was Rear Admiral Daniel Cheever, then commander, Carrier Strike Group FOUR. This is how we focused on and discussed the challenges:

> Operating from global sea-bases, with an ability to deliver a variety of lethal and non-lethal effects, from the insertion of Marines, to delivering strategic strike, from my perspective, in the era we have entered, the capabilities which the Navy-Marine Corps teams, indeed all the sea services, including the Military

Sealift Command and the U.S. Coast Guard, provide essential capabilities for the direct defense of the nation.

One key challenge facing training is the nature of the 21st century authoritarian powers.

How will they fight? How will their evolving technologies fit into their evolving concepts of operations? What will most effectively deter or provide for escalation control against them? There is no simple way to know this.

When I spent my time in the U.S. government and in government think tanks, I did a great deal of work on thinking through how Soviet and Warsaw Pact forces might fight. That was difficult enough, but now with the Chinese, Russians, and Iranians to mention three authoritarian regimes, it is a challenge to know how they will operate and how to train to deter, dissuade, or defeat them.

A second challenge is our own capabilities. How will we perform in such engagements?

We can train to what we have in our combat inventory, we can seek to better integrate across joint and coalition forces, but what will prove to be the most decisive effect we can deliver against an adversary?

This means that those leading the training effort have to think through the scope of what the adversary can do and we can do, and to shape the targets of an evolving training approach.

And to do so within the context of dynamically changing technology, both in terms of new platforms, but the upgrading of those platforms, notably as software upgradeability becomes the norm across the force. The aviation elements of the Marine Corps-Navy team clearly have been in advance of the surface fleet in terms of embracing software upgradeability, but this strategic shift is underway there as well.

The Admirals all emphasized the importance of the learning curve from operations informing training commands, and the training commands enabling more effective next cycle operations.

In this sense training, was not simply replicating skill sets but combat learning reshaping skill sets as well. Clearly, the Admirals underscored that there was a sense of urgency about the training effort understood in these terms, and no sense of complacency whatsoever about the nature of the challenges the Navy faced in getting it right to deal with the various contingencies of the 21st century fight....

There are a number of key drivers of change as well which we discussed. One key driver is the evolution of technology to allow for better capabilities to make decisions at the tactical edge.

A second is the challenge of speed, or the need to operate effectively in a combat environment in which combat speed is a key aspect, as opposed to slo mo war evidenced in the land wars.

How to shape con-ops that master C^2 at the tactical edge, and rapid decision making in a fluid but high-speed combat environment? In a way, what we were discussing is a shift from training preparing for the next fight with relatively high confidence that the next one was symmetric with what we know to be a shift to proactive training. How to shape the skill sets for the fight which is evolving in terms of technologies and concepts of operations for both Red and Blue?

In short, the Navy is in the throes of dealing with changes in the strategic environment and the evolving capabilities which the Navy-Marine Corps team can deploy in that environment. And to do so requires opening the aperture on the combat learning available to the fleet through its training efforts.[85]

---

85.   Robbin F. Laird, *Training for the High-End Fight: The Strategic Shift of the 2020s* (pp. 17–18). (Kindle Edition, 2021).

With the nuclear dynamic and the gray zone dynamic defining the spectrum of threats to be dealt with, how will our diverse authoritarian adversaries shape their evolving capabilities and concepts of operations?

The U.S. military approaches these challenges by prioritizing their ability to work with allies, and much of my work over the past twenty years has taken me to the Middle East, Europe, Asia and Australia, where I have discussed how the U.S. military is doing so. But allies and partners have their own agenda, diverse capabilities and interests. What will they do when confronting our peer competitors in a crisis, and how will we manage such crises both from an allied and adversary point of view?

It is clear that many of the Marines I have interviewed for this book get this and understand the importance of ramping up their understanding of the red side while working closely with allies and partners in shaping common capabilities. But training is one thing; actual combat and crisis management in the real world is very different from training or war games.

If we look at the recent Blitzkrieg withdrawal from Afghanistan, the difference between the real world and the planning domain is quite evident. The Blitzkrieg withdrawal was as much of a strategic shock as it is a strategic transition in that a generation of offices have really grown up in the Middle Eastern land wars, and the experiences and skill sets acquired in those wars are only partially transferred to the new strategic situation.

The Obama Administration promised a Pacific pivot, which largely did not happen because of the demands from CENTCOM and the Middle East, including the rise of ISIS and the Syrian civil war. In fact, it might be remembered that President Biden was Vice President Biden during the period of fighting the "good war" in Afghanistan. The military focus was on counterinsurgency, nation building and that most ambiguous of terms, stability operations.

Shifting from this skill set to preparing for full-spectrum crisis management and the high-end fight is significant. Will the U.S. shape a new counter-terrorism strategy in the Middle East which significantly reduces demand on U.S. forces? If not, then frankly, the demand side is beyond what the U.S. military can provide for a strategic shift.

In addition, CENTCOM's credibility is seriously in doubt given its performance over many years in the outcome—a failed Afghan military capability. And with that comes the question of why the U.S. Army is in any leadership role for preparing for full-spectrum crisis management and the high-end fight? The strategic shift prioritizes air and naval forces, and those land forces which can support crisis management which is largely about the USMC and its transition to the high-end fight.

And then there is this key question of the ability to manage crises, adversaries and allies.

The play-out of the Afghan withdrawal was hardly a textbook case in how to do escalation control or crisis management. As Dr. Bracken has put it: "If our actions in Afghanistan are indicative of U.S. competence in future crises, the world is in serious trouble."[86]

The allied piece is evident as well in the Blitzkrieg withdrawal. It is clear that for the U.S. military, either in the Pacific or in Europe, working closely with allies is the foundation for a credible crisis management or deterrence strategy. And working with allies means changing how the United States military integrates with allies and partners to shape a distributed force. Or put more bluntly, the United States is not in a position to compete with multiple authoritarian powers and to prevail without changing how the U.S. military works with allies.

In other words, the dynamics of three complex trend lines, the reshaping of the U.S. joint force, the evolution of the real warfighting strategies of our adversaries as well as the capabilities, stakes and positions allies will take in a crisis are all in play. The USMC as the nation's crisis

---

86.   Robbin Laird, "The Impact of the Biden Administration's Afghan Blitzkrieg Withdrawal Strategy on the Way Ahead for the U.S. Military," *Defense.info* (September 5, 2021), https://defense.info/re-shaping-defense-security/2021/09/the-impact-of-the-biden-administrations-afghan-blitzkrieg-withdrawal-strategy-on-the-way-ahead-for-the-u-s-military/

management force is at the vortex of sorting through its place in this complicated matrix of change.

The Configuration of the USMC Going Forward

A core focus of the force design effort is to shape capabilities for the Marines to operate more flexibly, rapidly and with agility to operate inside the adversary's Weapons Engagement Zone. Of course, the WEZ is a variable given where the adversaries might operate and at what level of conflict and with what escalation consequences.

Currently, the Marines are shaping ways to work C^2 and sensor systems in terms of flexible basing modes and have started with Naval strike missiles and the HIMARS as the launch point for working capabilities which could support Naval expeditionary operations as well.

In a December 2020 conference on future amphibious forces, held by DefenceIQ, there was a very robust and insightful discussion with regard to a key part of the challenge. As the moderator of the day, a noted former British general, highlighted at the end of the day, "We have had a very good conversation throughout the day about the future of amphibious forces." But as he also noted, the key challenge really was to sort through where one wanted to take those forces in terms of "what kinds of wars or conflicts were being prepared for or prioritized."

His question underscored the core challenge facing any discussion of the way ahead for maritime special forces or amphibious forces: What is their role in the high-end fight? What is their role in crisis management? And how related are the answers to these two questions?

Put another way, focusing on amphibious forces and their future quickly takes one into the realm of warfighting capabilities now, the next five years and the decade ahead. In turn, the question is posed as well with regard to what capabilities are desired and for which concepts of operations to shape what kind of warfighting outcome? In other words, there is no single force design which will easily embrace the range of options or be able to answer the question of prioritization for the warfighting approaches for the high-end fight. And this was clearly evident in the discussions during the day.

There was a discussion throughout the day of the advantages of shaping an inside force projected from the sea base to support operations in a denied environment. But it was clear for most presenters that the inside force was inserted to support an overall campaign effort, but it was important that the inside force did not compromise the capabilities of the outside conventional forces or the overall campaign.

As the moderator closed the conference, he highlighted the challenge of dealing with such a risk calculus. How much effort is required from the overall conventional force for Maritime Special Forces or an inside force to succeed? And in making that effort, how much do you drain from those conventional forces and with what effect with regard to its ability to operate and succeed?

The entire point of discussing the future of amphibious forces from the standpoint of the new strategic environment is the flexibility which sea-basing provides. Several of the presentations highlighted the flexibility which projecting special operations forces from the sea can provide for crisis management and hybrid warfare operations. With regard to peer competitors, the challenge is harder in terms of being able to insert force, and to ensure that it can survive and fight for another day. Much of the discussion during the day was with regard to what was required in order to be able to insert an inside force to work with the outside larger conventional force would require.

How to disaggregate for survival but be able to aggregate for combat effect? This requires the right kind of C^2, ISR accessibility, strike support, logistical support and an ability to be extracted. None of this is easy, and one should assume that the period where an inside force would be unobservable would be very limited indeed. Signature and sustainability would always be flashpoints for the inside force.

Much of the discussion during the day was about special force applications for the maritime force. Also addressed was the challenge of the blending of those missions with overall fleet operations. It was argued that the projection of this hybrid mix will be increasingly important in the thresholds below widespread conventional war.

Hence, the key question posed by the moderator: "What kind of war are you preparing for?" The assertion was that there would be more interest in shaping different types of inside force, but the ecosystem to support a wide use of such forces is simply not there. But for now, reorganizations are under way to shape new templates to use special forces and shape variant types of inside forces and to shape new templates for operations. New technologies would be inserted over time to enhance the ability to project robotic power forward to build out an inside force.

A key challenge is working through information sharing among coalition partners when operating in an area of interest. When you project force to an area of operation, how do you effectively work collaboration and cooperation, notably with regard to information sharing?

For those working on force design for an inside force, they face a significant challenge with regard to understanding how the overall conventional force capabilities will evolve, how the capabilities of the air, ground, sea, space and cyber components will intersect and how the inside force will fit into the overall redesign of the nuclear and conventional forces which nuclear countries like the United States deploy.

As a senior RAAF officer put it in a presentation made at a different DefenceIQ conference: "The detailed elements of force design can be extremely challenging as we can't predict the frameworks that future capabilities will be built around." This officer added a point facing the challenge of designing an inside force or a new combat capability more generally with regard to the evolution of an integrated force, namely, anticipating and knowing "the framework and environment these futures will nest within."

With the design of an inside force, the question is not simply reconfiguration for force insertion but also understanding the entire combat cycle envisaged whereby that force reinforces a conventional campaign rather than degrades it by putting hostages into the denied area with the commander's task being reset to save the inside force from destruction. It is a question of how to sustain the force forward and how to provide ways to extract the force back into the ramp-up of the conventional campaign.

At the same time, the ARG-MEU capabilities are being enhanced by the evolution of the amphibious task force capabilities of the U.S. Navy and the USMC. The evolution of the amphibious force and shaping amphibious task forces can contribute significantly to expanded capabilities for maneuver warfare at sea. By leveraging the new air capabilities, adding new defensive and offensive systems on the fleet, and expanding the C^2 and ISR capabilities of the fleet, the contribution of the amphibious task force can be reimagined and redesigned and thereby enhance the combat power of the U.S. Navy in maneuver warfare at sea.

There are two ways ahead with the build out of an amphibious fleet supportive of enhanced integration with the U.S. Navy. The current commandant of the USMC is focused on enhanced capabilities for the Marines operating as an inside force. In this context, he is focused on adding new smaller ships to the fleet to carry Marines and very specific and focused equipment to operate on points within the enemy's engagement zone. These ships have been labelled Light Amphibious Warships (LAW), which would form a separate small amphibious ship class.

According to Megan Eckstein in a June 8, 2020, article in USNI News:

"LAW would be among the biggest change to the amphibious force in decades. Marines typically deploy as a 2,200-strong Marine Expeditionary Unit aboard a three-ship Amphibious Ready Group. These ARG/MEU teams deploy from the East Coast, West Coast or Japan and go on rotational deployments, sometimes staying together as a formation and sometimes disaggregating to cover more exercises with partner nations.

"In contrast, the LAW ships would remain outside the ARG/MEU structure, an official at the Marine Corps' Combat Development and Integration (CD&I) directorate told USNI News. They would be based in areas where shore-to-shore movement of Marines and gear could be needed – places like the South China Sea if China were to fight for the islands and sea space it claims as its own, or the Baltic Sea if Russia were to make another land grab against a neighboring country – and would support the movement of Marine Littoral Regiments moving quickly from one piece of land to the next to conduct missions under the Expeditionary Advance Base Operations (EABO) concept.

"LtGen Eric Smith, the deputy commandant for combat development and integration and the head of the Marine Corps Combat Development Command, told USNI News in a recent interview that LAW "is a smaller version of a traditional amphib but much more able to hide in plain sight, much more affordable, much more numerous because of its cost."[87]

An example of what seems to be envisaged (given the reference to the Baltics) is what has been seen in recent North Atlantic exercises. According to Capt Kelton Cochran, 24th Expeditionary Unit, the deployment of HIMARS as part of the expeditionary force provides new options for that force. "MEUs operate globally, year around as the Nation's Force-in-Readiness," said U.S. Marine Corps Col Eric D. Cloutier, commanding officer, 24th MEU. "As we lean into the future fight, expanding our reach and flexibility by utilizing platforms like HIMARS gives us the ability to facilitate maneuver and freedom-of-movement for friendly forces, and our Allies and partners, while denying our adversaries the ability to do the same."

"HIMARS is designed as an affordable and adaptable theater force protection asset. The system has been in service with the Department of Defense since 2005 and was fielded by the U.S. Marine Corps in 2008 in support of operations Enduring Freedom and Iraqi Freedom. As the Corps looks to the future and refocuses on its naval roots, commanders are exploring the numerous options for employing the vehicle-mounted precision rocket system in more dynamic operations in the maritime and littoral environment.

---

87.   Megan Eckstein, "Marines Look to Two New Ship Classes to Define Future of Amphibious Operations," *USNI News* (June 8, 2021), https://news.usni.org/2020/06/08/marines-look-to-two-new-ship-classes-to-define-future-of-amphibious-operations.

"Embarking HIMARS platoons aboard Amphibious Ready Group ships and deploying them via surface connectors, such as landing craft utility vessels, is a concept of employment that West Coast MEUs have rehearsed and developed to a high level of proficiency. Maintaining a forward deployed land-based element of HIMARS that is attached to the MEU allows it to capitalize on strategic lift capabilities provided by USMC and Joint platforms in support of ARG / MEU missions.

"A HIMARS platoon, with strategic lift, can quickly infiltrate contested environments, prosecute targets, and depart before adversaries are able to detect or engage them. This technique is known as HIMARS Rapid Infiltration. The 24th MEU conducted HIRAIN in both live-fire and rehearsal events since early 2021 during pre-deployment training. Since deploying, the 24th MEU has engaged in multiple opportunities for sustainment through rehearsals with Joint units in theater, like the 352d Special Operations Wing, based in the United Kingdom."[88]

A second way ahead would be to reshape how the larger amphibious fleet would be configured. This would entail providing better C^2 and enhanced defense systems and leveraging the air systems onboard to support at-sea operations for sea control and sea denial, ship-to-shore insertion operations, supported with afloat assets, and perhaps expanding the F-35 lightening carrier concept. For example, older larger-deck carriers entering the twilight of their operational life could be reworked to operate as F-35B carriers and learn from the operations of the new British carrier class regarding how best to do so.

As Dan Gouré has put it: "While the Navy's and Marine Corps' vision of a new, integrated capability has some important positives, it has at least one major negative: its tendency to underplay or even diminish the role of airpower in future warfighting concepts. This is odd since airpower extends the operational reach of Navy platforms and Marine Corps units and allows them to conduct a range of complex operations. Advanced airpower, on ships

---

88.   Capt Kelton Cochran, "24th MEU, First to Deploy From East Coast with HIMARS," USMC (May 21, 2021), https://www.marines.mil/News/News-Display/Article/2627260/24th-meu-first-to-deploy-from-east-coast-with-himars/.

and at sea, will be critical in the initial period of a future high-end conflict, particularly in the Indo-Pacific theater.... Small amphibs may be harder to find and target, but they will not be able to operate either fixed or rotary wing platforms. Larger amphibs, such as those currently in production, can achieve survivability, reach, and responsiveness through their complements of fixed-and/or rotary-wing aircraft."[89]

There is also a challenge facing the USMC if it pursues the first future amphibious fleet approach rather than the second. And that is the Military Sealift Command (MSC) and its priority focus on logistical support. We have visited MSC many times over the past few years. When we visited MSC when Admiral Buzby was the head of MSC, he frequently made the point that he viewed the Littoral Combat Ship as a major challenge for any logistical support operation. Or put bluntly, he was not really interested in focusing on LCS logistical support when he had bigger fish to fry.

With the strategic shift from the land wars to full-spectrum crisis management, the sea services face the challenge of prioritizing maneuver warfare at sea. But it is impossible to execute maneuver warfare at sea if you have no fuel or go Winchester with regard to weapons. That challenge needs to be met by the logistical enterprise writ large. This means that as the fleet distributes across the maritime maneuver space and prepares to execute its offensive and defensive capabilities, a logistics enterprise has to function at full tilt to provide for the kit needed for operational effectiveness. As one senior Marine put it recently: "The Corps seriously needs to get on top of the force-wide logistics concerns. Logistics is the center of gravity for turning warfighting concepts into reality."

In the land wars, FedEx and commercial shipping could provide inputs to the land-based depots. This is hardly the support model facing high-tempo combat operations, where the supply chains themselves are key targets for

---

89.   Dan Gouré, "Force Multiplier: U.S. Fleet of Air-Capable Amphibious Warfare Ships," *Real Clear Defense* (October, 20, 2020), https://www.realcleardefense.com/articles/2020/10/20/force_multiplier_us_fleet_of_air-capable_amphibious_warfare_ships_581360.html.

adversaries. The situation now is even more pressing for any smaller ships to be supported unless they are part of modular task forces.[90]

In short, working the most effective balance between an inside force which depends on the overall joint force for combat effectiveness or operating itself as an outside integrated force which can operate from sea bases into the littorals and back again is a key challenge going forward.

Challenges Going Forward: The Perspective of LtGen (Retired) Robling

November 10, 2021

I had the chance to work with LtGen (Retired) Robling both when he was Deputy Commandant of Aviation from 2011-2012 and when he was the MARFORPAC commander from 2012 to 2014. We started by looking back at his time as the MARFORPAC Commander, and the beginning of the "pivot to the Pacific" and the challenges faced by the USMC at the time.

Question: Looking back, when you came to the Pacific command, the Osprey really was the key tool for USMC transformation in the region. In effect, it was the spear in the ground from which you built out a new way ahead. You also began the process of expanding the USMC relationship with Australia as well. How important was the Osprey in this transformation process?

LtGen (Retired) Robling: The Osprey was transformational for us. There are 25,000 plus islands in the Pacific and half of the globe in the INDOPACOM theater. We were actually the main air-enabled ground force at the time in the region. The Army brigade was coming back from the Middle East to establish the Brigade on Oahu, and they tried their Pacific Pathways approach which failed miserably.

---

90. Robbin Laird, "Sustaining the Integrated Distributed Force at Sea: The Military Sealift Command Challenge," *Second Line of Defense* (December 9, 2020), https://sldinfo.com/2020/12/sustaining-the-integrated-distribut-ed-force-at-sea-the-military-sealift-command-challenge//.

For us, the MV-22 opened the entire theater for us. We could air refuel the aircraft, we could island hop, and we could operate from Japan all the way to Australia. It was a game changer for how we approached theater operations and how the Joint Force Commander considered how he would use the Marines in the joint fight.

Question: Since you were there, and even though you were anticipating them, the F-35s are now operating in the theater. There are now two squadrons of Marines operating from Okinawa and they are operating every day in the first island chain. That is a big change from when you are there, and how would describe that change?

LtGen (Retired) Robling: It is a big change. Most importantly the Marines flying the F-35 will support the USAF's initial air campaign in any Korean contingency. This will give the Joint Force Commander unprecedented stealth capability until the rest of the joint force can close on the region. Secondly, the F-35's will support our partners and allies in the region by training and operating off of the ships in the 31st MEU. The F-35's ability to operate together and to distribute data to the joint force and operate in concert with the MV-22's has simply expanded how we operate in the Pacific and how the Joint Force Commander looks at the role of the Marines and their contribution to the joint force. Combing the two provides a unique airborne capability in the Pacific which can deliver force insertion throughout the region at significant speed and range.

Question: When I visited you in Hawaii during your time as MARFORPAC Commander, you and your staff were clearly focused on what you saw as an upsurge in "amphibiosity" with regard to our allies. Significant progress has been achieved along these lines since 2014. How should we view this progress?

LtGen (Retired) Robling: We were especially focused on Japan and Australia and since that time both nations have augmented their amphibious capabilities. We helped those nations to think differently about warfighting and how to defend their interests. For example, with the both the MV-22 and the F-35B operating from amphibious ships, the Japanese can think differently with regard to defending their outlying islands and, more generally, about the defense of Japan. The three – MV-22s, F-35Bs, and amphibious aviation ships – are transformational for both the USMC and our allies.

Question: For the USMC, the recent transformation process started in 2007 with the coming of the MV-22. Now General Berger, the current USMC Commandant, is adding a new chapter with regard to the next transformation module for the USMC. How should we understand the approach and how does it blend in with what has come before?

LtGen (Retired) Robling: I believe the Commandant was courageous in getting out ahead of the Joint force in facing what everyone is calling the pacing threat; China. Our nation has to face that threat and decidedly prepare for it now. But the challenge is that he is out *in front* of the other services in their preparation for a fight with China. I do not believe we as a country have decided what the strategy or that fight might look like and we don't have a full understanding of China's improved war fighting capabilities, how they will use them, how we will counter them, or what the USMC's role should be in that fight.

Question: The approach to building a more distributed USMC is certainly in line with past USMC practice, but the challenge is to ensure force cohesion and force integrability, first with regard to a deployed MEU or MAGTF, and with whatever joint or coalition partners are working with that distributed USMC force. How do you see the challenge of distribution and integration?

LtGen (Retired) Robling: The danger here is that we develop a niche force incapable of participating in high-end fights operating as some type of reconnaissance role or rear area security operation. In an escalatory war with China, I don't believe it would be long before North Korea starts looking seriously about taking South Korea and likely encouraged to do so by China. As a previous III MEF Commander and later MARFORPAC commander, I would argue that the Marine Corps' unique aviation and amphibious capabilities give it a decided advantage to the Joint Force Commander in other near peer campaigns. The redesigned force as envisioned by the Commandant will not necessarily support those type of activities.

While we work towards becoming a light force focused on forward positioning and persistent inside the weapons engagement zone activities, we do not have the kind of sensors which are needed for this type of operation. As a force that will collect and distribute data back to the joint force, we are woefully incapable of doing so much less operate low signature bases with low signature force structures. This requires the right kind of C^2, ISR accessibility, strike support, logistical support and an ability to be inserted and extracted at the time of our choice. C^2 will not be persistent, and neither will data transmission capabilities. We need a networked force that can operate even when we are not always tied into the joint force.

Logistical support is another weakness in our development of EABO operations that seriously needs overhauling. The Navy will likely need to prioritize their missions in full spectrum crisis management operations against China. Logistical support to small units of Marines on obscure islands will likely fall out of that their decision mix and the commercial capabilities to support the force in a maritime centric China fight will be sorely inadequate. The Commandant posed this weakness himself in remarks at the recent Marine Corps Aviation Symposium where he stated in the case of limited logistical support, the Marines may have to resort to foraging. How long can we forage on a pacific island?

I do believe however, that the Commandant is correct in his vision of investing in HIMARS and Maritime Strike Missile (both long and short range) to help in anti-access and aerial denial operations. These rockets and missiles are game changers and can significantly advance the Marines war fighting capabilities both in limited maritime and extended land operations.

I concur with the Commandant that the MAGTF cannot be the Marines only solution in warfighting operations. Yet we are building a force now that decidedly understates the role of aviation in all our warfighting activities, both in EABO operations and in our role in near peer conflict.

Over the last thirty years we have developed and acquired MV-22, CH-53K, and F-35 aircraft with significant capabilities not otherwise brought to the joint force. This aviation triad has increased our value to the Joint force tenfold. It has made the Joint warfighting commander think differently how he will prosecute a campaign because of our decided advantage this triad of aviation capabilities alongside our Marines gives us. Aviation cuts in constrained budget environments (we have always been in constrained budget environments) is inevitable, but once again, we must ensure the cuts are not so deep that we cannot recover from them if we are wrong about our role in the Indo-Pacific fight. We may be.

China may not care that Marines will be rooting around on islands inside the Second Island Chain. If our purpose is to be part of a naval force capable of ensuring sea control and denial operations, China may have already taken those considerations into their war fighting equation.

If I am right, then we need to give them pause to change their equation so our presence actually does what we say it will do. While I applaud the Commandant's focus on returning to our core mission of support to the Naval Fleet Commander through our role as the Fleet Marine Force Commander, our ability to work with the Navy in an ecosystem that requires insertion and support to focus inside the weapons engagement zone is not there now and will not likely be for quite some time. This will take a larger investment by the Navy in capabilities and training that they have so far been unwilling to do.

AFTERWORD

LtGen Brian Beaudreault, USMC (Ret)

The 38th Commandant of the Marine Corps (CMC 38), General David H. Berger set off a chain reaction in Washington, DC amongst defense analysts, Members of Congress, civilian leaders in the Pentagon, the Joint Force and certainly inside the Marine Corps when he published his *Commandant's Planning Guidance* (CPG) during July 2019. Informed and shaped by his previous general officer level command experiences, the depth, breadth, and speed of the institutional changes he was about to initiate were bold and aggressive.

No sacred cows were spared as he undertook a top to bottom, inside and out review of the current operating forces and their relevancy to deter and prevail against a peer adversary in contested, denied, disrupted, and degraded environments. General Berger clearly held the same opinion as his predecessor, General Robert B. Neller, that the Marine Corps was not organized, trained, or equipped to meet the demands of 21st Century warfare.

U.S. Marine MajGen James W. Bierman, the 3rd Marine Division commanding general, greets Gen. David H. Berger, the commandant of the Marine Corps as he exits an MV-22 Osprey at Camp Hansen, Okinawa, Japan, Nov. 16, 2020. III MEF was designated as the priority of effort per Berger's planning guidance. (U.S. Marine Corps photo by Cpl Hannah Hall)

Robbin Laird's work in this book closely examines the myriad opportunity costs that impacted the Marine Corps during twenty years of counterinsurgency and counter terrorism operations, primarily on land under U.S. Army leadership that contributed to the lack of 21st century readiness. Many have simply but accurately summarized the wicked problems the Nation currently encounters with the oft stated refrain, "we are at an inflection point."

Remaining action oriented during this inflection period, CMC 38's CPG was a catalyst in accelerating innovative thinking and brought greater urgency to the discussion about the Corps' role and readiness to operate effectively as a naval expeditionary force and the Marine Corps' role writ large within the Joint Force as the declared, "Inside Force" - the force that can persistently sustain effective operations within a peer adversary's weapons engagement zone.

The Commandant's Planning Guidance revealed his number one priority, Force Design, which was articulated in his March 2020 release entitled, *Force Design 2030*. *Force Design 2030* encompasses the programmatic, iterative, ten-year transformation effort across all elements of the three largest Marine Air Ground Task Forces, the Marine Corps Reserve and Marine Corps Special Operations Forces. General Berger established a dozen Integrated Planning Teams (IPT) led by field grade officers that analyzed the capability and capacity of the Fleet Marine Force (FMF), the operational arms of the Marine Corps that would constitute the "Inside Force." According to General Berger, "The "stand-in" forces will be designed to attrite adversary forces, enable joint force access requirements, complicate targeting, consume adversary ISR resources, and prevent fait accompli scenarios."

Chief amongst the IPT tasks was to identify options and produce detailed recommendations on how the Marine Corps, with a flat or declining budget, could generate the required resources to pursue a force wide transformation and begin to attack his modernization objectives. The approved IPT recommendations under the "divest to invest" approach serve as the aimpoint of the Marine Corps modernization goals. Those goals will be assessed annually as both material and non-material solutions get tested, accepted, dismissed, refined, or ultimately fielded as extant capabilities. The Commandant most recently updated *Force Design 2030* in April 2021. This update served as a quasi-scorecard on the near-term Force Design successes and a restatement of modernization and fiscal priorities that would yield the objective force circa 2030.

While the leadership of the Marine Corps remains focused on implementing *Force Design 2030* as resources allow, Robbin Laird has masterfully woven the transformation story of the Marine Corps that began well before 2019 with the 2007 fielding of the revolutionary, long-range, assault-support, tiltrotor MV-22 Osprey, followed by the fielding of the Fifth Generation F-35 stealth jet fighter and the future fielding of the CH-53K heavy lift helicopter.

Robbin has exhaustively interviewed current high-level commanders and consequential leaders across the Navy and Marine Corps enterprise and has pieced together a fantastic body of work that guides the reader towards a comprehensive understanding of the current challenges as well as the opportunities to be exploited by U.S., allied, and coalition forces within the Indo-Pacific and European theaters.

Robbin has crafted fresh ideas and makes solid recommendations throughout this work that can help the Commandant and Chief of Naval Operations reduce near and mid-term risk while enhancing the sensing, striking and sustainment power of naval expeditionary forces through more innovative employment of existing capabilities.

Robbin lays out creative options for additional Marine Corps contributions to reconnaissance and counter reconnaissance, sea control and sea denial while executing distributed operations, creation of more effective modular and resilient kill webs, leverages the Marine Corps as a deterrent force and a force that can play a leading role in helping to strategically manage escalation measures vis a vis nuclear-armed peer. But this assumes there is a consistent and agreed upon joint force view of employment of current and future Marine Corps and naval expeditionary force capabilities.

General Berger is committed to the USMC remaining the most ready force when the nation is least ready, able to assuredly operate in all climes and places. There are risks that lesser but still resource intensive contingencies could detract from Force Design and extend the timeline to achieve the objective force of 2030. That should stimulate even more thinking about innovative employment of that which we currently possess or could easily pursue through acquisition of commercial off the shelf technology while programmatic modernization remains ongoing. Robbin Laird does an outstanding job blending the conceptual with the practical.

One only needs to survey the security situation today to see a Russian Federation that is increasing its presence in Belarus, further threatening Ukraine sovereignty, expanding operations and infrastructure in the Arctic and is creating tensions along the border of our NATO ally, Poland. Xi Jinping continues to ratchet up military pressure and increase tensions with Taiwan and is positioned to retain authoritarian control of the Peoples Republic of China for a third term. While quantity is not quality, the PLA Navy has now surpassed the size of the U.S. Navy. Both the PRC and Russia continue to test hypersonic weapons delivery systems which adds urgency and importance to escalation management at the tactical and operational levels.

A "Stand-In" force equipped with longer range surface to surface engagement capabilities will certainly add to the difficulty of managing actions/counteractions along the escalation ladder once casualties are sustained. Hypersonic weapons call into question previous assumptions about indications and warning, available time or off ramps as space-based capabilities and other intelligence disciplines attempt to distinguish potential inbound conventional weapons from nuclear weapons. Robbin Laird's *The USMC Transformation Path: Preparing for the High-End Fight* could not come soon enough or at a better time while helping to craft innovative solutions to difficult challenges.

DR. ROBBIN F. LAIRD

D r. Robbin F. Laird A long-time analyst of global defense issues, he has worked in the U.S. Government and several think tanks, including the Center for Naval Analysis and the Institute for Defense Analysis. He is a Columbia University alumnus, where he also taught and worked for several years at the Research Institute of International Change, a think tank founded by Dr. Zbigniew Brzezinski.

Dr. Laird is a frequent op-ed contributor to the defense press, and he has written several books on international security issues. He has also taught at Queens College, Columbia University and Johns Hopkins University. He has received various academic research grants from various foundations, including the Fritz Thyssen Foundation and the United States Institute for Peace.

Dr. Laird is the editor of two websites, *Second Line of Defense* and *Defense.info*. He is a member of the Board of Contributors of Breaking Defense and publishes there on a regular basis. He is a regular contributor to the Canadian Defence magazine *FrontLine Defence* as well.

Dr. Laird is a frequent visitor to Australia, where he is a research fellow with the Williams Foundation in supporting their seminars on the transformation of the Australian Defence Force. Recently, he has become a research fellow with the Institute for Integrated Economic Research – Australia. The institute is focused on a number of key macro social/defense issues which revolve around establishing trusted supply chains and resiliency in dealing with the challenges posed by the 21st-century authoritarian powers.

He is also based in Paris, France, where he regularly travels throughout Europe and conducts interviews and talks with leading policymakers in the region.

Dr. Laird has published a wide range of books on defense and security, which can be found on his Amazon webpage:

https://www.amazon.com/Robbin-F.-Laird/e/B001HOMXEE%3Fref =dbs_a_mng_rwt_scns_share

Second Line of Defense Strategic Book Series

The Return of Direct Defense in Europe (2020)

The Return of Direct Defense in Europe: Meeting the 21st Century Authoritarian Challenge focuses on how the liberal democracies are addressing the challenges of the 21st-century authoritarian powers in terms of their evolving approaches and capabilities to deal with their direct defense.

As General (Rtd.) Jean-Paul Paloméros, former NATO Commander and head of the Allied Transformation Command, put it with regard to the book: "One of the many great values of *The Return of Direct Defense in Europe* is that (it addresses directly the need) to meet the challenge of XXIst century authoritarian powers. Because the great risks that lie in front of our democracies deserve to be named: national selfishness, divergence of strategic and economic interests, trampling on fundamental and commonly agreed values.

"*The Return of Direct Defense in Europe* is both a moving testimony to those who have built and defended our democracies for seven decades but as well a vibrant appeal to resurrect the spirit and the will of the democratic Alliance's founding fathers.

"It's true that the future is unpredictable, but nevertheless, it's our permanent duty to prepare for it and to learn from our history: as the Spanish-born U.S. philosopher George Santayana (1863-1952) put it: 'those who cannot remember the past are condemned to repeat it.'

"In writing this outstanding tribute to democracies and the crucial need to keep on fighting for their values, Robbin Laird and Murielle Delaporte do not only draw a very well informed and instructive historic perspective on the defense of Europe since the Second World War.

"They enlighten as well with regard to the crucial challenges of the present and even more of the future, with regard to the key choices that leaders of our democracies must make, and with regard to the key question that lies in front of new generations: How best to defend together democracy as a unique heritage built upon the sacrifices of their fathers?"

Professor Kenneth Maxwell underscored:

"This is a fascinating and very timely account of the major shifts and challenges which have transformed post–Cold War Europe and outlines in troubling detail the formidable challenges which lie ahead in the post-COVID-19 pandemic world.

"It is essential reading for all those who forget that history must inform the present.

"It illustrates the need for a hard-headed evaluation of the continuities as well as the ruptures of the recent past which has transformed both the scope of North Atlantic Treaty Organization (NATO) and the European Community, and which has also created opportunities for enemies of democratic government to thrive in a resurgent Russia under the leadership of Vladimir Putin.

"These challenges will not go away any time soon."

The book can be purchased directly from our website:

https://sldinfo.com/books/the-return-of-direct-defense-in-europe/

Or from booksellers worldwide, including Amazon, Kobo and Barnes & Noble

Joint by Design: The Evolution of Australian Defence Strategy (2021)

In the midst of the COVID-19 crisis, the prime minister of Australia, Scott Morrison, launched a new defense and security strategy for Australia. This strategy reset puts Australia on the path of enhanced defense capabilities.

The change represents a serious shift in its policies towards China, and in reworking alliance relationships going forward.

As one senior RAAF officer put it: "The Prime Minister of Australia, the Honorable Scott Morrison, has launched the Defense Strategic Update, which moved Australia's defense policy away from a globally-balanced approach under our Defense White Paper of 2016, towards a more regionally focused posture, founded in the principles of shape, deter, and respond. The new policy approach places great emphasis on the need for our forces to be well integrated, both internally to Australia, and across our strategic partners."

Joint by Design is focused on Australian policy, but it is about preparing liberal democracies around the world for the challenges of the future. The strategic shift from land wars to full-spectrum crisis management requires liberal democracies to have forces lethal enough, survivable enough and agile enough to support full-spectrum crisis management.

The book provides an overview of the evolution of Australian Defence modernization over the past seven years and the strategic shift underway to do precisely that. Although this is a book about Australia, it is about the significant shift facing the liberal democracies in meeting the challenge of dealing with the 21st-century authoritarian powers.

In this sense, the volume is very complimentary to our book *The Return of Direct Defense in Europe*, a book that concludes with a chapter that highlights the Australian contribution to the rethinking going on in Europe about direct defense.

The book is based on the biannual Williams Foundation seminars held since 2014 and includes insights and presentations by Australians and several key allies of Australia. In that sense, the book provides an Australian-led allied rethink with regard to how to meet 21st-century defense challenges. The two books read together provide a good overview of where key allies are with regard to rethinking defense.

As Anne Borzycki, director of the Institute of Integrated Economic Research – Australia, has highlighted: "Dr Robbin Laird brings a unique perspective to his analysis of the journey the Australian Defence Force (ADF) has been on over the last six years. As an American, and also a European resident, he understands the military and strategic realities of Europe and the United States and is therefore able to place Australia, as a modern middle-power, into the spectrum of Western Liberal Democracies. And importantly, this book highlights the lessons that Europe and the United States could learn from Australia as the first quarter of the 21st century draws to a close.

"This book is a modern history that begins in 2014. The year 2014 might seem recent – however given the upheavals wrought upon the world by changing global power dynamics, national domestic political challenges, military transformations and finally, the pandemic – it could just as well be 60, not 6, years ago."

And Andrew Carr, senior lecturer, Strategic and Defence Studies Centre, Australian National University, noted in a recent review: "Joint by Design offers a valuable overview of how Australia's defence force has been evolving, innovating and adapting. It tells a story that is typically only ever seen by the public in piecemeal. A new piece of equipment here, or training and doctrinal changes there. In Joint by Design, Robbin Laird shows, through dozens of interviews with the main participants, how these various parts all fit together.

"This book is therefore an important contribution to our understanding of both Australian defence policy now operates, but also how western armed forces are changing in light of the growing threat of the new authoritarians such as Russia and China. As such, it should be of interest to those concerned with the nature of modern warfare, security trends in Asia, and the evolution of western armed forces."

This book can be purchased directly from our website:

https://sldinfo.com/books/joint-by-design-the-evolution-of-australian-defence-strategy/

Or from booksellers worldwide, including Amazon, Kobo and Barnes & Noble

Training for the High-End Fight: The Strategic Shift of the 2020s (2021)

Training for the High-End Fight highlights the essential strategic shift for the U.S. and allied militaries from land wars in the Middle East to the return of great power competition. The primary challenge of this strategic shift will be the need to operate a full-spectrum crisis management force. That means training a force capable of delivering the desired combat and crisis management effect in dealing with 21st-century authoritarian powers.

The U.S. and its core allies are shaping new capabilities to deal with the various threats and challenges affecting 21st-century global theaters. Flexibility in operations and agility in inserting force with a proper calibration of effect will be enhanced as new systems come online in the years ahead.

But these systems will have the proper effect only in the hands of skilled warriors, who, today, have to face a radical disjuncture from traditional training approaches and thinking in order to address these new types of threats and work towards a seamless common operating picture.

This book looks at the further adaptation and evolution of the U.S. forces in preparing for conflict in a contested environment, variously referred to as the return of Great Power Competition, peer conflict or the high-end fight. The book is built around what was learned from a number of visits and discussions at warfighting centers in the United States during visits over the past few years, with the bulk of the interviews included in the book coming from visits in 2020. These visits have been to Norfolk, Virginia; Jacksonville and Mayport, Florida; San Diego, California; and Las Vegas and Reno, Nevada.

The book starts by providing a brief overview on the strategic shift and the crafting of the integrated distributed force to be able to deliver effective outcomes for our political leaders. The book then turns to the two key enablers of the integrated distributed force, namely, C^2 and intelligence, surveillance and reconnaissance (ISR), and with these terms being redefined in many ways in terms of how the force is evolving them, leveraging them and transforming them.

The setting is then in place to discuss what it means to train for the high-end fight. To train for and execute the capabilities of the high-end fight requires that training and exercises be well funded, and the innovations being generated by the warfighting centers drive force structure development.

The force that is evolving is a very capable one, but the reset in its combat approaches and combat architecture is crucial to enhancing its capabilities to provide for the skill necessary to master the puzzles and challenges of escalation management and to shape the skills needed for the world we are now in.

This reset in combat approach is pivotal to enhancing our escalation management skills and for protecting the liberal democracies against 21st-century authoritarian powers. Informed by interviews with officers at a number of U.S. warfighting training centers, readers will discover the future of 21st-century combat, and how our forces are preparing for it.

In his review of the book, this is what Air Marshal (Retired) Geoff Brown, RAAF, had to say:

"For the last 20 years high-end training has continued to be a feature of major USN/USMC and USAF exercises. However, the emphasis and the training has always been modified to take account of the operations in Afghanistan and Iraq. While this was a necessary requirement of the times, it did lead to a stagnation in high-end warfighting concepts as the exercises and training have remained largely unchanged for the last 20 years.

"The proliferation of 5th generation technology and the threat posed and encompassed in the cyber and EW domains has continued to evolve rapidly to the point that the latest generation SAMs are not necessarily or even the most significant threats posed to the deployment of Allied Air Power. The emphasis on operations in the Middle East has meant that the high-end exercises have not evolved as quickly as the technology or the threat.

"While the U.S. has continued to develop and deploy leading edge technology for the high-end fight, the training concepts and virtual environments have not necessarily kept pace with the requirements of this new technology. High quality and realistic training have always been and will continue to be the major determinant in military success. Training for the

High-End Fight is the only recent significant work that looks in detail at this issue."

This book can be purchased directly from our website:

https://sldinfo.com/books/training-for-the-high-end-fight-the-strategic-shift-of-the-2020s/

Or from booksellers worldwide, including Amazon, Kobo and Barnes & Noble.

2020: A Pivotal Year? Navigating Strategic Change at a Time of COVID-19 Disruption (2021)

2020: A Pivotal Year? addresses the impacts of the COVID-19 disruption on global politics and provides assessments of the ripple effects felt throughout Europe and Asia. We are looking at the significant changes we see in building out post-pandemic societies and how the conflict between 21st-century authoritarian states with the liberal democracies is reshaped. Authors based in Europe, the United States and Australia have all contributed to this timely and unique assessment.

The first section of the book provides a unique look at the impact of COVID-19 on the Western societies, with Professor Kenneth Maxwell's focus on the United Kingdom and Pierre Tran's on France. We continue our discussion by looking at a wide range of geopolitical dynamics, and more specifically Europe and Australia.

We have brought together a number of our essays on historical developments of interest, spearheaded by the outstanding work of Professor Kenneth Maxwell. We conclude by taking a look forward into 2021.

As one reviewer commented on the book:

"Robbin F. Laird's 2020: A Pivotal Year? Navigating Strategic Change at a Time of COVID-19 Disruption is a collection of essays and articles by numerous authors. As the world was unexpectedly and suddenly disrupted by COVID-19, which started in 2019 and became more severe in 2020, the world is in serious need of deep, rational, and objective analyses on the impact of COVID-19. The essays and articles included give such analyses. This is why 2020: A Pivotal Year? is such a valuable book at this point in time. "Edited by Robbin F. Laird, there are six chapters in 2020: A Pivotal Year? In each chapter, there are essays and articles covering a range of topics. I particularly liked the essay 'The War Against Coronavirus or Is It?' by Pierre Tran, which is in Chapter 1, 'Navigating the Covid-19 World'. Indeed, as we are trying to get the virus under control, should we use a strategy as if we are fighting in a war. The essay 'Is a War with China Inevitable?' by Paul Dibb in Chapter 2, 'Global Strategic Dynamics,' offers potent reading as the consequence is truly global. I found the essay '2020 a Pivotal Year?' by Robbin Laird in Chapter 6, 'In Lieu of a Conclusion,' deeply insightful. It states: 'The negative fruits of globalization were clearly demonstrated in 2020... after decades of relatively prosperity aided by a certain kind of globalization, that period of history is clearly over.'

"Yes, the post- COVID-19 world will be different. What will it be like? Laird's 2020: A Pivotal Year? points out the factors that will shape the post-COVID-19 world – a highly recommended read!"

This book can be purchased directly from our website:

https://sldinfo.com/books/2020-a-pivotal-year-navigating-strategic-change-at-a-time-of-covid-19-disruption/

Or from booksellers worldwide, including Amazon, Kobo and Barnes & Noble

Forthcoming Titles in 2022:

French Defense Policy Under President Macron: 2017 to 2021

Defense 21: U.S. and Allied Defense Issues 2021